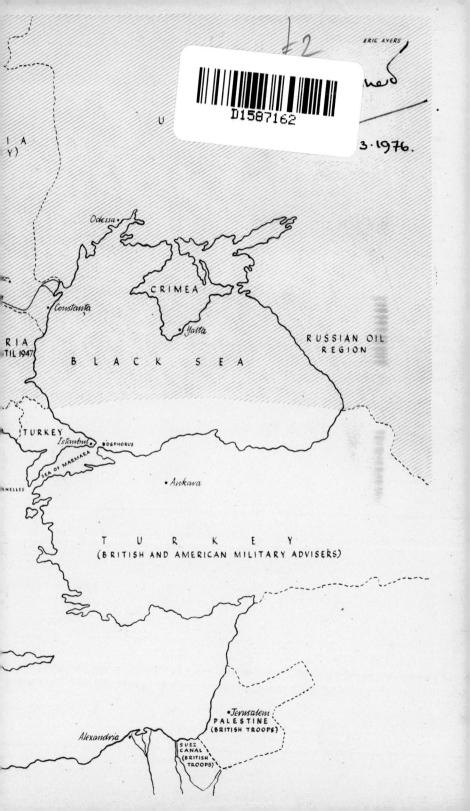

£2

ERIC AVERS

D1587162

3.1976.

U

I A Y)

Odessa

CRIMEA

Constanța

Yalta

RIA TIL 1947

BLACK SEA

RUSSIAN OIL REGION

TURKEY

Istanbul BOSPHORUS

SEA OF MARMARA

ANELLES

Ankara

T U R K E Y
(BRITISH AND AMERICAN MILITARY ADVISERS)

Jerusalem
PALESTINE
(BRITISH TROOPS)

Alexandria

SUEZ
CANAL
(BRITISH
TROOPS)

TRUCE IN THE BALKANS

TRUCE IN THE BALKANS

by *Elisabeth Barker*

LONDON

PERCIVAL MARSHALL

First published 1948
Percival Marshall & Company Limited
23 Great Queen Street, London W.C.2

CONTENTS

NOTE

THIS book is based as far as possible on first-hand observation, impressions, conversations and reading of current Balkan and Trieste newspapers. Unfortunately, there are inevitably many gaps in my first-hand knowledge. In these I have had to rely on second-hand information; but there I have tried to weigh up conflicting reports and views from conflicting sources.

There are perhaps far too many generalisations in the book. Although they may be given in dogmatic form, I would like to make it clear that they represent my personal views, often inevitably based on incomplete evidence.

So that readers can judge for themselves, if they want, just how far the book is based on first-hand knowledge, the following facts may be useful. I travelled in the Balkans in the early nineteen thirties. After that I always read what I could about the Balkans. In July, 1945, I set out there as a news agency reporter. I spent the month of August in Turkey; September, October and November, 1945, in Bulgaria; December, 1945, and January, February and half of March, 1946, in Rumania; a few days in March, 1946, again in Bulgaria. From the end of March to the end of May, 1946, I was travelling about Greece. I spent June and part of July, 1946, in Bulgaria, for the last time. From mid-July until mid-December, 1946, I was in Trieste.

My job gave me a chance to talk to a good number of politicians and many more ordinary people, and forced me to read the local newspapers carefully.

Because of visa difficulties I could not go to Yugoslavia, although before the war I knew it better than the other Balkan countries. That is why there is very little about Yugoslavia in this book. But other people have written or are writing first-hand accounts of Marshal Tito's Yugoslavia which will do much more than fill in the gap.

As for the four areas about which I have mainly written—Bulgaria, Rumania, Greece and Trieste—other people, starting with stronger political convictions, might have had the same experiences as I had but have reached very different conclusions. I might as well admit that one of the reasons why I wanted to go to the Balkans after the war was to acquire some hard-and-fast political convictions. But I did not succeed.

ELISABETH BARKER
January, 1948

I

Commonplace

IT is a commonplace that the Balkan countries are a border land
between East and West, between Asia and Europe. For four hundred
years they were the restless troubled borderland between the Turkish
Empire and the Austrian Empire. Then in the nineteenth century
Russia joined in to make the struggle a three-cornered one. But Turkey,
as an Empire, was growing old and losing her grip, so it soon turned
into a straight fight once again.

As, during the century before the first world war, Turkey slowly
shrank back from Europe towards Asia, the Austrian Empire pressed
south-east into the Balkans from Vienna and Budapest. Russia pressed
south-west into the Balkans from Moscow and Odessa. At first they
both used the political warfare of the period. There was a pro-Austrian
party and a pro-Russian party in most Balkan countries, each fighting
for power and getting its backing from its patron outside. Austria,
backed up by Germany, also worked on the Balkans through trade.
Russia also worked through the propaganda appeal of Pan-Slavism and
the Orthodox Church.

By 1914 both sides were impatient and ready for open war. It came
when a Balkan Slav student shot an Austrian Archduke, and Russia
stood by the small Balkan country, Serbia, on which Austria served a
humiliating ultimatum.

The 1914-18 war knocked out the Austrian Empire permanently, and
her backer, Germany, and her enemy, Russia, temporarily. This was a
startling and extraordinary situation for the Balkans. For the next
fifteen years or more the Balkan countries lived in a vacuum almost
free from outside pressure from East or West. For the first time in
centuries their people had a chance to breathe deeply and start working
out their own economic and political salvation instead of fretting and
fuming about foreign tyrants and patrons.

But the vacuum was rather uncomfortable and frightening. Fear and
hate had been forced upon them as part of their lives for so long that
when two big outside fears—fear of Austria and fear of Russia—
vanished overnight, they took to fearing and hating each other. This
left them not much time or energy for constructive planning and work
before the outside pressure started up again.

In the nineteen thirties Hitler's Germany stepped into the place of the old Austrian Empire and pressed from the West into the Balkans with trade pacts, propaganda, political warfare, bribes and threats. Russia, Soviet Russia, after years of isolation, began slowly to play a part in Europe and tried to penetrate the Balkans politically from the East.

By 1940 people in the Balkans either feared and hated Nazism and Germany or feared and hated Communism and Russia. A few feared and hated both, but there seemed then no way of escape from one or the other.

Very soon it did not matter much whom they feared and hated. By the summer of 1941 Germany had overrun nearly all the Balkans. Russia had only just been able to nip in and snatch Rumanian Bessarabia and Northern Bukovina out of the way of Germany's advance south-eastwards. Inside the Balkan countries the pro-German parties or cliques came out on top. The pro-Russians, mainly Communists, went underground. If they were lucky they started up partisan fighting. If they were unlucky they were hounded down and put in concentration camps or shot, or lived in hiding. Some escaped to Russia.

By the end of 1943 the East-West see-saw was beginning to tilt again. Italy's surrender had for the moment badly shaken the German occupation forces in the Balkans. It had shown that sooner or later the Germans would have to get out. Stalingrad had shown that the Russian armies would sooner or later come rolling back from the East and would reach the Balkans.

But a new and important thing had happened in the West. The British and Americans had landed in Italy and reached the Adriatic. At that moment they were much nearer the Balkans than the Russians were. They were taking a very definite if rather nervous and muddled interest in the Balkans. The British had liaison officers both with Mihailovic and with Tito in Yugoslavia, both with Zervas and E.L.A.S. in Greece. From Cairo the British had contact with the non-Communist Opposition in Rumania. They were preparing the way for liaison officers to make contact with the Bulgarian communist partisans.

People in the Balkans had for centuries thought and felt in terms of an endless struggle between East and West, over their lifeless or kicking bodies. It might be Turkey and Austria, it might be Russia and Austria, it might be Russia and Germany. It all fitted into the same old pattern. Now it was all going to fit in once again. Germany was going to drop out. The British and Americans—the new representatives of the West— were going to jump in and take Germany's place. In particular, they would try to nip in to the Balkans from the West before the Russians could roll in from the East. It would be the old shoving-match between East and West all over again.

Unfortunately people in the Balkans, although they were wrong over the military course of things, were not so far wrong over the main political lines.

Militarily, by top-level agreement, the British and Americans kept clear of the Balkans except for air bombing, commando raids in the Adriatic, and dropping arms, clothing, food and medical supplies to the Yugoslav guerillas. Greece was the big exception: here British troops landed and became a small occupation force staking out a claim for the strategic interests and political influence of the West at the southern end of the Balkan peninsula. Further north the Red Army rolled into Rumania and Bulgaria and lapped over for a short time into Eastern Yugoslavia. Big permanent Russian occupation forces were left in Rumania and Bulgaria.

Politically there was no such agreed clear-cut division of the Balkans between Russia and the West. Even before the war in Europe had stopped, the tussle for political power or at least for political influence had started. In the Russian-occupied countries there were already 'pro-Anglo-American' parties in opposition to the pro-Soviet governments. In British-occupied Greece there was a pro-Russian opposition to the successive pro-British governments. Every Balkan people was split once again between those who wanted the East—that is, Soviet Russia—to win in the Balkans, and those who wanted the West—the 'Anglo-Americans'—to prevail.

It was something new in the Balkans to have the Anglo-Americans playing a big rôle there, even if in the Russian-occupied countries it was only a negative foot-in-the-door policy.

England had, of course, made short sensational appearances before. The Greeks remember England for Byron and his part in the war of liberation in Greece. More typically, the Rumanians and Turks remember England in a different sort of part, an anti-Russian part which they think very up-to-date and topical. This England played when just under 100 years ago she suddenly decided to prop up an already faltering and decrepit Turkey and plunged, with France, into the Crimean war against Russia, a war to push a forward-thrusting Russia away from the mouths of the Danube and the Straits.

After that, lasting confusion, which still lives to-day, was created in the Balkans by the strange difference between the Englishman Disraeli—the man who shored up the Turkish Empire to protect British interests in the Suez Canal—and the other Englishman, Gladstone—the man who sympathised with the Balkan peoples' longing to get free from Turkey and condemned Turkish atrocities in Macedonia.

Then people in the Balkans, particularly Serbian veterans of the first world war, remember with friendship the British on the Salonika front and in the final drive up against the Bulgarian Army to liberate Serbia in 1918. Then, the British came as liberators of the Balkans from the Germans, Austrians and Turks. Even to Bulgarians this particular memory seems to have left curiously little bitterness. It was the Peace of Neuilly which followed the fighting and barred Bulgaria from Macedonia, Thrace and the Aegean that left unhealed wounds.

Even more curiously, the Turks now hardly seem to remember the Dardanelles fighting of that war. They like to forget that the British were ever Turkey's enemies.

On the whole, people in the Balkans have had mixed and muddled feelings about the British. Only the Greeks seemed quite certain that they liked them—or anyhow, they were certain up till the Greek civil war of 1944, which was really a war between the Greek left wing and the British. After that there was a fair minority of Greeks who resented the British.

For the other Balkan peoples the British have always been remote and mysterious. They liked the British because Britain was a long way off, and so was not likely to have any particularly grasping selfish designs in the Balkans. But at the same time they bore a grudge because Britain never wanted to take a practical interest in the Balkan countries, to buy their goods or sell them British goods, or to try to help them raise their standard of living. After launching the Salonika front in the first world war, the British cleared out of the Balkans very quickly. They left the Balkan nations to find their own way out of the post-war maze, and then seemed shocked and pained when later Germany became their chief market and supplier of goods.

Another reason for muddle was that people in the Balkans could never make up their minds whether in foreign policy England stood for progress or reaction, whatever those two words might mean at any given moment of history. Gladstone and Disraeli are still very much alive in the Balkans, where people talk about men who lived a hundred years ago as though they had seen them yesterday. Disraeli stands for reaction and imperialism, Gladstone for progress and a liberal foreign policy. Perhaps the meaning of these words has shifted; but, people ask, where does England stand to-day?

In the Balkans they also have very mixed ideas about England's social structure. To the very few intellectuals who have read serious books about England, have visited Western Europe to study social questions, or have been in touch with the Second Socialist International or the European trade union movement, England stands for social progress. They think of her as a pioneer in parliamentary institutions and in the development of trade unions and co-operatives. When Attlee's Labour Government came to power they expected it would give Europe a lead in parliamentary Socialism.

Many more have a quite different idea, drawn perhaps from reading Dickens and the early Galsworthy or perhaps merely from cartoons and hearsay. For them England is still the country of lords, big land-owners, rich business men and bankers, colonial governors, snobs, hunting and horse-racing, and the terribly poor. Nazi propaganda has sharpened this idea by labelling England the country of plutodemocracy and imperialist capitalism. Soviet and local communist propaganda, though usually distinguishing between 'reactionary circles' and 'the people', has very much followed the Nazi line and has also tried to show that the Labour Government has changed nothing.

This idea of a rich snobbish England acts two ways. It has a certain superficial snob appeal for the small middle-class and the well-to-do. English cloth, English tailoring, English dogs, all have a social value, or would have if they were any longer obtainable. Such people also hope that a capitalist England will be bound to stand up for the propertied classes everywhere.

On the other hand, the enthusiastic and often naïve left-winger hates this capitalist imperialist England as the symbol of what he is fighting against. Because it has been the party line, he has sometimes talked about friendship with all the 'democratic' nations including England.

He has carried portraits of Attlee—though never Bevin—in political processions. But underneath he resents bitterly an England which, he believes, has not really changed socially since the nineteenth century and which is the enemy of all modern left-wing movements.

Since the end of the war in 1945, some clever people have come to see that Britain is much weaker and poorer than she was, and so is unlikely to do anything very effective in the Balkans. The few who were idealistic about England, particularly the older Social Democrats, believe this will not last and that she will come back as a leading world power. Those who were counting on England to save the propertied classes from Communism have shifted their hopes and loyalties to the United States. The left-wingers have mixed their resentment with contempt for England's decadence, but think she is still machiavellian enough to do a lot of harm.

America, for most people in the Balkans, stands in a golden glow of fantastic riches, fantastic liberties and fantastic benevolence. Of the older men, many more know America at first-hand than have ever seen England. Until the United States imposed restrictions after the first world war, thousands emigrated from the Balkans to America every year. Surprisingly many of the emigrants came home again in middle age or old age, with great tales of wealth, modest savings of their own, but very few fortunes. Usually they went back to their own old village, perhaps built a small house, and became the big talkers in the village pub. Now, if ever they can get their hands on an Englishman or American, they burst into a flood of almost unintelligible American-English with a strong Balkan accent on top. Although they politely pretend they can, they understand very little English in return. It soon becomes clear that except for vague but glorious ideas about freedom for all and riches for the working-man, they got to know little of America except their own particular corner of their own particular town—Pittsburgh or Detroit or wherever it might be—and that they mixed mainly with their fellow-countrymen.

On their side, Americans came first to the Balkans not as traders or soldiers but as missionaries and teachers. Towards the end of the last century a number of American Methodist and other Protestant missionaries, men and women, came and did a lot of valuable practical social work, although they did not make many converts. Reuben Markham, the Christian Science Monitor correspondent who was expelled from Rumania by the Russians in 1946, started his career as a methodist missionary in Bulgaria and later became a schoolteacher. One State Department official who was posted in Greece and Bulgaria after the war had been born in Macedonia, the son of an American pastor.

The American schools in Istanbul, Athens and Bulgaria, have had a big influence on the boys and girls from middle-class families which could afford the fees. They taught them good English, American history and liberal ideas, American morality and American songs. Most important, particularly at the American college in Istanbul, where boys came from the different Balkan countries, they taught the idea of tolerance, brotherhood and collaboration among the Balkan peoples. Since the boys who went through this training were likely to become prominent civil servants or business men in their own countries, this American influence, though limited, was important.

The Americans have never fought in the Balkans, and so far, apart from their Rumanian oil interests, their trade relations with the Balkans have been very small. When they decided to go into the Balkans politically at the end of 1944, they started with a clean sheet and many moral assets. At first they followed rather nervously in the wake of the British, who were thought to have a priority interest in the Balkans so as to protect British Mediterranean and Middle Eastern commitments. Within a year the Americans, with a militant liberalism and a voluble disgust at Communism, had become the leading anti-Soviet force in the Balkans.

Balkan feelings about Russia are deep-rooted and powerful but mixed. Sometimes blind fear is on top, sometimes blind admiration wins. Russia is very close and very big. Some people feel that she casts a thick and sinister shadow, others that she sheds a protecting warmth.

In the last century Russia usually appeared as the big liberator, helping the Balkan peoples in their struggle to get free of the Turkish Empire. But, particularly among the peoples who were not Slavs, there was fear that if Russian armies came to liberate they might stay too long and cost too much. Russian culture was welcome enough, although it never seriously competed with French culture. But there was uneasiness about Russian political influence. It might lie too heavy on a small country. Even in Bulgaria, a little Slav country closely tied to Russia by language, culture and the Orthodox church, there was a revulsion of feeling against Russia within a few years of the Russo-Turkish war of 1877 which freed Bulgaria at last.

The Russian revolution in 1917 sharpened feelings in the Balkans to wild panic among the small possessing classes and to enthusiasm among those of the dispossessed who had any inkling of the ideas preached by the revolutionaries. Perhaps, if the new Russia had not been politically crippled by the Peace of Brest-Litovsk and if the British and French armies had not swept into the Balkans from the Salonika front, the fire of the Russian revolution might have run all through the Balkans, and not merely have dropped a spark in Hungary.

But this did not happen. Instead a good number of White Russian refugees seeped into the Balkan countries and were well received by the kings and governments. A diplomatic curtain fell between Soviet Russia and the Balkans and shut them off from one another for the next twenty years. Balkan governments with varying fierceness pursued, imprisoned and tortured their own Communists.

The most promising of the Balkan Communists escaped to Russia and were trained in Moscow for later work in their own countries. The two Bulgarians, Georgi Dimitrov and Vasil Kolarov, and the Yugoslav, Tito, were leading members of the Third International. The Greek, Nico Zahariades, and the Rumanian woman, Ana Pauker, also learned in Moscow.

Of the 'bourgeois' Balkan politicians between the two wars, a few, like the Rumanian Foreign Minister Titulescu, thought it would be wise to cultivate respectable relations with such a big neighbour as Soviet Russia, while at the same time keeping bolshevism out of the Balkans by all possible means. The rest were usually quite simply anti-Communist, anti-Soviet, and anti-Russian. They imagined that the Balkans could stay permanently cut off from Soviet Russia.

In 1939, the Molotov-Ribbentrop Pact brought Russia back into the Balkans as a formidable and active Power. Her return provoked the old rival feelings of panic and enthusiasm.

Nearly all Rumanians panicked, and within the year Rumania had had to yield Bessarabia and Northern Bukovina to the Soviet. Panic and romantic desire to win back the lost provinces made the Rumanians the willing helpers of Germany when she invaded Russia in 1941. At first the Rumanians were even fervent allies. Later, the deeper they were drawn into Russia, the more weary and gloomy they became, and the more resentful at the Germans' overbearing ways and their own heavy losses. But still blind fear of being swallowed up by Russia drove them on, and they fought loyally for Germany for over three years.

A good many Yugoslavs and Bulgarians who were far from Communists were rather pleased when Russia came on the scene again as an active force in 1939. After all, Russia was the great Slav power, and they themselves were Slavs. Russia might also be a counterweight to the Germans while the Western Allies were far away.

Whatever their politics—unless they were local Nazis—people in these two Slav countries followed Russian war victories with excitement. Some of this pro-Russian feeling still lived on, in a curious way, on both sides when local quarrels between pro-Communists and anti-Communists had become bitter and violent. To the end, the Yugoslav anti-Communist leader, Mihailovitch, and some members of the exiled governments of King Peter of Yugoslavia loathed Tito and the Yugoslav Communists but thought they could come to terms with the Russians. No Bulgarian government, however close to the Germans, ever dared break off diplomatic relations with Russia, right through the war.

Most Greeks felt a chill at having Slav Russia back as a power in the Balkans in 1939. Only the Greek Communists ever rejoiced sincerely over Russian war victories. By the end of the war, internal strife in Greece was so bitter and savage that thinking was hopelessly confused. For the average non-Communist Greek, the Greek Communists were all Bulgarians and the Bulgarians were bolshevik Russians and all were part of a great Slav plot to swallow Greece up in a Red Slav Empire.

The fighting ended. Russia by then dominated the Balkans militarily, except for Greece where the British had a foothold. The next question for the Balkan peoples was: could Russia now win a political victory and consolidate and make permanent the dominion she had won by military means? Could or would England and America do anything, politically, economically or otherwise, to undermine this dominion? Was the East going to win in the long struggle with the West over the Balkans?

Russia had a difficult job before her in the Balkan countries which had come under her occupation or influence in 1944. Three-quarters of the people were peasants. The industrial workers, Russia's natural allies, were few and badly organised. The peasants were mostly very poor, using primitive unproductive methods of agriculture on tiny plots of land; semi-educated or even illiterate; superstitious; obstinate; suspicious and credulous at the same time; mistrustful of authority and government as such; often with lively minds and argumentative tongues; capable of fierce loyalties in local politics and fierce national feeling; blindly individualistic and possessive.

Although the Balkan peasants are in some ways like Russian peasants or, in fact, any peasants living in backward conditions, certain of their special characteristics made them particularly thorny to handle. The long Balkan tradition of the struggle against the Turks right up till 1912, and the fact that the Balkan peasants had been smallholders owning their own scrap of land for at least one generation, usually much longer, made them more than commonly hedgehog-like.

During the war, it looked as though Russia had taken this problem into careful account, studied it and reached a sensible long-term plan for drawing the Balkan peasants into willing and productive collaboration with the industrial workers, or Communists, and for bringing them under Communist guidance though not under pure Communist rule.

There were also a few signs that Russia might have worked out similar plans for other backward peasant peoples on her borders, such as Mongolia and China.

To judge by Soviet wartime propaganda to the Balkan countries from 1942 onwards, the most important points of the Soviet plan were:

1. Peasants and workers must unite. (The local Communists must win over and co-operate with the local agrarian parties.)

2. Each country must be ruled by a coalition or front of all those parties, including 'bourgeois parties', which were not anti-Russian and were ready to co-operate with the Communists. The main base of the coalition would, however, be the 'union of peasants and workers', or of the agrarian and Communist parties.

3. There must be a new land reform. (This seems to have been a short-term vote-catching point, except for Hungary. In Rumania, Bulgaria and Yugoslavia there had already been land reforms after the first world war, and fresh division of land could not of itself produce any real economic betterment.)

4. Private property must be respected. (The peasants must not be panicked by too early collectivisation.)

5. The ruling front or coalition must make a strong national appeal. (It could call upon all those patriotic traditions which were not anti-Russian. In one or two cases, even patriotic claims embarrassing to a Communist party in a neighbouring country were permitted.)

It was of course not certain, during the war, whether Russia meant this as a long-term strategy, to hold good for the Balkan countries for ten years or a generation, or as a short-term stratagem to help the Balkan Communists seize sole power within a year or two. But it was in itself a moderate and sensible plan which took account of certain important psychological factors. For this reason it did not remain a mere paper or propaganda plan. By the end of the fighting, coalitions or 'fronts' had actually come into being in the Balkan countries with programmes which corresponded roughly with the plan's main outline.

If two more positive points were added, which in any case came in every Communist party programme—modernisation of agriculture through mechanisation, and industrialisation through electrification—the Russian plan gave hopes not only of peaceful political development but also of a steady rise in living standards in the Balkans.

There was only one condition: everyone concerned must really believe in the plan, must try sincerely to make it work, and must really believe that the other parties to the plan were also trying sincerely to make it work.

Scepticism and mistrust were the beginning of the trouble.

For example, practically no Rumanian, peasant or otherwise, believed anything the Russians said. Most thought the Russians' one idea, behind the scenes, was to ruin and swallow up Rumania. Most Rumanians mistrusted and despised their own Communists as no more than tools and agents of Moscow.

Practically no Russian believed that the big Rumanian peasant and 'bourgeois' parties meant to work sincerely with Soviet Russia or the Rumanian Communists. These parties were suspected of being hand in glove with the Anglo-Americans, of being British and American agents and spies preparing for the next war, against Russia.

Bulgarians usually had not the same suspicions about Russia as the Rumanians. But the rivalry between the Bulgarian Communist and Agrarian parties was old and very bitter. Soon each side suspected the other of plotting to seize sole power. In the usual way the Communists were mistrusted also as agents of Moscow and the Agrarians as agents of London and Washington.

There were two other big difficulties in the way of fulfilment of Russia's plan—human and economic.

Shortage of good human material to lead the Balkan Communist Parties was inevitable. For nearly a generation these parties had been suppressed and persecuted. The few leaders who had spent years in exile had lost something of the feel of their own people. Others who had spent years in prison had some hatred and thirst for revenge in their hearts, however much they might try to keep them down. There was no local network of tried and reliable party organisers throughout the Balkan countries.

In these circumstances, the outsider would have thought it would have been wise to keep each Communist Party as a small élite of carefully picked and trained men who had particularly studied the psychology and economic needs of their country and their peasants. By this means the Communists could best have fulfilled their task of guiding and providing dynamic force for the coalitions to which they belonged.

Presumably there were objections to this course, except in Yugoslavia, where it seems to have been followed. In Rumania and Bulgaria the Communist parties set out on recruiting campaigns to become big mass parties with vast voting power within a few months of their country's liberation.

This meant that opportunists, weaklings, frightened people or minor ex-fascists ran to join the Communist parties, to get an alibi and protection. They swamped the real old-time Communists and the real young idealists.

These dubious new recruits, who often started flinging their weight about to prove their new-found party zeal, were either despised or feared by the ordinary people. They discredited the work of the party leaders.

So also, in Bulgaria, did the few thousand very young and very inexperienced Communist partisans, mostly students, who when the Germans quitted Bulgaria came down from the mountains and paid off a number of personal grudges, sufferings and wrongs on policemen, local officials and villagers.

Because the Balkan Communists on the whole did not show themselves very wise, restrained or far-seeing, the whole Russian plan was badly shaken.

The economic difficulty, though not at first the sharpest, turned out the deepest of all. For if the sceptical Balkan peasants were to work in with the Russian plan, they must either get clear material benefits or at least be given good hope of them. They must get back fairly quickly their pre-war standard of living: must be able, by selling 10 kilograms of grain, to buy as many yards of cotton cloth, as much salt and paraffin, as they could in 1940. And, since their poverty even in 1940 was bad enough, they must have proof that their standard of living would soon get better. They must be made to believe that they would soon be able to grow more on their few acres and so get more money for their crops; that there would soon be new factories to turn out the cheap goods that they wanted to buy; that there would be new industries where those of their sons for whom there was no room on the land could find good jobs.

Russia and the Balkan Communists started off on the wrong foot in the economic field. Their plans were good, but circumstances were against them and the Russians seemed to go out of their way to make them worse.

In the last six years or so before the war, the Balkan peasants had found things rather easier because they had been given a safe market for their crops. Germany, for her own reasons, provided this market. Although she supplied luxury rather than essential goods in return, the peasants could at least depend on getting stable prices for their surplus produce. Even during the war, although the Germans tried their hardest to keep Balkan wheat prices down near the pre-war level, Balkan peasants still did reasonably well in terms of money. When they found there was little to buy with it, they just hoarded and hid their crops, and no one seriously interfered with them. At worst they could grow enough to feed their families.

When the Germans went and the Russians came, the peasants lost their one safe and stable market. Then they had a run of bad luck. Fighting in the Balkans upset the 1944 harvest, and two bad droughts damaged the 1945 harvest and ruined the 1946 maize crop. Maize is vital to the peasants both for their own food and as fodder for their animals. The peasants had very little surplus to sell and in bad districts had not even enough for their families. But grain was needed for the Red Army men stationed in the Balkans—in 1945 reckoned at 1,000,000 men in Rumania and 300,000 in Bulgaria. So grain was requisitioned, much more thoroughly than under the Germans. Yugoslavia though worse devastated was better off. After the first month or two she had no Red Army men, and she got help from U.N.R.R.A. But U.N.R.R.A.

help stopped at the end of 1946, and the drought hit Yugoslavia badly
too. By the beginning of 1947 peasants in the worst-hit districts of the
Balkans—particularly in the great Rumanian province of Moldavia—
were beginning to starve and famine and disease broke out. Russia, who
had suffered from an even worse drought in the Ukraine, could give no
help, and Rumania and Yugoslavia were forced to appeal to America
for grain.

As for positive progress in agriculture, a small start was made on
training 'agronomes' or agricultural experts to send to the villages, and
on forming tractor centres. But for the first two years at least Russia
could supply very few of the tractors or agricultural machines that were
needed, if only as propaganda to the peasants to convince them that
they could increase production and get rich by using modern methods.

Soviet occupation or Soviet influence did not help industry either.
Russia's first task was naturally to repair her own war-wrecked industry
and so she could do very little to help Yugoslavia's war-wrecked industry.
From the defeated Balkan countries Russia, as a conquering Power,
naturally claimed reparations and restitution of property. This meant
the removal of a good deal of industrial equipment from Rumania—
Bulgaria was more favoured and had little to remove—especially pipes
needed for drilling in the Rumanian oilfields. Further, Soviet requisitioning for Red Army needs was stretched, or so most people believed,
to requisitioning of manufactured goods such as silk stockings and
underclothes.

Russia could not supply the raw materials needed by industry. She
could only send fairly large amounts of raw cotton for manufacture in
the Balkans on condition that a proportion of the manufactured goods
was sent back to Russia in payment. But Balkan industrialists complained, rightly or wrongly, that it was poor quality cotton. Nor could
Russia replace outworn machines and equipment, nor supply the railway engines and trucks and motor lorries that were needed to get
industry on the move and distribute materials and finished goods. In
fact, the Russians were so short of transport themselves that they
requisitioned Rumanian transport and created even greater confusion
on the Rumanian railways than already existed at the end of the
fighting.

All this meant a sharp drop in production. Then again the psychological upheaval among the industrial workers, which followed Soviet
occupation and Communist labour agitation, meant that the workers
got through much less work than normally. Employers said this was
because the workers wasted so much time during working hours on
factory, union and party meetings that they had not much time or
energy left for work.

So Balkan industry, except perhaps in Yugoslavia, marked time or
even lost ground. For the first two years or more, it was no good
thinking of expansion of industry. The new governments could only

sketch out their big industrialisation plans on paper. Bulgaria launched a particularly ambitious long-term electrification scheme in the summer of 1946. Russia was to supply dynamos and equipment on a large scale to get things going. One symbolic power-plant, rumoured to be of American origin, arrived in Sofia. Apart from that the whole scheme seemed more in the clouds than on the hard earth, and few Bulgarians at that time believed it would ever come true. Bulgarian, Rumanian and Yugoslav experts got together at intervals to work out big joint Balkan electrification schemes, particularly for harnessing the water power at the Iron Gates on the Danube. But this again seemed then a beautiful dream: there was no money or machinery or equipment.

The hard fact was that war-stricken Russia, with her own immense tasks and needs, simply could not bring quick prosperity or even convincing promise of it to the Balkan countries, so as to make the new governments popular and solid during the first trial years. The Russians could not even make up their own minds whether to take what they themselves needed economically from the defeated Balkan countries, at the cost of unpopularity, or to forego their own economic wants in order to win political popularity and stability. To most people in the Balkans, it seemed that Russia took more than she gave, and that for their countries to be tied to Russia simply meant that they would get poorer and poorer—and they were poor enough at the start. They had so little faith that they irrationally blamed the Russians and their own Communists even for those difficulties that were really caused by the war and the droughts.

Another foolish but curiously strong reason why people in the Balkans had small faith in the Russians was that they could never forget the way the Red Army behaved in the first weeks or months in the Balkans. When the Red Army men came, worn by long months of fighting from Stalingrad westwards, they behaved like conquerors in small unimportant enemy countries. There was the childish if brutal bout of looting, raping and drunkenness, though far less in Bulgaria than Rumania, and very little in Yugoslavia. The Russian soldiers wanted watches, clocks, overcoats and women, and took them. Very soon in Bulgaria, some months later in Rumania, discipline tightened up. It became very good in Bulgaria, patchy but fair in Rumania. But people never forgot the early impressions and the fear, contempt and hatred for the Russians which then filled them. They soon started making jokes in pidgin-Russian—'Davai chas' and 'Davai palto', 'Give me your watch', 'Give me your coat'—but they were bitter nervous jokes.

What made things worse was that people found out that the simple Russian soldier had, according to superficial Balkan standards, an even lower level of 'culture' than the average Balkan peasant. That is, the Russian knew less about how to use a knife and fork or how to behave about the house. German soldiers in the Balkans had usually been remarkably clean and tidy and well-behaved about the house, with an obviously higher level of 'culture' than the Balkan average. The contrast was too much. So there was contempt and bitter resentment that men so 'uncultured' as the Russians should dare to lord it in the Balkans. Minor misdeeds that would probably have been tolerated or even laughingly admired in rich and sophisticated American soldiers were intolerable in the Russians.

One definite advantage the Russians did bring to the Balkans, though it usually passed unnoticed. This was relative freedom from inter-Balkan squabbling and strife within the Soviet sphere. (Greece, being outside the sphere, became the chief remaining legitimate target of hatred.)

It was treason in Bulgaria to criticise the settlement that restored Macedonia to Yugoslavia. It was treason in Albania to claim the Albanian-populated districts of Yugoslavia that had temporarily been joined to Albania during the war. Good relations between the new Balkan governments were religiously and actively fostered. Youth delegations, groups of journalists, women's delegations, sports teams, were always exchanging visits. Cultural associations linking up the Balkan countries were founded and long and learned speeches were made by bearded Balkan professors and writers, often under the approving eye of a distinguished Russian guest. Later, in 1947, a network of inter-Balkan pacts was woven under Soviet inspiration.

All this was genuine progress. But the common scepticism about anything run by the Russians or the communists cast a blight. People felt there was something artificial about it all. If the Rumanian Prime Minister, Petru Grozea, said that the Rumanians and Hungarians of Transylvania must live together like brothers, the average Rumanian would say to himself: 'Grozea is a fool. Therefore what he says is nonsense. Perhaps there is a trick behind it too. Probably the Hungarians are getting at us. We must look out and see that they don't do us down.' So people in the Balkans were not grateful to the Russians or their own Communists for trying to put a stop to quarrels among Balkan neighbours.

Many things, psychological, political and economic, particularly their own impatience, inexperience and suspiciousness, were against the Russians from the start. On their side they had military strength, an ideology which appealed at least to the small class of industrial workers, tenacity and stubbornness and perhaps a certain rough muddled good will and wish to help the Balkans—in the long run. Also in the long run, these things may be enough to make the Balkan peoples willing inhabitants of the Soviet sphere.

For the British and Americans, trying to stop the Soviet door closing on the Balkan countries, the task was simple. They were hopelessly weak in practical power to do anything; but they were strong through the mistakes and unpopularity of the Russians. They did not need to be constructive, but only to point out Russian or Communist blunders, whether through diplomatic notes or the press or more informal means.

The British and American Missions in the Balkan capitals found their impotence to influence the Russians or the new governments humiliating and frustrating. But just by existing, these missions were proof enough that Britain and the United States had not entirely handed over the Balkans to Russia and still had some interest in them. Even if their rôle was mainly symbolic and almost entirely negative, it was important.

They only needed to give a bare minimum of encouragement to the opposition groups in the Balkan countries. It would only have been foolish to dabble with underground organisations and clandestine plots, as they were often accused of doing.

Their favourite form of self-assertion, which was often criticised as futile but which did weaken the prestige of the pro-Soviet governments and send up the stock of the pro-Anglo-American oppositions, was to keep up a steady drip-drop of acid diplomatic notes complaining of the failure of the new régimes to be truly democratic or to hold truly free elections. As part of this policy, recognition of the Rumanian government was withheld until February, 1946, and then conceded grudgingly, with conditions attached. Britain withheld recognition of the Bulgarian government until after the peace treaty was signed in February, 1947, and the United States held out even longer.

To many outsiders, this stalling policy seemed pointless, foolish and possibly harmful. These people said that in practical terms it achieved nothing, but only irritated Russia and made her still more suspicious of the sinister aims of the 'Anglo-American imperialists'. It also goaded and frightened the new Balkan governments and made them even more suspicious and intolerant of the opposition movements, without softening their internal policies. Most dangerous of all, these people said, it made the oppositions stubborn and exacting where they should have been reasonable and realistic. It tended inevitably to compromise the opposition leaders and made it easier for their enemies to label them agents of Anglo-American capitalism.

Incidentally, it was also unfortunate that the British and American Missions mixed socially with certain small Balkan cliques which could hardly be called democratic and could more justifiably be called reactionary and which in some cases had mixed with the Germans during the war.

All these things were true. On the other hand, the foot-in-the-door policy of Britain and the United States did for a time keep alive, though sometimes in strange forms, the old liberal ideas of individual rights and freedoms and of the right of political opposition to any government in power. It delayed the total imposition of one-party rule and political and intellectual uniformity. From the point of view of the Balkan peoples, it could be argued that at that moment of their history the delay conferred few concrete benefits, and only held up economic reorganisation and progress. But from the point of view of British and American interest in combating Soviet influence, Anglo-American policy in the years 1944 to 1947 did at least for a time prevent Soviet Russia from establishing a complete monopoly of power in the Balkans.

In British-occupied Greece there was much the same situation in reverse, with some big differences. Soviet Russia, or her Greek friends, were even more, far more, successful in stopping the consolidation of a pro-British régime. On her side, Britain, in spite of all the money and men she poured into Greece, had very little that was concrete or solid to show at the end of two and a half years. Nevertheless, or perhaps for that very reason, the British managed to keep the tolerance or even affection of a much bigger proportion of Greeks than the Russians did among the peoples of the countries they occupied. Amiable inefficiency is a relatively endearing quality.

There were several reasons why after two and a half years of occupation the Soviet-occupied countries had got much further on the way of economic reconstruction, financial stability and political consolidation —in spite of the unpopularity of the pro-Soviet governments—than Greece.

One was that up to a certain point the new pro-Soviet governments could, by harsh methods at home and by using the Red Army as a bogey, enforce at least a grudging discipline. The centre or right-wing governments in Greece were weak, wavering and often corrupt, and though spasmodically harsh to their political enemies, they could never inspire or impose any sort of discipline, political or economic.

As for reconstruction, both the Greeks as individuals and also successive Greek governments merely folded their hands and waited for the rich British and Americans to pay their immeasurable moral debt to Greece and do everything for them. If they were criticised, they could always say that internal strife and threats from over the northern frontiers made things too tense for anyone to be interested in reconstruction. The pro-Soviet governments knew, or soon learnt, that in the early years after the war they could expect very little help from war-ravaged Russia: they had got to work their own way. The Greeks behaved like be-medalled war pensioners or remittance men, the pro-Soviet governments like eager novices anxious to appease a stern Mother Superior.

Finally, the friends of Soviet Russia in Greece, the Communists and their political allies, were by the nature of their political beliefs far better organised, far more ruthless and far more ready to push things to extremes, even to civil war, than were the friends of Britain and America in the countries of the Soviet zone. And no Greek Communist was ultimately afraid either of the British or of the various Greek governments, although he might face imprisonment, deportation, or, in rarer cases, execution; but the opposition in the Soviet-zone countries were truly afraid of the Russians and the pro-Soviet governments.

Politically, the British failed in Greece because they interfered in Greek politics either too little or too much; too little to be able to impose the kind of government they themselves wanted, a moderate liberal government of the centre; too much to be able to wash their hands of responsibility for the stupidities and outbursts of brutality of the right-wing royalist governments. However, even if the British had succeeded in keeping in power and consistently backing up a centre government, it is very doubtful whether such a government would ever, by its very nature, have been able to impose itself upon both Right and Left extremes. Even in this case, Britain would probably have failed to achieve real political stability or real consolidation of British influence in this important outpost of the Balkans.

When in the summer of 1947 the Americans took over Greece from the British, they had no more success.

There was another tiny area which was a doorway into the Balkans and a disputed borderland between East and West. This was Trieste, claimed by an 'Eastern' Balkan country, Marshal Tito's Yugoslavia, but occupied jointly for over two years by the British and Americans. Towards the end of the war, Trieste had become one of the most sensitive points of conflict between East and West. This was the reason for the undignified race at the end of the war, between Marshal Tito's IX Corps and General Freyburg's New Zealanders, to get into Trieste first. The Yugoslavs just won the race; but the British, bringing up diplomatic heavy guns, forced them to withdraw after forty-five days.

This did not settle the question. The fate of Trieste still had to be decided in the peace treaty. So for the following years the British and Americans had the joint task of stopping Yugoslav economic and political penetration of Trieste, and even sometimes, or so they imagined, of preventing Yugoslav military invasion.

In practical things, the British-American occupation of Trieste was more successful than the British occupation of Greece. This was partly because the Triestini by temperament dislike work rather less then the Greeks, partly because the British and Americans ruled the area directly, not through a local government. And whatever their natural prejudices and cumulative resentments against the Communists and the Slavs, the British and Americans did usually make a valiant if not very successful effort to be impartial administrators and trustees rather than political partisans.

All the same, the inner conflict between Eastern and Western political ideas and methods developed in Trieste in an intensive way. It was like a tiny political hothouse where exotic miniature plants sprouted and shot up. Or it was like a test-tube in which political germs, Communist, Liberal and reactionary, and racial germs, Slav and Latin, multiplied and fought each other with speed and violence.

Usually it seemed that the Eastern germs were the more potent, the more likely to kill off their enemies, the rather weakly Western germs.

But in spite of this inner political struggle, there was a certain sophisticated detachment and fatalism about many Triestini, both before and after the plan for a Trieste Free State was agreed. When the plan came, it seemed on the outside a compromise between the East and the West, who were to be joint guardians of this doorway into the Balkans. But the Triestini believed that the struggle for power would still go on in the Free State. In the end one side or the other would get the upper hand. Trieste would sooner or later become either a Western or an Eastern outpost and stronghold on the edge of the Balkans.

There were four ways of looking at the whole struggle between East and West over and inside the Balkans, according to your convictions or prejudices.

There was the lofty way. You could see it as a struggle between two rival ways of thought or ideologies; between Anglo-Saxon Liberalism and individualism, with their political virtues and inadequate and out-worn economic methods, and Soviet Socialism, with its logical but ruthless political methods and its forceful drive towards a defined social and economic goal. You could hope that, for the sake of the Balkan peoples, the two would in the end blend together like well-mixed oil and vinegar.

There was the Anglo-Saxon way. You could see it as a struggle between enlightened and progressive Western Liberalism and essentially backward, totalitarian, non-Socialist Soviet imperialism. In this case you could only hope progress would win.

There was the way of the Russians, the Communists and their friends. You could see it as a struggle between the new enlightened, truly progressive Eastern democracy and the exhausted, vicious, capitalist, imperialist pseudo-democracy of the Anglo-Saxons. Here again you could only hope that progress would win.

Last, there was the frankly cynical way. You could see it as a shoving-match between two rival imperialisms, Anglo-Saxon and Soviet, both in their own ways hypocritical, striving by methods which were superficially but not fundamentally different for mastery of areas which they thought strategically or politically important to their rival systems. Here you could only hope that after a lot of undignified scrambling and pushing the two imperialisms would reach some sort of lasting balance.

Then perhaps the Balkan peasant could forget the higher politics, except over an evening drink in the village pub, and like Candide could start cultivating his garden.

2

Turkish Sidelights: August, 1945

'IF the Russians try to force themselves upon us two million Turkish bayonets will leap out to meet them. Even if it is suicide we Turks will fight. Of course, we shall do our utmost to bring England and America in on our side in the first few days.'

It was a Member of the Turkish National Assembly for a district of south-west Turkey who was talking. He was lying on his back in the sand on the shore of the Sea of Marmora. It was a slightly sordid and overcrowded smart bathing-place for the well-off people of Istanbul. The Member, who had just been rollicking heavily in the choppy little waves, now had a small mountain of burning sand heaped on his comfortably curving stomach. He said it was to save him from sunburn. He had the strong high cheekbones and narrow merry eyes of a peasant and the good-tempered sly grin of a well-fed schoolboy.

'We cannot trust Russia. She has always wanted the Straits, even in Tsarist times, particularly in the nineteenth century. Now she says she wants to join in the defence of the Straits. That means she wants Russian garrisons in Istanbul, wants control of our fortifications on the Bosphorus and the Dardanelles. England in the past has always thwarted Russia's designs. That is why you fought the Crimean War. The Straits are strategically essential to the British Empire. That is why you will fight beside us in the next war. Nothing ever changes. Is not Turkey your most loyal ally? You cannot afford to desert us.'

'You may say that you do not want to fight, that England is tired out and weakened by the last war, that no one in England is ready for another war. That is stupid. Russia has been much more weakened than you. You should fight now, quickly, before Russia has time to recover. It will be much harder for you later on.

'Anyhow, we shall fight. All of us. I believe that some not very reliable or respectable persons have been trying to get at you in Istanbul. They may have talked about a fifth column. Don't believe what they say if they tell you that there are men in Turkey who would side with Russia if she attacked. Maybe there are a few traitors, but they are not real Turks. They are of Jewish origin or Greeks or Armenians. They do not count. They are powerless. Every real Turk, all our millions of

peasants in Anatolia, which is the real Turkey, are solidly together and
will stand firm against Russia.'

Anatolia: it seemed strange to think that anyone would want to fight
for any land so bare and naked, so inhuman and lifeless and unfriendly.
Or so it had looked from the aircraft flying over Turkey's southern
coast, northwards over worn mountains of rock, thinly scattered with a
little burnt soil, to Ankara, and then bumping westwards over the stony
ridges of the plateau. It was only quite close to Istanbul that there were
the first clumps of trees, the first greenish or yellowish patches showing
that there were real live growing things. But for most of the way you
wondered who had ever made or who would ever use the aimless-looking
winding tracks that twisted around the folds of the mountains and
ridges. They seemed to come from nowhere and go nowhere. Perhaps
the villages just melted into the dry brown rock; there were hardly any
to be seen from the aircraft. There was hardly any sign of life.

Still, if the Member said the peasants of Anatolia wanted to fight for
Turkey, he should know best. Certainly anyone who managed to scrape
a living off that rock must be as tough and wiry and undemanding
as a goat.

The Member was still talking. 'The Russians have no right at all to
ask for our north-eastern provinces of Kars and Ardahan. Why should
they join them to their Armenian Soviet Republic? There are no
Armenians in those provinces, or anyhow not since the 1918 war. I
cannot tell you where the Armenians are now. But certainly not up
there.

'If the Russians try to attack over that frontier they will have a hard
time. It is very bare difficult country. None of our people will give them
food or shelter. They will get held up, they will have to go very slowly.
That will give you British time to come to help us. Then everything will
be all right.

'Of course the Bulgarian frontier is not far from Istanbul. That can
be dangerous. The Russians can attack from there. But we have built
defences in depth, during the war. But you must not talk about those.

'The great thing for you to remember is that we Turks are very brave
and very good soldiers.'

A rather shy Turkish schoolboy wandered up treading gingerly on
the burning sand. The Member reared himself up and loped off to cool
himself in the sparkling glassy blue sea.

'I would like to be a pilot,' the schoolboy said. 'We have some of
your British planes, some Hurricanes, I think. Our pilots like them. But
the story is that they are not allowed to take up parachutes with them
any longer. They have been baling out when it was not necessary. Too
many planes were lost.'

After a little the Member came back, freshened and merry. 'Let us
stop talking about serious things. It is not suitable. Next May you must
go to Izmir, to Smyrna, to see one of our camel-fights. It is a great thing

only known in Turkey. There is a big sort of grass amphitheatre in the hillside, and two male camels are let into the open space—you know it is the mating season, so they are very fierce and very lively—and they fight each other with their legs, like boxing. They would like to bite but they are not allowed to. In the end one camel gets the other down on the ground, and then the winning camel suddenly produces what is like a fifth leg from his chest and starts beating the other with this fifth leg very savagely. But then the keepers come and drag the winner off before he has time to kill the beaten camel. You would like it. Turkey is full of strange and beautiful things.'

Three Turkish soldiers got on the little Bosphorus steamboat that was tethered below the big bridge that spans the thick and murky water of the Golden Horn. They looked very young, bewildered and startled, with eyes that stared but did not seem to understand things. They seemed a little like shaggy wild animals which had only lately been caught but not yet tamed; their spirits were partly broken but their temper was still uncertain.

They had the usual bright, shiny brown eyes, ruddy cheeks and rough brown hair of the country-bred Turk. Their uniforms were of crumpled, worn, shoddy greyish-green cotton. No one could possibly say they were smart. They were unbelievably shabby.

One had obviously been giving himself an extraordinary treat. He had bought himself a small bright pink comb, and a tiny tarnished pocket mirror, the sort of thing cheapjacks sold from trays in the poorer streets. He was staring at himself in the mirror—whenever he could manage to hold it at the right angle—in a blank surprised way as though he had never seen himself before and hardly recognised himself. Then he and his two friends would suddenly burst into a wild peal of laughter. Later he started trying to run the comb hesitatingly through his hair, rather as though it might hurt. But he seemed to like to look at the pretty pink thing better.

According to the old wives' tales floating about Istanbul, it was dangerous for a girl, or two girls, to go alone for a walk along the hills above the Bosphorus, because they were heavily guarded and she or they were bound to be set upon and raped by mobs of primitive and savage Turkish soldiers. According to some accounts, it was not so safe for young men either. Actual instances could seldom be quoted: even if they could have been, this would not have made the Bosphorus hills so very different from the woods around Aldershot and Farnham.

But it certainly looked as though the ordinary Turkish soldier, if not savage, was primitive.

One intelligent elderly Turk said: 'The Army is doing a very great

thing for our peasants. Not that it teaches them to fight, but that it
teaches them to read. In spite of the big progressive educational schemes
under the rule of Kemal Ataturk after Turkey became a Republic,
it is still so difficult to get enough teachers to go to the villages
that there are still millions of peasants who cannot read or write.
You will find men who still use notched sticks to count and reckon
with.

'When the Army calls up the peasants for their term of military
service, it opens a new world for them. It gives them a basic education,
teaching them to read and write and do simple arithmetic and know
something about Turkish history. Then it gets a peasant out of his own
village, where otherwise he might spend his whole life knowing nothing
of the rest of Turkey, and takes him to towns and cities and other
districts of Turkey. It breaks down the old narrow regionalism and
broadens his mind.'

At an elegant garden-party in Istanbul a British major, one of the
instructors or advisers who were teaching the Turkish Army how to use
British arms and equipment, said: 'They're fine chaps, tough all right,
may be brave. But my God are they ignorant and uneducated. Try to
teach them how a modern weapon works—it's no joke. Think how few
have ever seen the inside of a motor car. Even those that have had
anything to do with motors know very little about them. The usual
Turkish habit, if a piece of machinery goes wrong, is not to repair but
to scrap. They don't seem to have the feel.'

A charming-looking and intelligent Turkish girl of about twenty-two,
very sunburnt, with slim brown legs and arms, wearing a well-cut white
frock and high-heeled white shoes, pointed out a drab bundled-up
figure of a woman—obviously a peasant woman who had come to visit
the cheap Istanbul shops near the bazaars. She was swathed and looped
around in a sort of sack of dull black cotton and unlike most Istanbul
women had a fold of black stuff across her nose and mouth.

The girl said: 'You see her? That is the reason why I could never go
and live in a village. And that is the reason why I could never become a
teacher, or a doctor, although I once thought I would.

'I went to the American school here. That is supposed to be the best
education, except perhaps for the French school. Then I went to
Istanbul University. I studied literature and history. I thought I might
become a teacher. I like children.

'But everyone who becomes a teacher is compelled by the government
to go and work for two years in a village, probably somewhere in the
middle of Anatolia. They are quite right, really. How else will they ever
get schools going in every village and teach the peasant children to read
and write? Still, I could not face it. I may be a coward. I could not stand
life in a village. I could never wear a dress like this. I should always have

to keep my neck and arms covered up, even in the hottest weather. I could never go with bare legs as I do here. I could never sit in a café. I could never be seen walking down the street with a man. If I did any of these things, the village women who are very ignorant and very religious would say terrible things about me, perhaps do terrible things to me. I should be frightened. And there would be nobody for me to talk to or to make friends with, only the village women, and they are centuries away from me.

'It is no good, I could not do it. The gulf between a city like Istanbul and our villages is still too enormous. It takes too much courage to try to get across it. It was the same for a friend of mine who wanted to be a doctor. He could not face it either.

'That is why I am working as a secretary in a business office here in Istanbul. But that does not satisfy me. I want to go abroad and learn methods of teaching and child welfare. Then I might one day be able to start a nursery school of my own here in Istanbul. It would be something new. But never among our peasants.'

There had for several years been a movement among the younger Turkish intellectuals and university students to go and live among the peasants, study their way of life, and teach among them. Their aim was partly sociological, partly patriotic—to unite the Turkish nation more solidly by bridging the gap between the peasants and the educated classes. The peasants were said to number about 14,000,000 out of Turkey's population of 18,000,000, so the job was an important one. But the movement was still small, and, it seemed, rather superficial. The main problem remained. According to the 1935 Census only 23.3 per cent. of the male population and 8.2 per cent. of the female population could read or write. The situation had probably not changed much since then.

A gradual process of land reform was introduced in the summer of 1945. Before this, nearly two-thirds of the peasants were already small-holders living in close contact with the markets where they sold their produce. According to one estimate, about one-eighth were 'feudal peasants' living in a state of semi-serfdom under feudal lords or chief-tains in the particularly backward eastern provinces. In south-western Turkey in the districts of Antalya and Adana there was also a special class of share-croppers, working in conditions rather like those in certain of the southern states of the U.S.A.

The land reform was so moderate and gradual that it was not likely to produce any sudden or sweeping changes in the lives of these millions of peasants. For years they would still be cut off intellectually, socially and economically from the ruling class of bureaucrats, officers and business men.

But the peasants, thinly scattered over the bare wastes of Anatolia, did not seem likely material for revolution. Still, especially since the end of the war, there had been growing economic discontent, caused mainly by the muddled price policies and administrative inefficiency of the bureaucrats. With it had gone growing interest in politics. But if things developed quietly, it looked as though it would be a good many years before the peasants would, as an organised political force, represent their own interests in Turkish politics.

A young Turkish intellectual who had studied in Western Europe said: 'You want to know whether outside pressure from Russia speeds up or paralyses the development of our internal political life. I think it paralyses it. As long as Russia threatens, we must all stand together very closely. We must not let any foreigner see that there are any serious differences among us. Everybody sensible, including members of the government, including the President himself, knows that we must sooner or later have a real proper political opposition and real independent political parties. The Republican People's Party cannot go on ruling the country as a monopoly party for ever.

'Everyone knows that Kemal Ataturk himself wanted an Opposition and tried to start one up, but everyone was too nervous and frightened to be really independent, and he gave up the idea in 1930. Then during the war there was a kind of small unofficial opposition group inside the Republican People's Party. Now that the war is ended everyone, probably from President Inönü himself downwards, knows that some time Celal Bayar or Raouf Orbay will start up a moderate liberal opposition party, and maybe there will be other smaller parties too, though Turkey is not really ripe yet for class parties properly speaking.

'But they have to be very careful about it and go very slowly before they do anything because of the Russians. We mustn't let there be any split among us, we must not weaken ourselves in the face of the Russians or in the eyes of the world.

'That is why probably anyone who is ready to lead an opposition party—and nobody is very eager at the moment—will discuss things with the President before he takes any definite step, and may even try to get the agreement of the Republican People's Party too. Or anyhow of the more liberal and sensible wing of the Republican People's Party— some of them, I must admit, are very stubborn and rather stupid.

'This may seem funny to you, but you must remember three things. First that Kemal is still the great hero and saviour of Turkey for every Turk. Second, that our present President, Inönü, was Kemal's long friend and collaborator, that he is Kemal's successor, and that people look on him with some of the same reverence that they have for Kemal's memory. Third, that Inönü is not only President of the Turkish Republic but also President of the Republican People's Party, and as long as he is party leader some of his special glory falls upon the party. So simple or narrow people are still apt to feel that it is national treason to go against the Party, because the Party was Kemal's creation and Inönü is its head.

'But all this would ease up and develop much more quickly and naturally if it wasn't for the Russians.

'I will tell you a great secret. When I was very young, I used to sympathise with Communism myself. It is not a thing one likes to admit openly nowadays. But I wanted social justice and economic progress and I found great attraction in Communist ideas. I suppose I was foolish and idealistic.

'But now, though I have not lost all my ideals, I have been changed. I will tell you why. I found out that Communism is always anti-national; it is not only against Turkish national feelings but against all true national feelings everywhere—except possibly in Russia. You cannot be a Communist without being forced to betray your own nation. Although I may sometimes long to live abroad, to breathe freer air, I find I have very deep feelings for Turkey. It is my country and my nation, and even if I am critical and find some things terribly narrow, I could not bear to be disloyal. I shall always stand by my own people. By the way, I am a reserve officer, of course.

'Whether, supposing the Russian question is ever settled, we shall really be able to change and improve things here for ourselves, God only knows. We are ruled by a bureaucracy, and the bureaucracy is very strong, very firmly dug in, very stubborn, sometimes very stupid. Everything moves very slowly, sometimes it seems to move backwards. Sometimes I get depressed and cynical myself. There are still so few of us who are really educated. But I believe in the Turkish nation and I believe it will come out right in the end.

'Meanwhile our national duty is to stand fast against Russia. That is why the Turkish journalist and writer whom I like best and read most at the moment is Yalchin. You think he is terribly anti-Russian and reactionary. But he pulls the Turkish people together, he stops them getting muddled and going astray, all that he writes represents the true spirit of Turkey. You will find everyone says the same. In his way he is the most popular man in Turkey to-day.'

Huseyin Cahit Yalchin at that time wrote almost daily leaders in two Istanbul newspapers. They were fiery rhetoric, passionate polemics of a rather nineteenth century type. During the war all his polemising had been against Germany: apparently, in spite of Turkey's strict neutrality up till the very last months of the war, he had been given a free hand. Towards the end of the war an anti-Russian note started creeping in too. After Russia had formally demanded radical revision of the Soviet-Turkish Pact in March, 1945, and had started up a propaganda campaign against Turkey in April, Yalchin gleefully took off his gloves and got down to it. When, the same spring, it was reported that Russia wanted bilateral revision of the 1936 Montreux Convention regulating the Straits, a Soviet share in the defence of the Straits, presumably the posting of Red Army garrisons in the Istanbul area, and that Russia had even claimed the formerly Armenian-inhabited provinces of Kars and Ardahan, Yalchin was really in his element.

Nearly every article of his, and they came tumbling out in amazing profusion, was a strongly-flavoured, highly-coloured attack on 'Red Fascism' and Soviet imperialism. There was nothing to choose between German Nazism and Russian Communism, according to Yalchin. He also ran special lines in internal dissensions and weaknesses inside the U.S.S.R., and in Russian-imposed totalitarianism and terrorism in the Balkan countries inside the Soviet zone. No holds were barred, for Yalchin.

It was not really surprising that he quickly became the chief target for Soviet propaganda attacks against Turkey. He became Turkey's warmonger, well-poisoner and reactionary number one in Russian press and radio commentaries. He was for the Russians the forerunner of Churchill as Churchill became after the Fulton speech, a particular enemy of Soviet Russia.

While he may, as his very many Turkish admirers claimed, have stiffened Turkish morale in the face of an unrelenting Soviet nerve war, he must also have infuriated the Russians and greatly sharpened their suspicions of Turkey. Anyone would have deduced from Yalchin's articles that Turkey only wanted to be an Anglo-American base of operations in an imminent war against Russia—and, in the meantime, a base of political operations against the Soviet-controlled Balkan countries.

You would also have guessed, from reading his articles, that Yalchin must be a fiery, explosive and fanatical man; intensely narrow-minded and aggressive; a burning-eyed modern leader of a new holy war against the infidel, this time the Russian Communist infidel.

In real life he seemed very different.

An old acquaintance of his said: 'You do not really understand Yalchin. He is above all a writer: he adores writing. He finds that he can write most fluently and in the most lofty style if he is writing polemics. Polemics also provide him with the psychological stimulus he needs for his very prolific literary creation. So all his life he has been writing polemics. Of course, he is perfectly sincere in what he says about Russia; but in character he is really a very gentle, retiring man. You must not take a superficial view and imagine that Yalchin—or the Turks in general—are very warlike and aggressive and impulsive. They are prudent, cautious and reserved. Otherwise they would probably never have survived as a nation.'

Yalchin lived in a modest, rather dilapidated villa in one of the more fashionable outskirts of Istanbul. On the other side of the road was a piece of rough wasteland where a few goats were nibbling dry wiry grass in the light of a violent orange sunset. The stony path leading to the villa led through rough grass among unkempt fruit trees.

Yalchin's small study gave an impression of North Oxford Gothic. There was crimson and purple stained glass and a lot of heavily carved blackish wood, a big desk, books on all the walls. Yalchin himself was the type of the vague absent-minded professor. He seemed to belong to the Lewis Carroll period, a mild, remote, scholarly man.

He talked for a little in a melancholy way about Russia. There was none of the bombast and offensiveness of his articles. He became more violent when he went on to the Balkans.

'You are really going to the Balkans? You are very brave. Things are very disordered, even dangerous, there, I hear. These new Communist governments work through terrorism and violence. They have their secret police, modelled on the G.P.U. And behind them, watching everything and controlling everything, are the Russians.'

(Turkey had at that time one of the strictest, most complete and most irritating systems of police control, particularly of foreigners and of those Turks who mixed with foreigners, of any European or semi-European country, except probably Soviet Russia and Yugoslavia. Special permits were needed for foreigners to travel outside the very few cities; certain frontier areas were banned. But it did not seem a good idea to point that out.)

Yalchin went on: 'These new Balkan governments are in fact entirely Fascist in their methods. It is the new Fascism. Look at Tito, a typical Fascist leader. But the new Balkan Fascism is not efficient yet. There is a great deal of unrest and opposition, of hatred. There will be great trouble, perhaps revolt. The tension is increasing every day. And Britain and America are not going to stand aside. See what they have done. They have sent notes over the Bulgarian elections, pointing out that they could not be free and fair in present conditions, and they have succeeded: the elections have been put off at the eleventh hour.

'That is only a beginning. The Opposition has taken courage and will get stronger now that they see they are not alone. If Britain and America stand firm, it will not be possible to establish the Red Fascism in the Balkans.'

Two big happenings had just then made Istanbul buoyantly optimistic about an early Russian diplomatic and political withdrawal from the Balkans. These were Mr. Bevin and the atom bomb.

Mr. Bevin's first policy speech as Foreign Secretary in the British Labour Government delighted almost every Turk and certainly every Balkan *emigré* living in Istanbul. It was tougher and blunter than anything Eden had ever said. It was taken to mean that the Labour Government was not going to pander to Russia, as the Turks had feared, but was going to stand up more firmly than the Churchill Government had ever done, even perhaps at the risk of war.

Almost at the same time as Bevin came President Truman's revelation of the atom bomb. This was even better, the Turks thought. It was first and foremost a terrific diplomatic weapon for the Anglo-Americans to use as blackmail against Russia, to force her, among other things, to withdraw peaceably from the Balkans. Then, if war should after all be necessary, the atom bomb would make it a quick easy war, painless for everyone except the Russians—and perhaps a 'Red' Balkan capital or two, which might be useful as a testing-ground.

(These same two factors, Bevin and the bomb, had, it turned out later, a powerful and lasting effect in the Balkans as well as Turkey, producing an excitable and imaginative war mentality and a blank refusal to accept the *status quo* as lasting. This war fever and uncertainty made it particularly difficult for the Russians to consolidate their Balkan zone politically.)

The Turks, in spite of their heroic and suicidal attitudes, naturally did not want to have the next war fought on Turkish soil if they could help it. That was why the atom bomb did a lot to ease the tension of the last five years. During the past war they had stood up to fairly strong pressure from the big three to join in at a time when Turkey might perhaps have suffered invasion and air bombing. They waited until there was no longer danger of the Germans and Bulgarians marching on Istanbul and blasting and burning the city, with its thousands of flimsy old wooden houses, from the air. Turkey's rulers had very carefully preserved Turkey materially intact, even enriched.

Discreet Turkish two-way blackmail during the war had made both Germany and the Western Powers eager to buy up Turkey's goods at higher and higher and more and more uneconomic prices. At the end of the war, this process left Turkey with an artificially high price level which caused hardship and discontent at home among those who worked for fixed wages or salaries, and made it difficult to sell Turkish exports to countries which were no longer able or willing to pay exaggerated wartime prices. But apart from this awkward price situation, no one—except the Turks themselves—could say that Turkey had really suffered from the war. The Turks, of course, who knew little of devastated Europe, felt sincerely that they had made great sacrifices and suffered greatly in the Allied cause.

They felt that they had every right to rejoice, as much as any Allied nation, in victory, even the victory over Japan. On VJ Day all Istanbul was gloriously red, red with great fluttering sun-filled Turkish flags, on which the small Turkish sickle moon and star looked deceptively like the Soviet sickle and hammer. The big military parade, to celebrate Turkey's independence anniversary a few days later, was particularly solemn and festive; the young Republic, placed in such an important and tricky geographical position, had passed through great dangers, run great risks and had been saved—at least for the time being. Or as the cynical outsider would have put it: 'Let us rejoice: for Turkey backed the winning side after all, and just in time, too, to put herself in a strong position and give herself plenty of moral credit for use in the next round.'

Anyhow, in the powerful clear midday sun the military bands clanged and clashed (the Turks do not seem to be naturally musical), the cavalry, looking surprisingly smart, clop-clopped, and the mechanised infantry clattered cumbrously past the gay and many-coloured zinnias and dahlias of the Taksim Gardens, and past the grandstand where high officials of the Republic took the salute with becoming dignity in spite of the heat. On the pavements the crowds of sunburnt, muscular, voluble Turks, mostly men, filled with curiosity rather than enthusiasm, shoved, elbowed, jabbed and jostled violently but without malice, as Turkish crowds always do. The police kept them firmly in check.

Order was complete. Nothing indecorous, obviously, must mar this festival of the Republic. The Republic had been born from war and bloodshed. It had been the work of a violent, moody, imaginative and creative man, Kemal Ataturk. It had been the expression of a great national and social revolutionary movement, seeking to destroy the remnants of an outworn and rotten Empire, Caliphate and Sultanate. Like Soviet Russia it had tried to rebuild economically through the rapid industrialisation of a backward agricultural country and the rapid education of the backward peasant masses. After a quarter of a century, the Republic seemed to have stiffened and hardened, even mummified, until it had become the most anti-revolutionary, rigid and conservative of political structures.

In every public office or fly-blown café, two portraits hung side by side: Kemal Ataturk, who died in 1938, and his successor, Ismet Inönü. They were a great contrast. Kemal looked forceful and turbulent, with his bushy brows, deep-sunk eyes, prominent lower lip and jutting chin. Ismet Inönü, Turkey's second President, appeared to have small, correct, precise features—the face, an outsider would have guessed, of a timid but stubborn civil servant.

The spirit of Inönü rather than the spirit of Kemal seemed to be presiding over the big parade of August, 1945.

3

Bulgaria's Fatherland Front

A FEW days later Turkey's Balkan neighbour, Bulgaria, celebrated a big national day with a big parade, in the capital, Sofia. It was the day of a much newer revolution, which was not yet complete, in a State which was still formally a monarchy and was not to become a 'People's Republic' until a year later.

It was September 9th, 1945, first anniversary of the day when, with Russian troops already advancing into Bulgaria, the 'Fatherland Front', a group of mainly pro-Soviet politicians, seized power from a pro-Western government, which during its very few days of office had taken the first steps to break with Germany.

After one year of rule the Fatherland Front government, such as it had survived, could look back with satisfaction on the part the Bulgarian Army, after the switch-over, had taken in fighting the Germans in Yugoslavia and Hungary, even Austria. That was the Front's big achievement; every Bulgarian hoped it would redeem Bulgaria's reputation in the eyes of the Allies and get Bulgaria good treatment at the peace conference. At home, however, things had not gone so well during the year: the Front had already split and the chief leaders of the Agrarian and Social Democratic parties had left the government a month or two earlier. Already there was an Opposition.

On the eve of the anniversary, a solemn meeting of the Fatherland Front had been held in the National Theatre in Sofia, in a fresh smell of evergreen branches and under the eye of vast crudely-sketched portraits of Stalin, Truman and an almost unrecognisable lopsided Attlee. Bulgarian, Russian, British and American flags were draped around the platform. The four national anthems were sung by a choir.

The most popular foreign guests who were most loudly cheered were a delegation of Yugoslav partisans, young men and women, wearing their greenish-grey uniform and the red star in their caps. Official Russian representatives were there, but no British or Americans. The British and American Missions, after their notes of August complaining about the election preparations, were marking their displeasure with the Fatherland Front.

Practically the whole Fatherland Front government was there, although this was an inter-party rather than a strictly official affair.

The chief speaker was Tsola Dragoicheva, the woman secretary of the Fatherland Front National Committee. She had dark waving hair with chestnut glints in it and smallish bright brown eyes, and was dressed in nondescript black. She always was: it was almost a uniform.

Surprisingly, she was a rather timid, nervous and halting orator. This did not seem to fit in with the stories of her as a lifelong fanatical underground fighter for the Communist Party, or as the beautiful young student who had been sentenced to death by a Sofia court for anti-State activities, and had saved herself by becoming pregnant while in prison. To the outsider her speech would have seemed long-winded, academic and uninspiring; she flushed, stumbled and seemed unsure of herself. But she was cheered devotedly and devoutly by the audience, mostly youngish Bulgarians representing official bodies or Fatherland Front organisations, or ex-partisans wearing the orange-and-black striped Soviet war decoration.

After Tsola, the four secretaries of the four parties of the Fatherland Front coalition spoke. It was a big show of coalition unity. All were better orators than Tsola—small, tubby pink-faced Alexander Obbov, of the pro-government Agrarians, brawny, vigorous, youthful Traicho Kostov of the 'Workers Party' (Communists), smooth, urbane, handsome Peter Pop-Zlatev of Zveno, the 'bourgeois' party of the Front, and slight silver-bearded academic Dimiter Neikov, of the pro-Government Social Democrats.

The speeches grew longer and longer. Then came the second part of the programme—Slav music and recitations. The audience, except for one or two non-Slav intruders, seemed youthfully pleased and happy. They went on being pleased and happy till well after midnight. It seemed that the Bulgarians, like the Russians, liked things to go on for as long as possible. A party could not be a real success until after midnight.

Early next morning—it was a Sunday—the celebrations were carried on in the yellow September sun. Members of the government gathered in a leisurely way on rough wooden stands run up overnight in front of the badly bombed parliament building. It was all rather a country-town family party. From the stands you looked across to the Stars and Stripes over the American Legation and the bigger Red Flag over the Red Army officers' mess. Behind them was the massive shadowy purple mountain, Vitosha, which rules Sofia.

A small scattering of people turned up to line the broad 'Boulevard of the Liberator Tsar' along which the procession was to pass. There were no big crowds.

After about an hour's wait the parade appeared. At first it was a cheerful and merry business, though in the simple serious Slav way. There were portraits and banners and slogans—all giving thanks to the Fatherland Front—little bands of partisans, very youthful and earnest, farm wagons carrying tableaux showing Bulgaria's various industries, handicrafts and branches of agriculture, little companies of peasants from nearby villages in heavy embroidered costumes, mainly red on white. Some of the peasants were dancing to the music of a wooden pipe local village dances, with plenty of shuffling, twirling, leaping, clapping and laughing. There was a group of gypsies, looking half roguish, half rueful, carrying a banner saying, 'We thank the Fatherland Front for all it has done for the gypsies of Bulgaria.'

At one point several young Yugoslav partisans, some of those who had been cheered so eagerly the night before, were dragged down off the stands of honour to join in the dancing with Bulgarian peasants and partisans. One group of Bulgarian partisans carried a rough portrait of Frank Thompson, a young Englishman who was one of the very few British liaison officers to establish contact with the partisan movement in Bulgaria, and who was captured and shot by the Germans in 1944.

One part of the procession was more formal, more warlike. Units of the Bulgarian Army—infantry, cavalry and motorised—passed the saluting point, looking smart, physically tough and efficient. What made them even more impressive, if not alarming, was that as each unit approached—the infantry goose-stepping stiffly in German fashion—it suddenly burst into a deep full-throated roar, like a well-trained team of lions launched into the arena. But this, it seemed, was an old Bulgarian custom, not a Fatherland Front innovation. The lines of onlookers obviously felt real pride and pleasure in their Army—their traditional regular Army.

After them came units of the new Bulgarian police force, the People's Militia, wearing military uniforms of khaki with magenta piping. Many of the militiamen were on bicycles or motor-bikes or some even in armoured cars. All were armed with tommy-guns. Since during their one year's existence the Militia, a Communist-created and almost entirely Communist-officered body, had one way or another made themselves unpopular and feared by most Bulgarians, they probably brought a violent and sinister note into the procession for the non-communist and non-political onlookers.

Still, the parade would have been gay enough if it had not gone on so long. It lasted over five hours. The sun got very hot. The spectators wilted and melted away, the marchers in the procession grew jaded and listless. Soon after midday the members of the government and other distinguished people on the wooden stands grew hungry and slipped off to eat. They never came back. By 2.30 there were nothing but miserable and embarrassed-looking groups of employees from the various government departments or the national bank, drifting untidily down streets empty except for a few militiamen on duty, past an empty saluting base. The procession straggled to an ignoble close.

Opposition politicians by that time had an obvious excuse for saying: 'You see: there is nothing spontaneous about this at all. Everyone in the procession belongs to some Government institution or Fatherland Front organisation or party body, which forces its members to attend.

Maybe some go willingly, particularly the peasants who like a day trip to Sofia. But most are just afraid of losing their jobs or getting into trouble if they don't show up. It is roughly the same with the onlookers —only you saw how few of those there were.

'The Fatherland Front has lost all the popularity it had one year ago—and it was popular with almost every type of Bulgarian then. So were the Russians. But now the Front has become nothing but a one-party dictatorship—a Communist dictatorship, for the other parties are just stooges, just window dressing. And its power now rests on Militia terror and the fear of Red Army intervention, not on popularity any longer. You will soon find out for yourself.'

Even if this was a highly-coloured verdict, it was sad hearing for anyone who knew anything about the Fatherland Front in its earliest days. It had seemed to have the most solid foundation of all the fronts or coalitions formed according to the Soviet formula of the union of peasants and workers. Some sort of talks for collaboration were said to have taken place between Communists and Agrarians as early as 1941, before the Left-wing Agrarian, Dr. G. M. Dimitrov, had to flee from Bulgaria because he was threatened with arrest and execution as a British agent. These talks were supposed to have formed the secret basis for the later development of the Front.

Next year the other Dimitrov—the Communist, Georgi Dimitrov, who had made his name known throughout the world by his defiant self-defence at the Reichstag fire trial—inspired from Moscow the opening of a Soviet propaganda campaign for the formation of the Fatherland Front. It was to be both an inter-party organ of political opposition, with a constructive political programme containing the basic points of the Soviet formula, and the organiser of active resistance to the pro-German authorities in Bulgaria and to the German troops.

Later Georgi Dimitrov himself broadcast messages over the Soviet radio, or wrote articles which were broadcast, praising the ideas of the Fatherland Front, expounding its programme, particularly the unity of peasants and workers, and calling for resistance. His messages always sounded moderate and broadly based. One of his main themes, even after the Front actually came to power, was that the Communists could not rule Bulgaria alone; they must work together with the Agrarians.

During 1944 the British radio also, though much less intensively, called on Bulgarians to back the Fatherland Front.

Inside Bulgaria, the Fatherland Front never became a very powerful body so long as there were German troops in Bulgaria and pro-German governments in power. On the political side, leading politicians of the four parties—the Communist Neichev; the intellectual, Petko Stainov, and the masters in the art of *coups d'état*, Kimon Georgiev and Damian Velchev, for the Zveno party; Nikola Petkov and, when out of prison,

Boris Bumbarov for the Left Wing Agrarians; Grigor Cheshmedzhiev
for the Social Democrats—kept up rather loose contact in Sofia. During
1944 they also made occasional joint public protests against the pro-
German policy of the government.

The position was, however, not quite clear-cut: these 'Front' men
also kept up contacts with other anti-German politicians who were
leaders of other parties not regarded as belonging to the Front, for
instance, Nikola Mushanov, of the Democratic Party, and Dimiter
Gichev, of the Right Wing Agrarians.

Also, these other politicians themselves made public protests against
the pro-German policy of the government. This was important, since it
meant that the Front had not got sole monopoly of political opposition
and so could not claim sole right to rule the country when the Germans
left. So the opening of the 'Front's' rule was tarnished by petty strife
between two sets of politicians who could all claim to be anti-German
and pro-Allied, although some were more definitely pro-Soviet and
others more definitely pro-Western.

While the politicians of the Front spent the last year of the German
domination in political talks and combinations in Sofia, a partisan
movement had grown up in the hills and mountains both to the north
and south. It never became a very big movement: 15,000 is usually the
highest estimate for the men in the hills. Nor does it ever seem to have
been at all tightly organised; it was rather a loosely-linked series of
small bands. In so far as it was directed from the centre, it was obviously
directed by the Communist Party, not by the Fatherland Front as a
whole. Most of the partisans were young Communists or would-be
Communists, often students or other young townspeople. The Agrarians
subsequently claimed to have helped the partisans, rather than to have
fought themselves: this meant that in some districts, though not all, the
peasants gave food and shelter.

The partisan movement, although many of the young men were brave
and suffered hardship, even death, and although it left behind a valuable
myth, never became a really popular movement. Unfortunately there
were seldom more than a few thousand German troops in Bulgaria to
fight, and they kept out of the way; so the partisans usually had to
fight Bulgarians, which was a much less popular thing to do. Then, the
Bulgarian gendarmerie and Army were extremely efficient and ruthless
in their handling of the partisans, so that fighting was dangerous and
quite often fruitless. There were practically no stand-up engagements,
at most small-scale running affrays. Attacks on Bulgaria's few important
communications were difficult, and there were very few war factories to
sabotage. Reduced to less heroic actions, the partisans would usually
raid a village, possibly shoot the mayor and his clerk and the village
policeman, destroy the village land register and other records, loot the
village dairy, and make a few propaganda speeches to the villagers.
Then they would leave, perhaps having converted some of the villagers.

On the other side, even if the Bulgarian partisans did not do much useful sabotage and certainly did not hold down German troops, they had during the last year a big nuisance value. Bulgarian regular army troops had to be used against them as well as the gendarmerie, and successive Ministers of the Interior raged against them, and threatened harsher and harsher measures. This in turn made the pro-German governments more unpopular: even if the ordinary stolid Bulgarian was unenthusiastic about the partisans, he thought it a poor thing that they should be tortured or shot; it also showed that the government was incompetent.

All the same, it would perhaps not be unfair to say that the Bulgarian partisans were a good deal less important during the 'German era' than they became when the moment arrived for the Fatherland Front to seize power. Then the partisans came down from the hills into the towns and villages and set up in a day or two what was at least nominally Fatherland Front rule. While they often discredited the Front by the roughness and sometimes brutality of their ways, and by their acts of vengeance, they did impose the Front's authority throughout the remoter parts of the country very quickly. Without them, this process might have taken months, as, in different circumstances and without the help of partisans, it did in Rumania.

The main reason why, during the war, the Front's politicians and the partisans never formed together a big national resistance movement was that most Bulgarians suffered very little from the war and so saw no particular point in resisting. The country was not really occupied by the Germans. The few thousands of Germans stationed in Bulgaria behaved most correctly. The governments of the archæologist Bogdan Filov and his successors were pro-German and authoritarian, but not fanatically so. Few Bulgarians were oppressed except the Communists, the partisans, the very small Jewish minority, and a handful of Anglophils. Several Bulgarian divisions were sent to Greek Thrace and Macedonia and to Yugoslav Macedonia as occupation troops, and occasionally had to fight Macedonian partisans or quell disorders; but nearly all Bulgarians looked on these territories as belonging to Bulgaria, and so thought this job a natural one.

Most important of all, neither King Boris of Bulgaria nor his governments either dared (or probably wished) to declare war on Russia, and this was the one move that might have stirred the Bulgarian people to revolt. The King was ready to stand up to a good deal of German pressure on this point. His recalcitrance may even have had something to do with his unexpected death just after a visit to Hitler. The ordinary Bulgarian could look on his country as neutral: the war against Britain and America was only 'symbolic'.

Circumstances and atmosphere were wrong for the growth of a big national resistance movement like Tito's liberation movement in Yugoslavia. Nevertheless, when the Fatherland Front seized power in Bulgaria, the people hailed them joyfully, thankfully and sincerely, as the saviours of the country—from the Russians.

Up till August, 1944, the Bulgarians had always looked on the Russians, one way or another, as their protectors. Traditionally they were the big Slav brothers; throughout the war there had been a Soviet Legation with a large staff in Sofia. Even if the Anglo-Americans, particularly the British who loved the Greeks, should want to destroy Bulgaria at the end of the war, the Russians would surely stop them. In particular, there was Georgi Dimitrov in Moscow; he was powerful and could arrange things. But from the last week of August onwards there was a wave of panic. It looked as though the Russians were going suddenly to turn into avengers, to descend on Bulgaria, occupy and ravage the country and punish the people. Somehow, Bulgaria must be saved, must be lifted up and put down on the right side.

The signal for the panic was August 23rd, when Rumania suddenly switched over and turned against the Germans. The coup brought the Red Army unexpectedly to the Danube, where they could look across at Bulgaria. The Russians threatened the very small German forces in Bulgaria, who would obviously have to withdraw westwards into Yugoslavia. More serious, the Russians might decide to protect their own left flank by cleaning up Bulgaria before pressing on through Rumania to Hungary. They might cross the Danube and invade Bulgaria.

Everyone saw something must be done quickly. For weeks a Bulgarian delegate, Stoicho Moshanov, had been trying abortively to have peace talks with British representatives in Cairo, but this was no safeguard against Russian wrath. Anyhow, he had been cold-shouldered by the British who were clearly waiting for the Russians to take the lead over Bulgaria.

The three Regents, appointed on King Boris's death—Prince Cyril, General Mihov and Bogdan Filov—summoned to consultation all the Opposition politicians, both the pro-Western moderates like Nikola Mushanov, Dimiter Gichev and another Right Wing Agrarian, Muraviev, and also the more pro-Soviet leaders of the Fatherland Front. The idea was to form a combined government of both groups.

But the Front leaders were not prepared to play. They could not be found or did not turn up. Either they had private information that the pro-Western moderates would not be acceptable to the Russians, or else they saw no reason for sharing power when their big chance had come. The moderates were very uneasy. They would have felt happier if any government they formed could have included a Communist or two, as safeguards. One of them, Atanas Burov, an independent financier of Conservative leanings, wanted at first to refuse the Foreign Ministry because he could not be sure of appeasing Russia if there were no representative of the Front among his colleagues.

The Front kept away. The military situation outside Bulgaria was pressing. At the beginning of September the pro-Western moderates formed a cabinet, without the Front, under Muraviev. Their aim was to break with Germany as quickly as possible but at the same time to avoid any fighting on Bulgarian soil. A particular difficulty was how to extract the Bulgarian occupation forces from Yugoslavia, where they were closely controlled by the Germans, without loss. Getting the Germans out of Bulgaria was relatively simple.

There was a day or two's inevitable delay, while Bulgarian military leaders were consulted and made their dispositions, before the Muraviev government could declare war on Germany. By that time the Russians had lost patience and crossed the Danube into north-eastern Bulgaria in small numbers, and had declared war on Bulgaria. The Russo-Bulgarian war was a matter of hours. The Muraviev government hastened to offer surrender, and according to its members, Marshal Tolbukhin, the Soviet commander, had accepted this surrender by radio before the government was ousted by the Fatherland Front.

The Russian declaration of war caused surprise and uneasiness to the Western Powers who apparently had not been consulted in advance. It was assumed Russia had acted to secure herself full right to the lion's share in control of Bulgaria, which otherwise would have fallen to Britain and America who had long been at war with Bulgaria. Later, the last-minute Soviet declaration of war on Japan seemed a rather similar gesture, although in this case it had been agreed with the Western Allies in advance.

In Bulgaria the Russian action brought panic to its highest pitch. Bulgarians lost all faith in the power of the pro-Western Muraviev government to save the country. So when on the night of September 8th-9th the Fatherland Front seized power, through a silent *coup d'état* at the War Ministry and in certain Army formations stationed near Sofia, smoothly executed by the veteran military conspirator, the sphinx-like Damian Velchev, the first reaction was a wave of glorious relief and enthusiasm throughout the country.

'We are saved, but it was only the Fatherland Front that could have saved us,' people felt, as they turned out to hail the Red Army as friends and liberators instead of enemies and avengers.

That was how the Fatherland Front took power on September 9th, 1944.

It started off in an atmosphere of rejoicing and reconciliation. The Front was perhaps rather too exclusively pro-Soviet, too far to the Left, for the normal tastes of the more conservative Bulgarians. But after all it was the Red Army that was occupying the country, so it would be foolish to grumble and wiser to accept the obvious advantages of a 'reddish' government.

Anyhow, its political and social programme, based on the general Soviet formula for the Balkans, was reassuringly moderate and quite un-revolutionary. There were parties in the Front which were far from Communist. Zveno was a definitely bourgeois party which in the past had been outspokenly authoritarian and had even been accused by the Left of being semi-fascist. It was basically a group of reserve officers and middle-class intellectuals who wanted a sound and strong-handed administration. The Agrarians were a good way to the Left and under the Stamboliski régime over twenty years earlier had been ruthless towards the middle-class; but they had always quarrelled off and on with the Communists, in the natural suspicion and antagonism between country and town. The Social Democrats had also had a steady squabble with the Communists for the last twenty-five years, over the usual split between reformists and revolutionaries, between the Second and Third Internationals.

It did not look as though the Communists would have things all their own way. There might well be a certain balance of forces inside the Front which would make it really representative and national. If in foreign policy it was most concerned with winning Russia's trust and benevolent patronage, that was natural in the circumstances; given the Front's party make-up, it could be expected to try to restore at least amicable relations with Britain and America as well. Everyone was hopeful.

Perhaps the first disillusionment was the coldness of the Russian troops. The Bulgarians, recovering quickly from their panic, expected the Russians to behave as big brothers and fellow-Slavs. After all, Bulgaria had never fought Russia: what bar was there to friendship? But the Russians showed no signs of fraternising. They kept aloof and quite obviously thought little of the Bulgarians, a paltry people of seven millions. They did not seem interested in Slav brotherhood. There was much less looting and raping in Bulgaria than in certain other countries invaded by the Red Army; but inevitably there was some. All in all, the Bulgarians were chilled.

At the same time came the excesses and stupidities of the more inexperienced Bulgarian Communists, would-be Communists and their hangers-on. The Fatherland Front coup was the signal for the partisans and the small-town and village Communists to seize control of the countryside. In this process, there were summary killings of police, gendarmerie, local officials and personal enemies. Old wrongs, feuds and grudges were paid off.

A year later huge figures were circulating in Sofia of the number of violent deaths that followed the Fatherland Front's seizure of power; 100,000 was quite a common rumour in more extreme Opposition circles. A senior British officer suggested 20,000, estimating roughly that three people on an average had been killed in every village in the country. The real figure may well have been very much lower, but there was no means of checking. On the Fatherland Front side, some of its responsible members would sometimes admit that there had inevitably if regrettably been a 'spirit of vengeance' among those who had suffered persecution during the war.

At the very start of the new régime, the theory was that a Fatherland Front committee, made up of representatives of all the Front parties, was to be formed in each town and village to carry on administration for the time being. These committees were very important, since it was not until over a year later that it was finally decreed that they were to be advisory only, and no longer executive. In practice party representation was very uneven. Zveno and the Social Democrats had in the early days practically no provincial organisation outside Sofia, and the Agrarians, though they had a very wide following, had not kept country-wide cadres and had let party affairs get into a chaotic state. Only the Communists had maintained an efficient underground organisation. So for the first year or more the local Fatherland Front committees consisted mainly of Communists, with Agrarians coming a bad second and the other two parties far behind. Since the Communists had not been trained in tact or the art of self-effacement, this unbalance made for bitterness and friction in the countryside.

Even when mayors and other local officials took back the administration from the committees, the Communists somehow got the majority of these posts. This preponderance was shown by figures given in the Bulgarian parliament as late as summer, 1946. So, in general, the theoretical Fatherland Front balance of forces was even less of a working reality in the countryside than in Sofia.

One of the lesser causes for complaint in Sofia during the earlier days was unauthorised requisitioning of houses, flats, cars and other private property, and some looting, by Communists, partisans or the new-born Militia. This was all distressing to the Sofia middle-class, who were not rich enough to bear philosophically any threat to hardly earned property.

Most of the Sofia middle-class were even more distressed and scared by the People's Court trials of war criminals at the beginning of 1945. In these the three wartime Regents, practically all members of all Bulgarian governments which had held office during the 'German era' from 1941 onwards, and even members of the would-be peacemaker government of Muraviev—together with a number of Royal Court officials and political hangers-on—were condemned. One hundred and one men were executed, including the Regents.

These executions alone would have shocked but not alarmed moderate Bulgarians. What was alarming was the sentences of imprisonment on the highly respectable members of the pro-Western Muraviev government. They were accused of having helped the Germans to quit Bulgaria unharmed and continued the persecution of the Bulgarian partisans during their few days of office. But many felt that the real charges against them were that they were mistrusted by the Russians and were pro-Western. This seemed an unhappy omen for the future.

There were many other People's Court trials against alleged war criminals and collaborators. The total figures of People's Court sentences, given by the Minister of Justice, were: 1,880 death sentences, 1,900 life sentences, 960 sentences to 15 years' imprisonment, 684 to 10 years, 129 to 8 years, 999 to 5 years, 330 to 3 years, 300 to 2 years, 747 to 1 year; 1,497 acquitted. For a country as small as Bulgaria these figures seemed high, and as there were a good many people with uneasy consciences, added to general nervousness.

The most serious cause for disillusionment and opposition was the splitting of the Fatherland Front itself. This had already started by the end of 1944, soon after the exiled Agrarian leader, G. M. Dimitrov, came home, and reached a climax when the main leaders of the Agrarian and Social Democratic parties left the Government in July and August, 1945. By the time this painful, confused and sometimes sordid process was complete, most of the glory was gone from the Fatherland Front. It could still be argued that it was the only practicable government for Bulgaria in the circumstances, that it was more efficient than any alternative government could have been, that it had kept the country's economy stable, and that its loss of popularity was unimportant.

On the other hand, it could also be reasonably argued that the Front had lost some of its best men, that it had become an unconvincing camouflage for rule by the Communist Party, and that at least a big and talkative minority of Bulgarians was disillusioned and frightened.

What was certain was that a great deal of dirty linen had been washed in public, that there was an utter breakdown of unity and trust, and that Bulgarians were roughly divided again on the old line—'Easterners' against 'Westerners', at this time, pro-Russians against pro-Anglo-Americans.

4

Feuds and Rivalries in Bulgaria

THERE were at the end of the war two men capable of becoming
national leaders of Bulgaria—the two Dimitrovs. Neither was
in Bulgaria in September, 1945. The Agrarian Dimitrov had
already come and gone—rejected by the Fatherland Front, or
at least by the Communists, because he was regarded as a British agent.
The Communist Dimitrov was still in Moscow, where he was said to
have a fine flat and an influential position. In Sofia he had been nick-
named 'Telegram Georgie' because, people said, he was trying to rule
Bulgaria by telegrams from Moscow. Certainly there was a stream of
public telegrams and messages from Georgi Dimitrov to various Fatherland Front and Communist Party organisations, in which greetings,
advice and directives were delivered in statesmanlike tone. It was not
until November, 1945, that the Communist Dimitrov, perhaps worried
by the increasing confidence of the Opposition, came home to Bulgaria.

There were no outward traces of the Agrarian Dimitrov in Sofia in
September, 1945, although he had only just left the country—no
portraits, though Bulgarians love portraits of politicians, no banners,
no slogans. Less than a year earlier he had been one of the most popular
men in the country. Now he might never have existed. But the Communist Dimitrov brooded over Sofia in absence. A twice-life-size statue
of him in rough plaster, wearing a long frock-coat, carrying a scroll in
one hand and looking noble in the style of Beethoven, towered before
the gateway of the disused royal palace. Photographs of him, with a
flowing Edwardian moustache, and books about him were in the main
shops. Portraits of him and banners hailing him as founder of the
Fatherland Front were carried in all processions. Messages were sent
to him from nearly all political gatherings. It was impossible to be in
Sofia for forty-eight hours without feeling his brooding presence.

It might have seemed reasonable that if the Fatherland Front was to
be based on the union of peasants and workers, that is of the Agrarian
and Communist parties, there should be room for both Dimitrovs in
Bulgaria. This was not possible. It was not only a question of the old
rivalry between the two parties, of the hostility and mistrust between an
'Easterner' and a 'Westerner': there quite simply was not enough room.

One of the banes of Bulgaria has been overcrowding: bad over-

D

crowding of the agricultural population, for whom there is too little cultivable land, overcrowding of politicians for whom there is too little constructive outlet. The two kinds of overcrowding are linked.

Every Bulgarian, if not a peasant, is the son or grandson of a peasant. A peasant's son, if he has much energy, does not want to stay on the land: all he can normally hope for is a fraction of his father's very few acres to work. If he is lucky he somehow gets to the university and becomes a lawyer. If he is less lucky, he will become a town worker of some kind, although industry itself is so small and undeveloped that it offers him very little scope. If he becomes a lawyer, the peasant's son gets involved in politics. If he becomes a worker, he gets involved in labour agitation, and so again in politics.

This means there are too many politicians. It is the result of ambition and surplus energy. So few careers are open to men of energy. The civil service is wretchedly paid; the professions are small, overcrowded and unprofitable; trade, industry and banking are small-scale and offer very few openings. All that is left is to become a politician. Although this calling is also overcrowded there is more attraction in it and more chance of rising to greatness. It gives a chance for self-assertion and the rhetoric which most Bulgarians possess. Vitality—the Bulgarians are a physically strong and healthy people—can find an outlet at last. You may become a Minister. This does not mean riches, but probably the use of a large car and chauffeur, possibly the loan of a house, certainly a policeman or militiaman at your door to guard you, and perhaps he will help wash up or mind the baby. Later as an ex-Minister you will have always a certain social position and respect, and also all the pleasure of intriguing in cafés to get back into the government. There are a great many ex-Ministers.

Because Bulgaria is overcrowded with politicians, and also for other reasons, feeling between politicians, even politicians of the same party, is often very bitter, sometimes violent, sometimes spiteful. In the endless game of musical chairs it is only the few who get the comfortable chairs while the rest have to stand around in the cold. This makes for pushing, scrambling and back-biting, if nothing worse.

(The back-biting is not confined to politicians but seems the curse of Bulgarians in general, probably caused by an instinctive sense of social insecurity and overcrowding. A girl from a small Central European country who married a Bulgarian said: 'They are kind and friendly but I have never known such people for saying horrible things about each other, often without any rhyme or reason. In my own country it is bad enough, but here it seems something quite special.')

This overcrowded overheated Bulgarian air explains partly why there was not room enough for both Dimitrovs in Bulgaria at once. Each was too forceful a personality, too capable of arousing mass devotion, for mutual toleration.

The Agrarian, Georgi Mihailov Dimitrov, was known affectionately by his followers as 'the Doctor'. Surprisingly he was a real doctor of medicine, not a doctor of laws. A man in his forties, he was tall, impressive, with a fine head. He first became known as organiser of the Left Wing Agrarian youth movement in the late 'twenties. He became its recognised leader, and was said to be loved and admired by its members, students, peasants' sons and young peasants. He tried not to stay mewed up in Sofia but to travel around the countryside and get to know the peasants. He was a rousing speaker.

The feuds among the various fractions of the Agrarian Party were so complicated that the Doctor, up till the war, never became a recognised leader of the Party as a whole. But during the 'thirties he became leader of a left wing fraction of the Party known as the 'Pladne' group after its newspaper. This had the reputation of being a progressive and radical group although, owing to the suppression of normal parliamentary life after 1934, it was impossible to say how big a proportion of the peasants it had behind it.

In 1941 when the German invasion of the Balkans was threatening, the Doctor and his friends made contacts with the British in Sofia, to plan underground resistance, with British support, in case of German occupation. At about the same time he claimed to have had talks with the Communists and to have reached with them some sort of understanding which later was the basis of the Fatherland Front. When the German move into the Balkans started, the Doctor escaped to Istanbul. He was later tried in Sofia and sentenced to death in absence as a man who had taken British gold.

During the war years he advised the British military authorities in the Middle East on Bulgarian affairs, much as Georgi Dimitrov presumably advised the Soviet authorities, though far more influentially, in Moscow. The Doctor also did propaganda work through British channels and tried to keep some sort of contact with his friends inside Bulgaria. Towards the end of the war, the Communists became suspicious of him for some reason, perhaps because in the days when Mihailovitch was generally accepted as a real resistance leader in Yugoslavia, the Doctor had sent him friendly messages and a letter. This letter was later used against Dimitrov by the Communists. Anyhow, in 1944 stories were put around in several countries that the Doctor had become anti-Soviet, anti-Communist and an agent of Mihailovitch, and was under the influence of 'reactionary Poles' in Istanbul. But he was never attacked by the Soviet Press or radio.

Then came the Fatherland Front coup and the first rosy weeks of honeymoon between the Communists and Agrarians in Bulgaria. The Agrarians who had become Ministers in the Fatherland Front government were personal friends of the Doctor's and looked to him as their leader. They suggested he should come home. The Communists did not object, although, when the Bulgarian armistice delegates went to

Moscow, Georgi Dimitrov told one of them that he mistrusted the Doctor, that he was a British agent, and that he would therefore do no good to the Agrarian Party.

An invitation to the Doctor and one or two other Agrarians in exile to come home was broadcast from Sofia. The Doctor came by train from Istanbul. After he had crossed the frontier, peasants with flowers and banners welcomed him enthusiastically, all along the way to Sofia. He had to stop and make speeches to them. They cheered. In a moment it seemed that he had become perhaps the most popular man of the Fatherland Front régime then in Bulgaria.

The Doctor accepted the Fatherland Front, its political programme and its emphasis on Russian friendship. He regarded himself as one of its founders. But he did not enter the government. He only became secretary of the Agrarian Party. Perhaps he wanted to keep his personal independence. He said his first job must be to reorganise the Party, as one of the two chief parties of the Front, throughout the country. This was urgent since, owing to Party divisions ever since the murder of the Agrarian leader Alexander Stambuliski in 1923, and also to wartime suppression, the Agrarian organisation was chaotic. The Doctor may well have thought this was unhealthy if the Agrarians were to play their rightful part and were to hold the excessive zeal of the Communists in check. He certainly had in his mind the idea of balance—a balance between the Communists and Agrarians, a balance between Soviet and Western influence in Bulgaria. In the overheated atmosphere of the moment, this idea was dangerous. It could too easily be distorted and misinterpreted as disloyalty, even treason. But the Doctor was too simple, perhaps too narrow and stubborn, to dress up his views.

He toured the country for several months, organising and speaking to the peasants. He was welcomed everywhere. Soon trouble started. Stories got around that in his speeches he was saying that the Agrarian Party, not the Fatherland Front, should rule the country, that Bulgarians must remember the British and Americans, even that British and American troops were coming to Bulgaria. In the end he was accused of spreading pacifist slogans, such as 'Peace, bread and work', which were sapping the morale of the Bulgarian soldiers fighting against the Germans. His friends denied these stories or said they were distortions, and declared the Doctor was perfectly loyal to the Front. But somehow he made a bitter personal enemy of the powerful woman Communist, Tsola Dragoicheva, and that was dangerous. Already in January, 1945, he had to resign his post as secretary of the Agrarian Party.

In the spring of 1945 open attacks on him came out in the Communist press. Inside the Front relations between Agrarians and Communists grew strained. Suddenly the Communist Minister of the Interior, Anton Jugov, placed the Doctor under arrest. He was closely guarded by Militiamen in his flat in Sofia. Several of his most trusted followers were arrested, among them his woman secretary, who after long interrogation was killed falling out of a window at Militia headquarters in Sofia. Officially it was said she had committed suicide after admitting her guilt. The Agrarians said she had been horribly tortured before her death: by some oversight her corpse had been sent to her family and there was clear proof.

The charges against the Doctor were not formulated and at that time remained obscure. But obviously the real accusation against him was of being an Anglo-American agent working against the interests of Russia.

After a time the Doctor escaped from house arrest. The British Mission said they could not give him protection. He took refuge with the United States political representative, the irrepressible and mercurial Maynard Barnes, who gave him hospitality in his villa on the outskirts of Sofia. For the first day or two there was some awkwardness with Bulgarian Militia and Red Army troops around the Barnes villa. After that the Doctor was left in quiet, under American diplomatic protection. At the end of August, 1945, after American intervention, the Minister of the Interior gave him a passport to leave Bulgaria. He left on the same plane as Maynard Barnes who was going on leave.

That was the political end of the man who might have been a big Agrarian leader, perhaps a big rival to the Moscow Dimitrov. His name was still remembered and occasionally mentioned in public by those Agrarians who had quit the Front, and especially by the revived Agrarian Youth organisation, which was fanatically devoted to him. He was still often attacked in the Communist newspapers. They invented a new word, 'Gemetovtsi', or 'G.M.-ites', formed from the Doctor's initials, meaning any particularly nasty brand of neo-fascist. In November, 1945, detailed and lurid charges against him and certain of his followers were published by the Public Prosecutor. In June, 1946, a court with a Communist prosecutor and a Communist judge tried him in absence and condemned him to death, just as a pro-German court had done five years before. The Doctor was in the United States and said nothing.

It seems that he was a stubborn and inflexible man, hating compromise and concession, rather narrow in his party loyalty. He and his friends firmly believed that the Agrarian Party was by far the biggest party in numbers in Bulgaria. Though they were ready to work with the Communists, they thought their party's size ought to be taken into account in setting the political balance. The Doctor also believed that Bulgaria had a lot to learn from Britain and America and that America could help her materially in ways Soviet Russia could not. This meant that Bulgaria's foreign policy should be based more or less equally on both East and West, on Russia, Britain and America jointly, not on Russia alone.

These were all things which were probably unrealistic and which it was certainly impolitic and tactless to stress in Fatherland Front Bulgaria. Perhaps if the Agrarian Dimitrov had been more pliant and opportunist he might have survived. But he was not; so the Communists decided against him. Whether this decision was taken in Sofia, or whether the Communist Dimitrov in Moscow had something to do with it, is not known. It was a decision which meant the break-up of the original Fatherland Front coalition.

The struggle between the Agrarian and Communist parties, which was the basic problem of the Fatherland Front in 1944 and 1945, dated back to the years immediately after the first world war. In 1919 the Bulgarian Communist Party, called the 'Workers' Party', developed, as a result of the Russian revolution, out of the 'Narrow' wing of the Bulgarian Social Democratic Party. The new party started its career with a spate of revolutionary dynamism.

The Agrarian Party was older but first became important at about the same time. The Agrarian, Alexander Stamboliski, a fiery peasant orator with warlike moustaches, entered the first government formed after Bulgaria's defeat in 1918. Soon after, he became Bulgaria's first Agrarian Prime Minister, and started a series of reforms to help the peasants. His idea was that Bulgaria should be a peasant State; townspeople were to have little say in it. Stamboliski's Orange Guards, bands of peasants acting as a sort of volunteer party militia, were said, when excited, to beat up townspeople just because they were townspeople.

Although the Agrarians and Communists, two young and radical parties of the Left, should have been natural allies, they were not. No formula for harmonising country and town interests had then been found. They bickered over the monarchy: the Communists wanted to overthrow it at once; the Agrarians, though republican in principle, wanted to keep it—in its place—for the time being. Stamboliski optimistically thought he could train up the young King Boris the way he should go.

The year 1923 was typical of the parties' quarrel. When in June a plot was staged (partly by the men who later became the leaders of Zveno) to overthrow Stamboliski's Agrarian government, the Communists stood aside and let the Agrarians go under in bloodshed and torture. Stamboliski himself was horribly murdered. A strong-hand reactionary government took power. In September, 1923, the Communist leaders, Georgi Dimitrov and Vasil Kolarov, were prime movers in an abortive revolt of workers which also ended in bloodshed and brutal repression. At that moment most of the Agrarians stood aside.

The two parties were at odds, off and on, for the next twenty years. The talks leading to the foundation of the Fatherland Front gave hope that they had matured enough to trust each other. For the first month or two of power it seemed they had. Then came the quarrel over G. M.

Dimitrov in the winter of 1944-45. At the same time there was friction in the countryside. The Agrarians said the Communists seized the power in the town and village Fatherland Front committees and tried to interfere in the internal affairs of the local branches of the Agrarian Party. The Communists accused the Agrarians of disloyalty to the Communist Party and the Front and of hostile feelings towards Soviet Russia.

In May, 1945, trouble came to a head. According to a public statement made a year later by a leading Agrarian, which was not contradicted, the Communists formally demanded that certain nominees of their own should be included in the leadership of the Agrarian Party. The Communists also forced through the holding of an Agrarian Party Congress, against the will of the Agrarian leaders who declared the Congress unrepresentative, and got their nominees into power. From this moment Alexander Obbov, one of the very few Agrarians whom the Communists at least thought harmless, gained more and more power inside the Agrarian Party organisation, of which he was now secretary.

Soon after the Congress, Boris Bumbarov, a close friend of G. M. Dimitrov, who had spent part of the war in a Bulgarian prison, had to resign his seat in the Fatherland Front government. In July and August, when difficulties over the election campaign got acute, Nikola Petkov and the other original Agrarian members of the Fatherland Front government also resigned. So did the Social Democrat Ministers. Nikola Petkov and, later, Kosta Lulchev, secretary of the Social Democratic Party, became the leaders of the Opposition—the first Opposition in Fatherland Front Bulgaria. In less than a year the Front had split.

The departing Agrarians and Social Democrats were replaced in the Fatherland Front Cabinet by other Agrarians and Social Democrats on whom the Communists felt they could rely, notably Alexander Obbov. In this way the theoretical balance of parties in the Front could be kept unchanged. But it was commonly said that only a small and opportunist fraction of each party remained with the government. The mass of real party supporters followed the leaders into opposition.

Everyone wanted to see how much freedom the Opposition—which had not been foreseen in the Fatherland Front scheme of things—would be allowed in Soviet-occupied Bulgaria. At first they had no legal status and no newspapers. They started by other means an agitation against the way the electoral campaign was being run—the Fatherland Front's first election had been fixed for August 26th before the split happened—and accused the Communists and Militia of terrorism.

Certainly when the Opposition tried to put up candidates they met all kinds of technical difficulties. Curious things happened. Often a day or two after the candidate's nomination, a statement of retraction from the candidate would be published in the government press, saying it was all a mistake and he had never really approved his own nomination.

One Opposition candidate in the provinces said later: 'It was too much of a strain on the nerves. The Communists met outside my house every evening and shouted "death to the traitor". Slogans saying the same thing were painted up on the walls, and they made public speeches against me, inciting the people. Also there were mysterious telephone calls to my wife threatening that if I didn't give up she would lose her husband. I was not beaten up. But it was too much. I quit and went to Sofia.'

Nikola Petkov wrote a letter of protest against electoral terrorism and sent copies to the British and American political representatives. For this he was bitterly attacked in the government press as a betrayer of his country inviting foreign intervention. He was still more angrily attacked when, towards the end of August, first the United States and then the British Government, seizing their first chance of exerting influence after a year's impotent ineffectiveness, sent notes complaining about electoral conditions and proposing a postponement. Nobody expected the Fatherland Front to take any notice; it was believed that the Russians wanted early elections in Bulgaria as a good advertisement for democratic rule on the Soviet formula.

There was a long and stormy last-minute session of the Allied Control Council at the end of which the Soviet representative was supposed, unexpectedly, to have washed his hands of the whole business. (It was just after the Potsdam conference, so perhaps concession was the directive of the day.) At the eleventh hour—on the morning before election day—the Fatherland Front government suddenly announced the postponement of the elections.

This was the first and only definite diplomatic success won by the Americans and British in their dealings with the Fatherland Front and the Soviet authorities in Bulgaria. It gave an immense fillip to the Opposition. They felt, rightly or wrongly, that they themselves had achieved something. They knew it was dangerous to appear to be agents of the Anglo-Americans, and they wanted to avoid this charge, but it was stimulating to feel they were not alone. Their followers took courage; and a good many well-off and middle-class people, who had never had anything to do with Agrarian ideas or Social Democracy, and who sometimes had shady political pasts, became loud and noisy supporters of the Opposition.

Nikola Petkov became something of a hero. His father and brother, both Agrarians, had died violent deaths during earlier upheavals. He himself had lived for years in Paris and had tended to keep out of politics. He was a broad-shouldered, thick-set man, polished and urbane but at the same time vigorous and sincere. He was not a peasant type, but a man of Western European culture. He was accused of being a 'very rich man'. Actually, he had a smallish house, by Western standards, in the middle of Sofia, where he lived with his sister and her husband. The house was always overflowing with Agrarians, a good many of them real peasants wearing rough woollen peasant clothes. There was often a knot of them standing patiently waiting in the tiny front garden. Inside, the telephone was always ringing, usually with messages from local branches of the Party. Petkov was a daring and tenacious man, but he felt the strain of being an Opposition leader. His right hand trembled badly.

The next big success of the Opposition, or concession by the Fatherland Front, was permission to start three Opposition newspapers. After delays and hitches, these opened up in September, 1945: one belonging to the Agrarians, one to the Social Democrats, and one, surprisingly, to the Democratic Party of Nikola Mushanov, which had never formed part of the Fatherland Front and was officially classed as thoroughly reactionary. There was no censorship before publication, although there was always the danger of suppression by one method or another. The Opposition could now launch a violent press campaign against various aspects of Fatherland Front rule. Very soon the Opposition Agrarian newspaper, *Narodno Zemedelsko Zname*, had a circulation well over ten times as big as the pro-government Agrarian newspaper and rivalling the two biggest government newspapers. Nikola Petkov, its editor, claimed it could easily have passed this level if the government had allowed extra newsprint.

These newspapers came in useful to the Opposition when the government announced that the postponed elections would be held on November 18th. They could now denounce supposed electoral terrorism much more effectively: they did so, with a great deal of drama and probably a good deal of poetic licence. They launched a formal demand for the replacement of the Communist Ministers of Interior and Justice by 'neutrals', as a guarantee of fair elections. There was no response. It was said that the Russians were against any change. After a good deal of dithering, the opposition Agrarians and Social Democrats announced jointly that they would boycott the elections. Everybody started speculating: would America and Britain try their strength again, and request a second postponement of the elections? If they did, and if the government had to yield again, it would be a dangerous blow to the prestige of the whole Fatherland Front system.

Perhaps that was why, twelve days before election day, the Communist Georgi Dimitrov suddenly arrived by air in Sofia from Moscow.

Georgi Dimitrov was born and bred in a revolutionary atmosphere. He was born on June 18th, 1882, in Kovachevtsi, a village in the Radomir district of Bulgaria. According to the official Communist account, his father, a worker, had 'revolutionary ideas' which his son learned from him. Georgi's eldest brother, Constantin, became secretary of a printing workers' trade union; he was killed in the Balkan Wars. Another brother, Nikola, also a revolutionary, went to Russia in 1905, and became involved in the revolutionary movement there. In 1908 the Tsarist police arrested him at an illegal printing press in Odessa. He was sent to Siberia where he died in 1917. A third brother, Todor, took part as a Communist in the Workers' revolt in Bulgaria in September, 1923, was arrested and held without trial. He died in 1925. The youngest sister, Elena, yet another revolutionary, escaped by underground route from Bulgaria to Russia in 1925.

Georgi's mother, who from her photograph was a simple but very strong-minded woman, had so much courage that when her son was being tried at the Reichstag fire trial in 1933, she travelled with Elena to Paris and addressed a French workers' meeting asking for help for her son. The two women then went on to Berlin.

With such a family, Georgi had a lot to live up to. He started work at a printing press at the age of twelve. At fifteen he became an 'activist' in the Sofia printing workers' union. His first political article was printed that year in the paper, *The Printing Worker*. At eighteen he became secretary of his union. At twenty he joined the Social Democratic Party and fought, in the internal party struggle, for the revolutionary or 'Narrow' wing against the reformist or 'Broad' wing. He became secretary of the Sofia branch of the 'Narrow' wing, and at the age of twenty-seven was a member of the Central Committee of the 'Narrows', who in 1919 developed into the Bulgarian Communist Party.

During the same years Georgi carried on his trade union work on a widening basis and was mixed up in a series of strike movements in Bulgaria before the first world war. He also was fired with the idea of establishing links with the workers of other countries—an idea which he could develop, over twenty years later, in his work for the Third International. In 1912, it is said, he called on Bulgarian workers to 'help the miners who were on strike in England'.

In 1913, at the age of thirty-one, he was elected to the Bulgarian Parliament. His group did not want Bulgaria to take part in the first world war. Georgi went to prison for a year and a half on a charge of undermining discipline in the Army.

In 1919, when the 'Narrow' wing formally transformed itself into the Communist Party, the new Party wanted to send Dimitrov and Vasil Kolarov to Russia for the Second Congress of the Comintern. They set out 'illegally' by boat on the Black Sea, but a storm drove them on to the Rumanian coast. They were arrested by the Rumanian police, but released. In the end, late in the next year, Dimitrov reached Russia by a roundabout route through Italy. In Moscow he met Lenin and Stalin, whose devoted disciple he became.

Back again in Bulgaria, he was one of the leaders of the Workers' revolt in September, 1923. When it failed he escaped to Yugoslavia.

Then started long years of political exile. At home two death sentences were passed on him because of his Communist activity. Return was dangerous. He worked mainly in Vienna and Berlin, loyal to his father's revolutionary ideas.

In 1933 Dimitrov was arrested in Germany in connection with the Reichstag fire case. At the Leipzig trial his defiance, courage and eloquence and his provocative and scornful replies to Goering made him known all over the world. Anyone who has watched Bulgarian political trials would say that these things not only showed the spirit of Dimitrov the Communist: they were typically Bulgarian.

When all the world had admired his bearing at the Leipzig trial, it was wounding for Dimitrov that the Bulgarian government of Nikola Mushanov—later Opposition politician under the Fatherland Front— apparently took no interest, gave him no support and offered him no hospitality after his release. Dimitrov probably did not want to go home at that moment. He had higher things on hand. But he would almost certainly have liked a pressing invitation. Its absence seemed to have left a certain personal rancour against the 'bourgeois' politicians of Bulgaria.

After the trial Dimitrov went to Moscow. In 1935 he became secretary-general of the plenary committee of the Third International and kept this influential job until the International was formally dissolved in May, 1943.

The immediate pre-war years were the period when the Communist order of the day, outside Russia, was the Popular Front. It was no longer an exclusive appeal to the proletariat. It was an appeal to intellectuals, *petit bourgeois*, peasants and 'patriots' to unite with the workers against Fascism. This was the broadened basis of Dimitrov's work in the Third International. It was also, with certain changes, the basis of the later Soviet formula—for which Dimitrov himself may have been partly responsible—for the wartime and post-war Balkan 'fronts' or coalitions.

No one expounded the need for this broadened basis more eloquently or reasonably than Dimitrov, both on the international plane and in relation to Bulgaria itself. His wartime and post-war messages and exhortations to Bulgarians were moderate, constructive and statesman-like. The Communists, he said, must not imagine they could rule alone; they must work with the Agrarians, since Bulgaria was a peasant country; the Fatherland Front must be a permanent basis of political life; there was no need for hasty revolutionary methods. But later it sometimes seemed that Dimitrov, however big the international rôle he had played, however statesmanlike he could be from Moscow, had always remained a Bulgarian, with the limitations of a man from a small overcrowded country. At heart he was always the intolerant champion of the 'Narrow' wing.

There was great excitement in Sofia when on November 8th, 1945, a special midday edition of the Communist newspaper announced in big heavy block letters that Dimitrov had come home at last.

He could presumably have returned in triumph at any time from September 9th, 1944, onwards. People assumed that he had more important work of an international character in Moscow; or that he could help Bulgaria better while in direct contact with the Kremlin; or that he could keep a more lofty and statesmanlike control of the Fatherland Front from afar off than near at hand.

About a month before his return he had sent his old friend and colleague, Vasil Kolarov, home from Moscow. Kolarov, a square-built man with heavy jaw and kindly eyes, gave an impression of greater solidity, stability, depth and tolerance than the mercurial and fiery Dimitrov. Kolarov spoke slowly, evenly, always measuring what he said; he had an air of wisdom and seemed immovable but not passionate in his decisions. During October, 1945, he had had a few informal talks with Opposition leaders, particularly Nikola Petkov, to see if they could be brought back into the Front on the Front's terms. It appeared that he had a genuine liking for Petkov, but thought him quite extravagant and unrealistic in his demands. The Opposition, elated by their recent successes, held their ground and refused concessions. Nothing was achieved. Now many Bulgarians, even the Opposition, thought: perhaps Georgi Dimitrov, as an elder statesman above party bickerings, has come to find a way of conciliation.

The afternoon of November 8th was grey, with ragged low clouds and gusts of wind and rain. In the big square or tiny park in front of the National Theatre, a crowd of tens of thousands gathered. Mostly they represented Fatherland Front and party organisations, particularly youth organisations; some came spontaneously, partly out of curiosity, partly out of real enthusiasm. For this was a man who had won more international fame than most Bulgarians. Boys were spreadeagled in the black wet branches of the trees. Everywhere there were soggy banners with roughly scrawled slogans: 'welcome home', 'welcome to the founder of the Fatherland Front', 'welcome to the darling of our people, the pride and glory of Bulgaria'. In front of the theatre was a strong guard of mounted Militiamen. The crowd stood in the rain, not knowing for certain whether Georgi would come at all.

Inside the theatre everything was set for a solemn celebration of the anniversary of the Russian October Revolution. Flags, palm trees, a massed choir on the stage, the diplomatic corps (except for any British or American representatives), high government officials, cabinet ministers, representatives of the partisans and war-wounded filled the theatre. There was a long wait: would the great man come? Then a bluish spotlight was thrown on an empty box to the right of the stage. The choir burst into the anthem. General Biryusov, Soviet representative on the Allied Control Council, walked in, in full and glorious uniform, leading a small slight man with a lush and curving grey moustache, wavy grey hair, waxen cheeks with flushed high cheekbones, very bright, fixed, black eyes. It was probably the theatrical effect of the spotlight, but Georgi Dimitrov looked somehow artificial, like a wax-work, perhaps, of a nineteenth-century villain of melodrama. Third member of the party was Damian Velchev, the silent conspirator, now War Minister of the Fatherland Front.

There was terrific cheering and clapping and rhythmic shouting of the three syllables, Di-mi-trov. It lasted nearly five minutes. Dimitrov did not smile or look moved or pleased. He stayed stiff, his eyes un-winking. Only General Biryusov smiled.

The ceremonies went their way, sometimes interrupted by a sudden burst of applause for Dimitrov. Everyone wanted to know whether Dimitrov would consent to speak. At the very end, after much pressing, he did. His speech was relayed by loudspeaker to the wet and waiting crowd outside the theatre.

To all except his most fanatical partisans, it was a shock and a dis-appointment. It was not, for the most part, statesmanlike or above party strife. It was hotly personal, even egotistic. There was a flavour of bitterness. He spoke of his long exile and the death sentences that had awaited him in Bulgaria, recalling Mushanov's failure to invite him home in 1933. He told how that morning he had stepped out of the plane on to his native soil: the first thing he had asked for was his country's newspapers; the first thing he saw, in this moment of emotion after so long an exile, was the filthy rags of the Opposition, indulging in vulgar abuse of that great institution, the Fatherland Front. Then came sarcastic and biting attacks on the Opposition, in the old Leipzig trial vein. These were most effective oratorically, but disappointing for those, both in the Fatherland Front and in the Opposition, who had hoped for conciliation.

Outside, the listening crowd cheered. But some on the outskirts looked black and drifted away. Still, at the end of speech the faithful shouted so long that Dimitrov appeared, dwarfed by a vast bouquet of white chrysanthemums, on the balcony in front of the theatre. Beside him was Tsola Dragoicheva, smiling, flushed and gratified by reflected glory. The applause grew hysterical. Superficially, the homecoming was an immense success.

After that the electoral campaign went according to plan. It was clear that Dimitrov had no idea of making concessions to the Opposi-tion or to the Anglo-Americans. A United States note of protest duly arrived a few days before the elections, but this time there was no British note to back it up. No notice was taken of the American note. The Opposition stepped up their appeal for a boycott of the polls. Their newspapers printed more and more bloodcurdling reports of beatings and terrorisation of Opposition men in the provinces, by the Communist Youth or by the Militia. Rather late and not altogether straight, denials of these reports were issued by the Ministry of the Interior or printed in the government press.

One week before election day, Vasil Kolarov and Alexander Obbov travelled to Karnobat, a market town in the agricultural plain of Eastern Bulgaria, to address a big and important Fatherland Front meeting. The Opposition Agrarians had boldly decided to hold one of their rare public meetings in Karnobat the same day; usually they held that public Opposition meetings led to beatings and terrorism and so lowered morale.

It was a rainy November Sunday. Early in the morning special trains started bringing Fatherland Front supporters into Karnobat from bigger towns within a fifty-mile radius. Opposition supporters, on their own account, had to make their way by horse-cart or ox-wagon or on foot.

From the special trains men, women and children, often family parties, came tumbling out cheerfully enough, though many had been travelling in cattle-trucks or open trucks. They had brought with them their banners, portraits and flags, which soon got sopped in the rain. A fair number were wearing embroidered peasant clothes. Many were carrying baskets or bundles of food, mostly hunks of bread and paprikas, to last them out the day. There was a good-tempered bank-holiday atmosphere with an underlying strain of grim earnestness.

The visitors marched the two miles into the town up a muddy road, to make up the bigger part of the crowd of 15,000 or so which was soon tightly packed into the square in front of the town hall. Here they stood devotedly for well over four hours in the soaking rain, listening to powerful but rather repetitive political speeches. A very few managed to put up umbrellas, many more held folded copies of government newspapers over their heads to keep off the rain. Sometimes, not often, a child would burst into howls and be angrily shushed.

The crowd clapped and cheered loyally and energetically at regular intervals during the speeches. Alexander Obbov, who was the most personal and least ideological of the speakers, got most applause. After all the speeches were over, there came recitations and dramatic representations, all still on the little wooden platform in the rain, in front of the town hall. Then at last the family parties, tired and hungry, began to drift away. But the younger ones, the really faithful, stayed to the very end, cheering all the louder as the crowd dwindled.

Meanwhile the Opposition's supporters had been herded into a large open cattle market outside the town, fenced in all round by a wall. A few armed Militiamen stood at the gateway into the enclosure, possibly to note down the outstanding members of the audience as they went in. Outside, to encourage their supporters, very young men of the Opposition Agrarian Youth organisation galloped up and down on horses brandishing the green banners of the party. People trickled slowly and a little nervously into the enclosure. Inside, not more than 3,000 people stood in the rain around a wooden platform from which, under streaming orange and green banners, Boris Bumbarov and the Agrarian Youth leader, Peter Serbinsky, a freckled young man with fiery red hair, a fiery temperament and a gift of fiery oratory, made bold speeches. The cheering was enthusiastic, but thin and ragged in comparison with the mass meeting of the Fatherland Front. There was no heckling; in this instance, the Opposition was being let well alone.

Slight trouble came early in the afternoon when small groups of Opposition Agrarians, carrying their banners, daringly marched through the town itself. The Fatherland Front supporters, who by that time were scattered through the town, turned out to shout, boo and hiss and throw bits of wood or rubbish at the marchers. The marchers dared not retaliate. There was no bloodshed. The most serious damage of the day would probably be a lot of colds in the nose, except that Bulgarians are so tough and hardy that they may have escaped even these.

To judge by these two rival meetings, it might have been deduced that the Fatherland Front was five times as strong as the Opposition in this district of Eastern Bulgaria. This estimate would, however, probably have been seriously wrong; to judge fairly two other factors—travel facilities and the psychological atmosphere in the surrounding towns and villages—would have to be taken into account.

The second factor was most difficult to estimate. But it seemed certain that, even if Opposition reports of physical terrorism were exaggerated, many Bulgarians were frightened. Perhaps they were imaginative and had little real cause for fear. But so long as they were frightened the whole apparatus of public meetings and voting was unreal and bore little relation to the true political wishes of the people.

On the eve of the elections, most of the middle-class of Sofia seemed determined not to go to the polls. 'No one in this block of flats will go,' a professional man said. 'I have made up my mind: I won't go, even though I have a government job which I may lose. But my mother is nervous,' one officer's daughter said.

They had, of course, the choice of going to the poll and handing in a blank or spoilt voting slip—perhaps drawing on it a black cat, the unofficial mascot of the Opposition—but they thought this would be a mistake since it would make it easier to juggle with the count.

Some of these would-be abstainers, the next day, told how they had had several telephone calls, or personal calls from relatives or Fatherland Front officials, urging them or warning them to vote. Some had taken fright and gone to the polls, though all claimed to have put 'black cats' into the voting box.

Whether this last-minute change of heart was just a display of middle-class nerves, or whether they had any real reason to fear losing their jobs or their livelihood, it was almost impossible for an outsider to say.

In general it seemed that, among the middle-class, the better off a man was, the more confident and defiant he was in his Opposition attitude. The more insecure he was economically, the more wavering he was apt to be.

On polling day, in Sofia and the neighbourhood, everything went off perfectly smoothly, in perfect order. There were no outward signs of terror or disturbance. There were two or three armed Militiamen outside each polling station, and usually one inside; but it was difficult to complain of that. The Fatherland Front directive had been that election day should be made a national holiday, a day of national rejoicing. Particularly in the villages, this directive was followed faithfully. Powerful loudspeakers blared out national dances and songs, with their insistent tricky rhythms and semi-oriental harmonisation. Peasants were encouraged to come to the polls in their best national costumes. 'Agitkas', small propaganda units of young men and women, were sent round the countryside in lorries, to start up dancing in the mud of the village street. Queues of waiting voters formed outside the polling stations. Squads of troops marched in formation to the polling stations, in cases where they did not vote in their own barracks. Women had the vote for the first time; old, old peasant women, staring and bewildered, were led to the polls and went through the formalities as devoutly as if it were a religious ceremony.

Bands of foreign journalists were motored around the countryside in cars supplied by the Ministry of Information, accompanied by Ministry officials as interpreters. There was no other means of transport. As far as they were concerned, there was nothing to criticise. Once a poorly-dressed woman slipped furtively up to some journalists and said: 'Why have you abandoned us: it was only you who could have saved us.' Outside another polling station a boy of seventeen protested loudly that the election was unfair, but could not or dared not explain why.

As far as the foreign journalist could tell, all he could say was that the election seemed perfectly orderly. Next day he was prominently quoted as saying so in the government press, often with the addition that he had also said it was fair and free. That, of course, it was much less easy to judge.

Also, he had no check on the methods of counting the votes. The Opposition, as they had boycotted the election, were naturally enough not represented on the electoral committees in each polling station. There was no independent control of the count. The way in which the preliminary results were issued by the Ministry of the Interior and the government press was confused and contradictory. It was difficult not to deduce there had been juggling with percentages of abstentions. Cynical outsiders looked on the final results as inartistic. According to the Foreign Minister, who presumably came in to the picture in an attempt to clear up the muddle over figures, out of a total of 4,378,314 possible voters, 3,757,596 had cast votes and 3,311,962 had voted for the Fatherland Front. This meant that over three-quarters of Bulgaria was solidly behind the Fatherland Front. Maybe it was true, but it seemed too high a figure to be really convincing.

The Opposition quickly came out with their own rival, unofficial and considerably different figures for the results, particularly for Sofia. But naturally these were impossible to check. However, on the basis of these figures, the Opposition refused to accept or recognise the election as valid and immediately started a campaign for a fresh election to be held with 'neutral' Ministers of Interior and Justice, and separate party lists. The British and Americans expressed incredulity about the election results. But there was no proof, either way.

In any case, Bulgaria once again had an elected parliament, and every member of this parliament was a member of the Fatherland Front. The Front had won the first round in the struggle to consolidate an 'Eastern' democracy or pro-Soviet régime. But the struggle was not over. Bulgaria still had no peace treaty and the Fatherland Front government was still unrecognised by Britain and America. Western intervention was still a menace.

E

5

The Big Three in Bulgaria and Rumania

THE system of the three-power control commissions set up to supervise Bulgaria and Rumania (and Hungary) during the period between the armistice and the peace treaty never worked smoothly. The principle of the commissions was a gain to the Western Powers. It gave them a formal right to take some interest and have some say in the political and economic affairs of the Soviet-occupied countries. In theory, it kept open the door to the West and prevented a Soviet monopoly. In practice, the British and American representatives on the commissions found that they had remarkably little power to get themselves heard. They could protest stiffly, after the event, to the Soviet representatives and deliver snubs to the Balkan governments, but they could be snubbed much more effectively in return.

The armistice terms of September and October, 1944, merely said: 'An Allied Control Commission will be established which will undertake until conclusion of peace the regulation of and control over the execution of the present terms under the general direction and orders of the Allied (Soviet) High Command acting on behalf of the Allied Powers.' The rights and powers of the British and American representatives on the Control Commissions were not defined.

Still, the British and American representatives imagined that they would have the right to be consulted in advance by their Soviet colleagues on all questions of importance, to express their own views and to make their own proposals. In practice, they soon found that meetings of the Commission as a whole were rare and spasmodic, that they were only consulted after the event, if then, and that their views were not particularly welcomed. Orders were issued in the name of the Control Commission of which the British and American representatives knew nothing.

The Russians on their side presumably felt that as, during the early months, a war was still being fought not far from the Balkans, and as they were militarily responsible in the area, it was up to them to get on with the job. If the Anglo-Americans wanted to take reactionary or near-reactionary Balkan politicians under their protection or to help ex-enemies to evade justified economic requisitioning and compensation, that was their business: the kindest and easiest thing the Russians could do was to ignore them.

It also seemed likely that in the early months there was a genuine misunderstanding between the Russians and their Western opposite numbers about the terms of reference of the Commissions. There was some talk of private verbal assurances given by Mr. Eden in Moscow in the autumn of 1944, which left the British and Americans without a foot to stand on. If these assurances existed they were never published.*

In February, 1945, at the Yalta Conference, the Western Powers sought a wider and firmer basis for Western participation in the Balkans. They achieved the Yalta 'Declaration on Liberated Europe'. This said that the Big Three 'jointly declare their mutual agreement to concert during the temporary period of instability in liberated Europe the policies of their three governments in assisting the peoples liberated from the domination of Nazi Germany and the peoples of the former Axis satellite States of Europe to solve by democratic means their pressing political and economic problems.'

The three governments would jointly assist any European liberated State or former Axis satellite, among other things, 'to form interim governmental authorities broadly representative of all democratic elements in the population and pledged to the earliest possible establishment through free elections of governments responsive to the will of the people; and to facilitate where necessary the holding of such elections.'

The Declaration added: 'When, in the opinion of the three governments, conditions in any European liberated State or any former Axis satellite State in Europe make such action necessary, they will immediately consult together on the measures necessary to discharge the joint responsibilities set forth in this declaration.'

Although this Declaration gave the Western Powers a vague general right to interfere anywhere in Europe they felt inclined, it did not give them the right or the power to outvote or overbear Soviet Russia in those instances where they were at odds with her—and that was nearly every instance, in the Balkans and Eastern Europe. The best they could hope for, on the basis of Yalta, was a series of dissatisfying and unreal compromises.

In any case, Yalta did not do much to improve British-American standing on the control commissions. The Western Powers' representatives got more and more frustrated and humiliated.

At the Potsdam Conference in July-August, 1945, the working of the Control Commissions was discussed afresh between the Big Three.

---

* James Byrnes, former American Secretary of State, in his book, *Speaking Frankly*, published in 1947, said that when Churchill and Eden visited Moscow in the autumn of 1944, there was an 'informal understanding' that, if the British found it necessary to take military action to quell internal disorders in Greece, the Soviets would not interfere; the British would in return recognise Russia's right to take the lead in maintaining order in Rumania.

The only published result was: 'The three governments take note that the Soviet representatives on the Allied Control Councils in Rumania, Bulgaria and Hungary have communicated to their U.K. and U.S. colleagues proposals for improving the work of the Control Councils, now that hostilities in Europe have ceased. The three governments agreed that the revision of procedures of the Allied Control Councils in these countries would now be undertaken, taking into account the interests and responsibilities of the three governments, which together presented the terms of armistice to the respective countries, and accepting as a basis the agreed proposals.'

Many people interpreted this as meaning that in principle the Russians had agreed to give the British and Americans a bigger share in the working of the Control Commissions. This interpretation turned out rather optimistic.

The Potsdam declaration also for the first time directly linked the two questions of peace treaties for the satellites and Western recognition of the satellite governments. This opened the way to endless but futile haggling of the one against the other.

The declaration said:

'The three governments have charged the Council of Foreign Ministers with the task of preparing peace treaties for Bulgaria, Finland, Hungary and Rumania. The conclusion of peace treaties with recognised democratic governments in these States will also enable the three governments to support applications from them for membership of the United Nations. The three governments agree to examine separately in the near future, in the light of the conditions then prevailing, the establishment of diplomatic relations with Finland, Rumania, Bulgaria and Hungary, to the extent possible prior to the conclusion of peace treaties with those countries.

'The three governments have no doubt that in view of the changed conditions resulting from the termination of the war in Europe, representatives of the Allied press will enjoy full freedom to report to the world upon developments in Rumania, Bulgaria, Hungary and Finland.'

Theoretically, this declaration put Britain and America in a strong bargaining position. Russia immediately recognised the Rumanian and Bulgarian governments; but they could say to the Russians: 'You want us also to recognise your protégé governments and sign peace treaties with them. We do not like these governments and will not recognise them until they are changed to suit our tastes. And we will not sign treaties with them until we have recognised them. So you had better get these governments changed as soon as possible. It is all laid down in Potsdam.'

In actual fact, America and Britain could not take up this attitude strongly or sincerely for two reasons: First, they wanted to get the Italian treaty signed, and Russia would not sign until the Western Powers signed the Balkan treaties. Next, the British and Americans thought that the most important thing for the Balkans was that the Russian occupation troops should withdraw: this was more likely to lead to a change in the governments than any diplomatic bargaining. Before the Russian troops would withdraw, the peace treaties must be signed. And signature would mean recognising the existing governments.

So from the long-term point of view the Americans and British did not gain much at Potsdam. From the short-term point of view, however, the general feeling was that their position in the Balkans was strengthened. It was in this atmosphere that, just after Potsdam, the British and United States Governments delivered the notes that got the Bulgarian election postponed from August 26th. Also in August, 1945, inspired by Potsdam and with the moral blessing of Britain and America, King Michael of Rumania 'broke off diplomatic relations' with his government—the National Democratic Front government of Petru Grozea. In a letter of August 21st, 1945, King Michael 'asked the advice' of the Big Three on the broadening of the Rumanian government in the spirit of Potsdam. Since the Grozea government had been imposed on the King by Soviet Russia, acting through M. Vishinski, in March, 1945, King Michael's letter meant, in fact, that he was appealing to Britain and America to intervene and to reverse or modify M. Vishinski's action.

The next step was the removal of press censorship, both in Bulgaria and Rumania, on British and American newspaper correspondents, early in September. Also in September came the Bulgarian government's permission for the publication of three Opposition newspapers. This step was not taken by the Rumanian government until the next spring, after the visit of a three-Power commission to Bucharest.

Towards the end of October, 1945, there was great excitement. President Truman had decided to send to Bulgaria and Rumania, as his personal envoy, Mark Ethridge, a distinguished American journalist. He was to report back to the President on political conditions, after a personal investigation.

He came first to Sofia. All the simple-minded—particular the Opposition rank and file—thought that he would settle Bulgaria's fate.

He turned out to be a charming and urbane man, a liberal from the South, with a great gift for telling funny stories to avoid answering awkward questions. He was amiable to everyone, both the Fatherland Front and the Opposition. It was at first hard to guess what he thought.

On October 25th he gave a dinner to journalists from both Government and Opposition newspapers, and asked both the Minister of Information and Nikola Petkov, as editor of the chief Opposition newspaper. Outside the hotel hundreds of members of the Opposition youth organisations gathered to cheer him and shout over and over again, 'We want freedom, we want freedom.' Anyone recognised as British or American in the crowd was warmly shaken by the hand and told that only British-American help could save Bulgaria. The British political representative, who happened also to be dining in the hotel, was carried in shoulder high from his car.

But very soon after the Opposition Youth had gathered, the Communist Youth came hurrying up, more and more of them, carrying Fatherland Front banners and shouting Fatherland Front slogans. There developed a great shoving and pushing match between the two rival crowds, for possession of the road in front of the hotel and of each others' flags and banners. But though the scrimmage went on for well over an hour, it was surprisingly orderly: no one was seriously hurt, no one let off a gun, the Militia, though badly jostled, did not use force; one big pane of glass was broken. In the end the Communists won by weight of numbers.

Whether this exemplary non-violence was meant to impress Ethridge, or was caused by fear of Militia reprisals, or was due to the Western spirit of bland good humour somehow spread like soothing balm by Ethridge, it would be hard to guess.

Later Ethridge went to Rumania, without having settled Bulgaria's fate. There he carried on similar talks and took part in similar festivities and was greeted with similar hopefulness by the Opposition. His ultimate report to President Truman on the two governments, Bulgarian and Rumanian, was unfavourable. But it had little practical effect in the two countries.

Anglo-American prestige fell again soon after the Ethridge visit. In spite of Ethridge and in spite of Anglo-American displeasure the Bulgarian election was held on November 18th as arranged. In Rumania Petru Grozea refused to yield to the King, the Anglo-Americans seemed to have no influence on the Russians, and the political deadlock was unbroken. In December, 1945, the British and Americans made a new effort to wring concessions over the Balkans, at the Moscow Foreign Ministers' Conference.

The results, on the surface, seemed a compromise favouring the West. In reality, Russia had yielded very little. The Moscow communiqué said:

'RUMANIA: The three Governments are prepared to give King Michael the advice for which he has asked in his letter of August 21st, 1945, on the broadening of the Rumanian government. The King should be advised that one member of the National Peasant Party and one member of the Liberal Party should be included in the Government. The Commission referred to below shall satisfy itself that: (*a*) they are truly representative members of the groups of the parties not represented in the government; (*b*) they are suitable and will work loyally with the government.

'The three Governments take note that the Rumanian government thus reorganised should declare that free and unfettered elections will be held as soon as possible on the basis of universal and secret ballot. All democratic and anti-fascist parties should have the right to take part in these elections and to put forward candidates. The reorganised government should give assurances concerning the grant of freedom of the press, speech, religion and association.

'A. Y. Vishinski, Mr. Harriman and Sir Archibald Clark-Kerr are authorised to proceed to Bucharest immediately to consult with King Michael and members of the present government, with a view to the execution of the above-mentioned tasks. As soon as these tasks are accomplished and the required assurances have been received, the government of Rumania, with which the Soviet government maintains diplomatic relations, will be recognised by the government of the U.S.A. and by the government of the United Kingdom.

'BULGARIA: It is understood by the three governments that the Soviet government takes upon itself the mission of giving friendly advice to the Bulgarian government with regard to the desirability of the inclusion in the Bulgarian government of the Fatherland Front, now being formed, of an additional two representatives of other democratic groups who (*a*) are truly representative of the groups of the parties which are not participating in the government, and (*b*) are really suitable and will work loyally with the government. As soon as the governments of the U.S.A. and the United Kingdom are convinced that this friendly advice has been accepted by the Bulgarian government and the said representatives have been included in its body, the government of the U.S.A. and the government of the United Kingdom will recognise the Bulgarian government, with which the government of the Soviet Union already has diplomatic relations.'

A clear and invidious distinction was drawn between the Bulgarian government, which was so independent that it merely needed 'friendly advice' from Russia, and the Rumanian government, which was to be told what to do by a three-Power commission on the spot. But as things turned out, this distinction worked in favour of the Rumanian government, which got Western recognition a few weeks later, and against the Bulgarian government, which did not get recognition until over a year later.

Between the great Powers, the Moscow communiqué meant that the Soviet Union bargained the admission of two representatives of the Rumanian and Bulgarian Oppositions into the Rumanian and Bulgarian governments, respectively, against recognition of these two governments by Britain and America. Russia gained more than she lost. She lost, for the time being, the right to ban the Oppositions as fascist and reactionary or to declare them illegal, either directly or through the existing governments. On the other hand, such a move would in any case have been very unpopular and possibly dangerous, so that Russia probably would not have considered it seriously at so early a stage.

Also, it was easy to keep even legal Oppositions under reasonable control, and two Opposition representatives in a government of fifteen or more Ministers would be powerless. On the profit side for Russia, the British and United States Governments, by recognising the governments of Rumania and Bulgaria, would lose much of their diplomatic bargaining power and their grounds for interfering in these two countries.

In all, the Moscow communiqué seemed a device for saving face for Britain and America, rather than a serious attempt to solve the very real political problems of Rumania and Bulgaria. It gave no sincere working compromise between the 'Easterners' and 'Westerners'.

For Rumania, things moved fast. The three-man commission—Vishinski, Sir Archibald Clark-Kerr, then British Ambassador in Moscow (now Lord Inverchapel), and Averill Harriman, then U.S. Ambassador in Moscow—arrived in Bucharest on December 31st. With such lofty mentors, a solution had to be found quickly. The Opposition tried, rather querulously, to state conditions for entering the government of Petru Grozea, but although they were heard sympathetically by Clark-Kerr and Harriman, they were told they must rely on the assurances which Grozea would have to give after they had entered the government. This made them even more querulous. But they put forward their nominees. There was some desultory haggling between Vishinski and his Western colleagues over the names submitted by the Opposition. In the end they all agreed on Emil Hatieganu, for the National Peasant Party, and Mihail Romniceanu, for the National Liberal Party. They were to enter the government without condition.

On January 7th, 1946, the new government was sworn in. King Michael returned to Bucharest from his country home at Sinaia and resumed relations, if rather frigidly, with Petru Grozea. Vishinski left via Sofia for London on January 8th. Clark-Kerr stayed a day or two longer, trying to extract or cajole written assurances of the four democratic liberties out of Petru Grozea—with very modest success. The two Western members of the Commission left amid mutters of 'Runciman' and 'a second Munich' from the more excitable sections of the Opposition. In mid-February the British and United States Governments recognised the Rumanian government of Petru Grozea, though in a conditional form. The men of the Grozea government, except for the two Opposition Ministers, were triumphant.

After that, although more diplomatic notes passed on the subject of democratic liberties, the delay in holding the promised democratic election and the methods of holding it, the Western Powers had lost much of their power of pressure and their formal ground for intervention. Very little if anything was changed in the methods or aims of the pro-Soviet government of Petru Grozea. The Opposition Ministers were powerless, except to make plaintive protests against the actions of the government of which they were nominally members. Since they were suspected, not without justice, of reporting what went on in the government to the representatives of the Western Powers, they were allowed very little share in the actual work of the Cabinet.

The Opposition won the right, after entering the government, of publishing a limited number of newspapers, under government censorship occasionally reinforced by Soviet intervention. They also had the right to carry on a certain limited political activity and organisation, subject to the risk of incursions or occasional terrorism by local pro-government enthusiasts. Finally, they had the right to contest the long-promised election, in November, 1946, as legally recognised parties. But all these rights were of little practical use. Even responsible government supporters, when speaking frankly, did not suggest that the election either would be, or had been, conducted on anything like Western methods: their argument was that no Rumanian election ever had been. The Opposition were allotted only 37 seats out of a total of 414 in the new parliament.

There were the usual American and British notes or expressions of disapproval both before and after the event. The Yalta and Moscow declarations were invoked, but sounded hollow by that time. No British or American official representative attended the opening of parliament by King Michael on December 1st, 1946, nor did any Opposition deputies. Dr. Iuliu Maniu, leader of the National Peasant Party, announced that his party, the main surviving Opposition group, did not recognise the November election and consequently would not participate in the work of parliament. The Moscow compromise seemed to have worked in a very one-sided way.

In Bulgaria things developed differently. So as to save the face of the Fatherland Front, Russia had arranged that there should be no three-man commission. Instead, Vishinski, stopping off in Sofia for the night of January 8th, 1946, apparently thought he could fix things in an hour or two.

Negotiations had already started 'to implement the Moscow decisions' between the Fatherland Front prime minister, Kimon Georgiev, and the Opposition leaders, but had got nowhere yet. Still, Kimon Georgiev was not Vishinski, who had all the authority of a big three decree behind him.

At two in the morning, Vishinski summoned Nikola Petkov and Kosta Lulchev to him. Petkov, the story went, said he was celebrating one of the days of Christmas, Orthodox style, and so could not leave his home. In any case he refused to go to Vishinski until the next day. Kosta Lulchev, a simple, tough, old-time Socialist of Second International connections, with a venerable iron-grey beard, went in the middle of the night but remained obstinate. Petkov went the next morning.

Both Opposition leaders stuck to the same terms. They told Vishinski that they of course wished to fulfil the Moscow decisions of the three foreign ministers. But they could only enter the government on certain conditions: removal of the Ministries of Interior and Justice from communist hands, and the holding of fresh genuinely free elections. They considered these conditions in accordance with the spirit of Moscow.

Vishinski, it was said, got very angry and banged on the table. (The story in the Balkans was that Vishinski, discussing one of his stormy Balkan interviews with an acquaintance, said: 'It is a shameful lie. I did *not* bang on the table'—bringing his fist down with a terrifying thump to emphasise the '*not*'.) In any case, Vishinski told the Opposition leaders that they were defying the Big Three Foreign Ministers and misinterpreting and sabotaging the Moscow decisions. They had no right to make conditions. Petkov asked who had decreed this interpretation of the Moscow decisions. Vishinski said that, in Bulgaria, the Soviet interpretation alone was binding. Petkov said that he could not agree, but would accept any joint interpretation by the Big Three.

That was the end. Vishinski left Sofia. The Opposition stayed outside the government, and were strongly attacked by the Fatherland Front press for sabotaging Bulgaria's chances of Anglo-American recognition and a lenient peace treaty. The Moscow decisions on Bulgaria were never fulfilled. Although the Western Powers had stood aloof—they could hardly instigate the Opposition to prevent the execution of an agreement to which they themselves were partners—they gained on the whole from this non-fulfilment. They kept, for some months longer, a slightly broader foothold than they now had in Rumania.

In March, 1946, there was a fresh attempt at concilation in Bulgaria. The government of Kimon Georgiev formally resigned, and there were prolonged negotiations between Georgiev—who was a 'bourgeois' politician and far from a Communist—and the Opposition leaders, for their entry into the government. The United States government stepped in with an oral communication on March 28th, saying that they hoped to see the Bulgarian government broadened in accordance with the Moscow decisions.

At one moment, according to Nikola Petkov, agreement was almost reached. The Ministry of Justice was to go to an Opposition representative. The Minister of the Interior was to remain a Communist, but under him an Opposition Agrarian was to be put in charge of the Militia and an Opposition Social Democrat in charge of the administration of the Ministry. Free elections were to be held with separate party lists.

Suddenly everything changed overnight and the agreement fell through. The Opposition's explanation was that Russia stepped in to stop it. Nikola Petkov's newspaper printed under a small-type headline, 'Why the Negotiations Failed', a short official announcement that Kimon Georgiev had visited the Soviet Minister in Sofia, Stefan

Kirsanov, late at night. The newspaper was suspended for ten days, it was said at Russian request. A new practically unchanged government was formed, without the Opposition. It was stated that the United States would not recognise it because of its failure to include Opposition elements. The British attitude was roughly the same.

When the three Foreign Ministers met again in Paris in June and July, 1946, for preliminary talks on the satellite peace treaties, it again looked as though there might be changes in Bulgaria. Vasil Kolarov was in Paris as leader of a Bulgarian delegation. He was refused permission by the British Government to visit London to discuss the recognition of the Bulgarian government. But he saw Ernest Bevin in Paris, and was told that Britain wanted the Bulgarian Opposition to be given 'a fair and reasonable share' in the government of the country.

Kolarov was said to have sent home reports saying that the British and American Governments would not sign a peace treaty with Bulgaria until the Fatherland Front government was broadened. Everybody in Sofia expected there would be new negotiations between the Government and the Opposition. But at that moment the Communists were feeling uncertain and nervy about several things: the loyalty of the Army, the loyalty of the Zveno Party, the chances of revolt when the Red Army left Bulgaria. They were in the mood for toughness and purges, not concessions. Georgi Dimitrov said flatly: 'There can be no turning back or even checking of the democratic development of our country. It is moving forward to an even greater strengthening of the Fatherland Front.' In other words, no compromise.

So things trailed on until the second Bulgarian election—this time for a constituent assembly—was held on October 27th, 1946. A Communist was still Minister of the Interior. The Opposition, perhaps concluding that Anglo-American intervention got nowhere in the end, decided to make the best of a bad job and fight the elections. The Fatherland Front contested the elections as a united bloc, but voters could make known their preferences among the various parties of the Front.

Again the election was held under the cloud of Anglo-American displeasure, but by this time the cloud was becoming small and far away. A few days before the election there was a tiff between the United States Government, which had sent communications to the Bulgarian government about the election, and General Biryusov, Soviet representative on the Allied Control Commission, who had banned publication of this correspondence in the Bulgarian newspapers. America got no satisfaction.

The results of the election were interesting, if not representative of the real state of feeling. The Opposition—Agrarians and Social Democrats—together got 101 seats out of a total of 465 seats in the Assembly. The Fatherland Front got the remaining 78 per cent. of the seats; but inside the Front all the non-Communist parties had practically melted away. The Communists got 277 seats, and all the other Fatherland Front parties together only 87.

Petkov claimed that electoral irregularities had reduced the Opposition vote from a genuine figure of 60 per cent. to the announced figure of 22 per cent. British and American spokesmen expressed scepticism about the results. The Fatherland Front, in its new distinctly lopsided form, carried on.

The Communists had a clear parliamentary majority. The obvious thing was for them to form a government that was either purely Communist or at least majority Communist. But no. A new Fatherland Front government was formed on the basis of the old Fatherland Front coalition formula. There was roughly the same distribution of seats among the parties, although three of them had dwindled into tiny parliamentary fractions.

The only serious change was that Georgi Dimitrov, who so far had formally been no more than president of the Communist Party and chairman of the Foreign Affairs Commission of the Assembly, at last took over open responsibility as Prime Minister, in place of the Zveno leader, Kimon Georgiev, who became Foreign Minister. This at least cleared the air: with Georgi Dimitrov ruling Bulgaria in practice but behind the scenes, no one had ever known quite where he was.

A Bulgarian ex-partisan girl, a Communist, was indignant when it was suggested that, under normal parliamentary practice, the Communists might have formed a government alone. She said: 'You do not understand. Bulgaria is not ripe for Communist rule. The people are not yet educated up to it. They are not ready. We need the Fatherland Front for a long time yet, so that the whole nation is represented. It does not matter that the other Fatherland Front parties are very small: they stand for certain elements in the nation. Anyhow, before the election there was an agreement among the Front parties to share out the seats in the government on the old basis, whatever the proportion of party preferences marked. We could not go back on our word.'

The new Assembly opened. The Opposition members took their places; although they had stayed outside the government, they had done better in the election than the Rumanian Opposition. The old purely Fatherland Front Assembly had been a very dull, monotonous sleepy affair. Every measure had been passed practically unanimously and automatically, with the bare minimum of polite criticism—except from one obstreperous and incorrigible old peasant who was nominally a government Agrarian. The new Assembly was very different. The Opposition protested violently and dramatically against a series of alleged electoral irregularities. They were howled down, threatened with suspension, in one or two cases actually suspended. It was quite like old times. The business of the House went on. There were quarrels over the policy and tone of the Opposition newspapers. The Opposition stood their ground. Occasionally they voted for a government Bill if it was in line with their own party principles.

In February, 1947, Georgi Dimitrov said that his government was examining the possibility of a working agreement with the Opposition parties. 'We know that in the last election at least a million electors who are neither fascists nor reactionaries voted for the Opposition lists, for very different motives,' he added rather surprisingly. Among his conditions for co-operation with the Opposition were: the Opposition must not comment publicly on certain questions in such a way as to disturb Bulgaria's relations with her neighbours or the Great Powers; no 'calumniators' must speak in parliament; the Opposition must stop 'calumnies' in the press and 'incitement of discontented elements'.

The Opposition had little to gain by bargaining on such terms.

On February 10th, 1947, the treaties of peace with Bulgaria, Rumania and the other satellites were signed in Paris, by Britain and America among the rest. In both Bulgaria and Rumania—less loudly in Rumania —this was hailed as a great triumph for the pro-Soviet 'Eastern' governments in power. The Western Powers had at last seen reason.

A few days later, although America still held out, Britain took the last step and formally recognised the Bulgarian government. The British note added a number of parting pinpricks:

'His Majesty's Government wish to make it clear that the grant of *de jure* recognition in no way implies that they consider either the past methods employed by the Bulgarian government to consolidate their position or the conduct of the recent elections to have been in keeping with the spirit and intentions of the Yalta declaration on liberated Europe. But they have taken into consideration the obligations accepted by the Bulgarian government in Article 2 of the Peace Treaty, and have decided to accord them *de jure* recognition in the hope that it is the intention of the Bulgarian government henceforth to fulfil in the spirit as well as the letter their pledge to secure to all persons under their jurisdiction the fundamental freedoms, including freedom of expression, of press and publication, of religious worship, of political opinion and of public meetings.

'His Majesty's Government sincerely desire the well-being of the Bulgarian people. They will watch with close and friendly interest the course of future developments in Bulgaria, the disposition of the Bulgarian government towards His Majesty's Government and the spirit in which the Bulgarian government fulfil all their obligations under the peace treaty, and they will thereby determine their attitude to the Bulgarian government.'

A reply from the Fatherland Front government, expressing satisfaction at the British decision, said that the British, in criticising the methods employed by Bulgaria in the past, had not taken into account the special conditions in which the Fatherland Front was formed.

Perhaps, looking back on the whole story of Anglo-American inter-

vention in Bulgaria and Rumania in the years between the armistice and
the peace treaties, people will say that it had about as much effect as a
badly-worn brake on a heavy bus hurtling downhill. Yet it did something to slow down Russia's political impetus—for the time being.

The postscript to the record of Anglo-American intervention is a
pitiful, even tragic, story. During the spring and summer of 1947 relations between East and West grew quickly worse. The Moscow Council
of Foreign Ministers in March broke up in disagreement; George
Marshall, presenting the Truman doctrine of anti-Communist aid in a
broader and more constructive light, had his offer of American support
for European reconstruction brusquely rejected by Russia. The pro-
Soviet governments of Eastern Europe, among them the Grozea and
Dimitrov governments, willingly or unwillingly followed Moscow's
directive.

In consequence, these governments no longer had anything to hope
from America, and had no further reason for pandering, however
mildly, to the sensibilities of the Western Powers. The Oppositions, on
their side, reached a state of desperation in which follies might have
been committed.

On June 6th Nikola Petkov was arrested and charged with promoting
a military conspiracy against the Fatherland Front government. A few
days later over twenty of the leading members of his Opposition
Agrarian Party were deprived of their seats in Parliament. The brief and
stormy trial of Petkov was closely watched by the British and United
States Governments; Dimitrov declared that Anglo-American intervention would make Petkov's fate worse. On August 16th, Petkov was
sentenced to death by hanging. In the face of British and American
protests, the sentence was executed on September 23rd. The Opposition
Agrarian Party had by this time been formally dissolved.

A few weeks later Dimitrov produced an alleged confession of guilt
by Petkov, saying that he had been given courage in his opposition to
the Fatherland Front government by his connections with the British
and United States political representatives in Sofia. The authenticity of
this document was questioned in the Anglo-American press, which
quoted the following passage from Petkov's final speech in court:

'I declare that I am not afraid of whatever fate awaits me, nor am I
perturbed by shouts of "traitor". For both my father and my brother
were murdered in the streets of Sofia, denounced as traitors, only to be
recognised as national heroes by the Bulgarian nation afterwards. I have
never been of any service to foreign or internal reactionaries. I ask you
to judge only on the basis of the evidence brought before the Court and
your own conscience as judges. I ask for a verdict of "Not Guilty".'

When on January 13th, 1948, nine members of the last relic of the
Bulgarian Opposition—the Opposition Social Democratic Party—

refused to vote in Parliament for the Fatherland Front budget, Georgi Dimitrov recalled the fate of Petkov and his group, and said: 'You must think over whether you want to share the fate of your allies.'

He warned them not to count on intervention from London and Washington and added:

'Of course, if they had not intervened from abroad, and if some had not ultimately attempted to dictate to our sovereign court, Petkov's head could have been saved. The death sentence could have been commuted to other punishment. But when I came to the question of blackmailing the Bulgarian nation and infringing on the right of our sovereign people's court, the death sentence had to be executed. And it was executed.'

As a final touch, it was announced on January 26th, 1948, that the government wing of the Social Democratic Party and the Bulgarian Communist Party were to fuse together. This fusion would close another, perhaps the last, possible channel for contacts with the West.

In Rumania the story was much the same. In July, 1947, Ion Mihalache and several other leading members of the Opposition National Peasant Party were arrested as they were trying to escape from Rumania by air. A few days later Iuliu Maniu himself was also arrested, and the National Peasant Party was formally banned. All were charged with plotting to overthrow the Grozea government by force. The trial started, after unexplained delay, at the end of October. The Public Prosecutor particularly accused the defendants of maintaining contacts with four members of the United States Mission in Bucharest, and with the British Minister, Adrian Holman. They were also charged with passing information to the Anglo-Americans. Even more forcibly, they were accused of forming a 'military group' led by Mihalache, in consultation with the United States Mission. A further charge against Maniu was that he had sent abroad two former cabinet ministers of pro-Western convictions, Niculescu-Buzeşti and Vişoianu, to work against the government.

On November 11th, Maniu and Mihalache were sentenced to solitary confinement for life. Niculescu-Buzeşti and Vişoianu, together with the former Rumanian Foreign Minister, Grigore Gafencu, and the wartime Rumanian Ambassador in Turkey, Alexander Creţianu, were sentenced to fifteen years' imprisonment *in absentia*. These four men were by that time all in the West, in Switzerland or the United States.

British views on Maniu's sentence were given in mild terms in a written reply in Parliament by Hector McNeil, over two months later. He merely said that most of Maniu's 'offences' were not crimes in democracies and that others were unproven. He added that as Rumania had been under an armistice régime, Britain had been entitled to keep in touch with Rumanian political leaders.

November, 1947, was a big month for the Rumanian Communist Party. In addition to the trial of the National Peasant Party leaders, it was announced that Titel Petrescu, leader of the Opposition Social Democratic group, was to be tried by a military tribunal. This section of the Opposition was also soon to be leaderless.

The Rumanian Communists also took steps to bring their own associates into line, or else to eliminate them. The pro-government wing of the Social Democrats, led by Voitec and Radaceanu, held a joint meeting with the Communist Party to adopt the programme of a new 'United Workers' Party', to be formed to fuse the two parties. On November 29th, local committees were set up to prepare the ground for the new party. So the pro-government Social Democrats, the only element within the Communist-led coalition of the National Democratic Front with any show of independence or any contacts with the Western world, gave up their individual existence as a party.

The pro-government wing of the National Liberal Party, led by the National Democratic Front Foreign Minister, Georges Tatarescu, met a sterner fate. At the time of Maniu's trial it was strongly attacked by the government press, which accused the Foreign Ministry of being 'a source of secret information for the British and United States Missions'. Tatarescu himself was accused of 'serving Anglo-American imperialism'; this was surprising since he had always been particularly unpopular with the British Mission, at least. On November 5th, Tatarescu and the three other National Liberal Ministers in the Grozea government resigned. Tatarescu was succeeded as Foreign Minister by Ana Pauker, one of the top-ranking Communists in Rumania.

One of Ana Pauker's first major acts was to reply to a United States note of November 17th complaining of the unrepresentative character of the Rumanian government. She said:

'The accusations contained in the indictment of the leaders of the former National Peasant Party, which referred to the part played by certain former representatives of the U.S.A. in Rumania, or by members of the U.S. Missions, in preparing the violent overthrow of the Rumanian government and the democratic régime, are based on the declarations of the defendants.

'True to the fundamental principles of the Yalta, Potsdam and Moscow agreements, the Rumanian government cannot consider as legitimate the associations and actions of the kind proved in the course of the trials, namely, against the Rumanian government and the democratic régime. The Rumanian government deems it unnecessary to refute the opinion expressed in the Note about its character.'

So by the end of November, 1947, the pro-Soviet government of Rumania had shown clearly enough that it would not permit any Anglo-American intervention or influence in Rumanian affairs, and that any Rumanian politician suspected of associating with the British or Americans would be treated as a traitor. But there was still King Michael, who had been honoured by the Soviet government for his share in the 1944 coup against the Germans, and who had been too popular in Rumania for the Communists to consider it wise to attack him. Throughout the armistice period, his name had been a rallying point for the Opposition. It still was, when the Opposition no longer had any political leaders.

On December 30th, 1947, just in time to round off a year that had been highly profitable for the Grozea government, King Michael abdicated. Rumania was declared a People's Republic, like Bulgaria. On the surface, at least, it thenceforth fitted neatly into the general pattern of the Eastern sphere. There was no official Anglo-American protest over King Michael's abdication. The British and United States Governments maintained normal diplomatic relations with the Grozea government.

The period of uneasy political truce in Rumania and Bulgaria, from 1944 to 1947, ended with the virtually complete elimination of the pro-Western Oppositions and the erection of a high and spiky barrier against Western influence or intervention.

In the way of personal contacts, the British and American Missions in Sofia and Bucharest only came across a small number of Bulgarians and Rumanians. Social relations with the governments were, presumably on instruction from London and Washington, chilly and standoffish. They were confined to the bare necessities of official dealings. Members of the governments were only rarely invited to British or American social gatherings.

With the leading members of the Opposition relations were delicate. The Opposition—in Bulgaria at least—did not want to get themselves labelled as agents or hangers-on of the British and Americans, although this was in fact inevitable. In Rumania they had fewer inhibitions. The British and Americans on their side did not want to give the impression that they were giving direct support to the Opposition. So a good deal of discretion was observed over any meetings, whether informative or social, with the Opposition. But the spirit of such meetings, when they did take place, was much more friendly than at meetings with members of the government. No one had any doubt where the natural sympathies, or prejudices, of the British or Americans lay.

As for unofficial contacts, the people whom the British and Americans met socially, and with whom they even became intimate, were usually a very small circle of the upper and well-off classes, mostly the remnants of the old pre-war diplomatic or cosmopolitan set. Nearly all of them were naturally violently anti-Russian and anti-Communist. But they were people who spoke English or French and were agreeable. Probably the laws of social gravitation made these contacts inevitable. What would have been avoidable were the careless or unwitting contacts, in the early days, with people who may have been socially desirable before the war, but had got themselves blatantly known as pro-German or pro-Fascist during the war.

F

Some officers or officials, more enterprising than the rest, would go and spend week-ends in the mountains, climbing or shooting, and, if they had picked up enough of the language, would get talking with the peasants or villagers in a friendly way. They would get a rather broader view—except that the peasants, whether sincerely or to please their guests, would usually talk as violently against the government as did the fine people in the capital. In Bulgaria, there were also one or two officers who tried genuinely to have serious discussions with younger Communists; but they were exceptions.

The N.C.O's and other ranks at the British and American Missions all had their local girl-friends, or popsies. Usually each man had a 'regular'; usually they were charming nice girls of solid middle-class families who had managed to learn a little English. The families made no objections, presumably hoping against hope for marriage. There were, in fact, a small number of marriages.

Otherwise, there were few contacts between the Missions and the Bulgarians and Rumanians. On those they met, the Missions must have left the impression that the Anglo-Americans were fabulously rich, believers in good living, irresponsible and lighthearted, pleased with themselves, drinkers who usually only got merry or sentimental, very anti-Communist. It was perfectly safe to make anti-Russian remarks to them.

The Russians naturally made a different impression. But in their case there was even less contact with the population as a whole. Although in 1945 there were believed to be upwards of 1,000,000 Russian troops in Rumania and upwards of 300,000 in Bulgaria, they lived a life apart from the people. Non-fraternisation was nearly absolute.

Russian officers mixed very little with the middle-classes, presumably by their own wish. One wealthy but would-be progressive young Rumanian woman said, 'Of course, in the first weeks we tried to invite the Russians to our houses, but it was really too embarrassing. They didn't know what to do with their knives and forks and glasses. They were clumsy. They couldn't talk. We felt it was really too uncomfortable for them, we thought it would be kinder to stop asking them.' More probably the Russian officers had received orders not to accept any more invitations.

A Russian officer practically never took a local girl out dancing or to a restaurant, as the British and Americans did. If he wanted to dance, he had either to take out one of the few Red Army girls, or, when sitting with other men in a dancing place, to walk over to another table, bow formally and invite a local girl for a single dance—usually to the thinly veiled annoyance of her own party. The single dance did not lead to conversation.

What Russian other ranks did when they wanted feminine company, is not known. Presumably strictly unfraternal one-night affairs were not banned. But they cannot have been easy to arrange.

There were rare exceptions to the non-fraternisation rule. One lower middle-class Rumanian family of German origin, living in the provinces, had, most exceptionally, a single young Red Army officer billeted in their house. Although they themselves were violently anti-Russian and anti-Communist, they became very fond of this young Russian, called him by his Christian name, and had long talks with him, in German, about life in general and even politics. The woman of the house said she often told him she felt as though he were her own son.

This must have been a very rare case. Usually there was no mixing; and the Russians bore themselves, not with the arrogance, but with the aloofness of a higher class of beings. Perhaps as a result, they seemed singularly uncontaminated by the bourgeois softness of life. Only a few of the Red Army woman officers in Bucharest seemed to have been carried away: these went about in uniform, with long flowing peroxided hair, Hollywood style, and were very heavily and crudely made up. At a hairdressers, a simple, pleasant Russian peasant girl, who had not yet taken to make-up, would hold out her fingers rather nervously to an extremely sophisticated, highly-groomed Rumanian manicurist, and, blushing, would shake her head violently to stop the Rumanian from painting her nails purple. But at least half the Russian girls seemed as unmoved by Balkan sophistication as the Russian men. You could see no outward sign that their faith in the Soviet way of life had been shaken or undermined.

In Bulgaria, in 1945 and 1946, it was exceptional to hear of any open trouble between the troops and the population. There was, of course, the standard complaint that the troops ruined any house or building where they were billeted and were unhousetrained in their habits. From those parts of the countryside where there were concentrations of troops, there were also complaints of forcible and excessive requisitioning of food at a time when food was scarce for Bulgarians. But open quarrels seemed rare, although after the early days the average Bulgarian had little love for the Russian troops.

In Rumania, where Red Army discipline was less strict, there were more stories of misbehaviour and friction. There still seemed to be revived outbursts of looting from time to time, and more drunkenness. At the Transylvanian town of Sibiu, in the spring of 1946, a Russian officer was sitting very drunk in a café after the curfew hour imposed by the Red Army. A Rumanian lieutenant of gendarmerie, whose duty it was to enforce the curfew in accordance with the Red Army order, came and most politely reminded the Russian of the hour. When the Russian got angry, the Rumanian was discreetly going away, but the Russian pulled out his gun, shot the lieutenant dead and wounded a Rumanian private who was with him. At the lieutenant's funeral a crowd of about 3,000 Rumanians gathered and shouted: 'We don't want the Russians. Let them get out of here.' The Russian authorities did not interfere.

That, at least, was the story told by the townspeople of Sibiu. There are probably a number of parallel stories from parts of Europe occupied by the Anglo-Americans.

The Rumanians, however boldly they might talk against the Russians behind their backs, did not dare to contradict a Russian to his face. In a small bare Bucharest eating-house, a young Russian soldier, fairly drunk, was making a great row one evening. He had been sitting drinking with another Russian for some time; his friend had left earlier; now he himself wanted to leave, but his overcoat had vanished. He was very sad and very angry: it was bitterly cold, and anyhow he dared not go back to barracks without the coat. He loudly and violently accused the landord of stealing his coat, shouted at other people eating there, seized chairs and brandished them above his head, and threatened to break the place up. The landlord tried to be very soothing, but the Russian was not appeased. A Rumanian gendarme came at intervals with an interpreter and did some more soothing, in the most honeyed fatherly way. Nothing was any good. No one dreamt of chucking the young Russian out. After about three hours of recurring outbreaks of wrath and threats, he became tired and sad, and sat down in front of the stove. He started crooning a long dirge-like improvised chant, addressed at times to his lost overcoat, at times to a plate of green tomatoes on the table beside him. The Rumanians all breathed again. The situation was saved.

It was often hard to understand why the Russians were quite so unpopular. In spite of their occasional bad behaviour, there was something childlike and fundamentally good-humoured about them that was disarming, if you were not afraid of them. That was probably the bottom of the trouble. The Balkan people were blindly, exaggeratedly afraid of them, and at the same time despised them for their lack of 'culture'. This combination of feeling provoked maximum resentment.

In many ways, Russian occupation was far less obtrusive and all-pervading than British occupation. In Sofia you saw very few Russian troops in the streets, no Russian notices or signposts. The only time the Russians were noticeable was when companies of them marched down the main street, singing a rousing marching-song and carrying their towels rolled under their arms, on their way to their weekly bath. Normally their uniforms were so drab and inconspicuous that they melted into the background of the city. In the countryside they were usually kept out of the main towns and off the main roads. The few Russian signposts on the main roads were small and dirty.

In neither Sofia nor Bucharest had the Russians taken the best hotels, though they had one or two good buildings, usually not in the centre of the town. In Bucharest, and also in Rumanian provincial towns, there were more Russians to be seen than in Bulgaria, but they were seldom in the best restaurants or the best shops. They looked like strangers from a long way off, not like colonisers.

In Greece, the British occupation—or the invited presence of British troops—was far more conspicuous and outwardly irritating. The British had all the best hotels in every town where there was a garrison, and some of the best flats. They ate and shopped in the best restaurants and shops. They walked the streets as though they were patrons or colonisers; their clean khaki drill uniforms and white belts and pink faces stood out loudly against the Greek background. They had parades in the main square or the main street at the most crowded hours. There were enormous shiny black-and-white notices and traffic signs everywhere, not only in towns but also on the country roads. British traffic police and military police with their red hats looked efficient and formidable, although they could not stop army drivers from driving madly—British dangerous driving was a favourite grievance with the Greeks. The British, outwardly, appeared far more the conquering and dominating race than the Russians.

British intervention and control of Greek affairs was also outwardly far more striking than Soviet intervention in Rumanian and Bulgarian affairs. In Greece there was a large British economic mission, financial advisers, labour advisers, a British Ambassador on whom the Greek Prime Minister called very frequently for authoritative guidance. There was a British police mission to train up a new Greek police force on the British model. There was a British military liaison mission to train up the new Greek Army on the British model, with British drill, with British handbooks, and with British equipment.

Outwardly, the Russians indulged in none of these things. There were no Missions, although there were naturally Russian representatives on the commissions for securing the fulfilment of the armistice terms. As far as could be seen, there was no direct Russian interference with the armies or the police. The Russians in their propaganda laid great stress on non-intervention in the internal affairs of other countries.

Behind the scenes things were clearly different. The Russians could rely on, and work through, governments which were unreservedly loyal and docile. Comparatively few instructions or directives would be needed to see that they ran things the right way, from the Russian point of view. In view of the lack of skilled Soviet administrators, it was obviously more efficient to employ local talent. More important still, there were the local Communist parties, whose members held key posts in the Governments and Ministries, in the Police, and to a lesser extent in the Armies. They would also be detailed informants. With these helpers, the Russians could impose their wishes quietly, behind the scenes, not openly and blatantly. If the Soviet commander found it necessary to call the Prime Minister to book when he had unwittingly strayed, this could be done without publicity.

Open interference was only needed at moments of serious political crisis, as when Vishinski had to make a lightning descent to get King Michael to accept the Grozea government, or to try to impel the Bulgarian Opposition to enter the government. These were exceptional cases. But they cancelled much of the effect of the normal Soviet show of non-interference.

The Rumanian and Bulgarian publics, or a big part of them, were always sceptical about this non-interference. There were endless and usually quite unfounded stories about Russians running the police, Russian instructors in the Army, Russian officials in the Ministries. It was all part of a general anti-Russian complex in the public mind. Behind it lay the deep-embedded conviction that Bulgaria and Rumania, so long as they were occupied by the Red Army and probably also after the Red Army left, were quite powerless to defy the wishes of victorious neighbouring Soviet Russia.

The Russians and the Anglo-Americans had very little to do with each other in Bulgaria and Rumania, apart from strictly official business and strictly official functions. On the Russian side, presumably, fraternisation was discouraged. But the natural feelings of the Russians seemed friendly enough, if hesitant and doubtful.

For instance, this as a chance conversation in a Bulgarian train in the autumn of 1945. There were five junior Russian officers in the carriage, all very hot, one or two sitting in their coarse cotton vests mopping themselves. The senior officer there was a dark-eyed, dark-browed Ukrainian major. He did most of the talking.

'Oh, so you are a journalist. Tell me, which is the newspaper of the people, in England?'

'*It is difficult to say. I believe the daily with one of the biggest circulations is the "Express", which is owned by a big Tory, what you would call a reactionary. But it was the Labour Party, not the Conservatives, who won the elections. Yet the Labour Party newspaper, the "Herald", has not the biggest circulation.*'

'You do not understand. I mean, what is the real newspaper of the People?'

'*If you mean, what is the Communist Party newspaper, it is the "Worker". But it has a relatively very small circulation. So I don't know whether you could call it the newspaper of the People.*'

'Ah, of course, I forgot. There is no People in England. Everybody is bourgeois. The English live on the labour of the coloured people of the British Empire. It is these who are really the People.'

'*Well, that is one way of looking at it. But a lot of us work quite hard.*'

'Yes, your workers have been terribly oppressed. Tell me, do you have holidays with pay?'

'*Most workers do now, but not all.*'

'That it is terrible, we have all had holidays with pay for a long, long time. (Pause.) How many children have you?'

'*None, I am not married.*'

'Why are you not married? That is extraordinary.'

(Pause for reflection.) '*Perhaps partly because, before the war, if I had married I should have had to give up my job.*'

'But that is terrible. Such a state of things could never exist in Soviet Russia. Every woman has a right both to a job and to marriage, and to children, all at once. That is very bad. . . . But, Liza, I can see you are a Lady' (using the English word).

'*No, indeed, I assure you I am not a Lady. I work.*'

'Yes indeed, Lady, Lady. It is no good your saying anything, Lady. I am going to call you Lady.'

All the Russians had firmly, obviously on instructions, so far refused brandy, raisins or Turkish milk chocolate, although there was no food on the train or at the stations and they had none themselves. At this point there seemed some sign of weakening. The Ukrainian was prepared to make a concession and have a small swig at a bottle of Turkish cognac smelling of scented nail varnish. But he would only drink second.

'*Very well then. I drink to Anglo-Soviet friendship.*'

(Long pause for thought. A doubtful, testing glance from under the dark brows.) 'I drink to *sincere* and *non-lying* Anglo-Soviet friendship.'

There was one other conversation which nobody believes, but which happened at a frontier town on the Danube. It had been difficult to get across the Danube; there was some hitch over the permit to leave Rumania, which was finally cleared by a Red Fleet officer, who then kindly laid on a tug with a crew of twelve for the trip across the river from the Rumanian to the Bulgarian side. On the Bulgarian side there was equally a hitch about the permit to enter Bulgaria. It was only the Soviet colonel in command who could give a verdict.

The Soviet colonel said: 'Of course, I have seen you before. I remember you went through over three months ago. Well, I am sorry, I have no permit for you to enter. Nothing has been notified from Sofia. I do not know what I can do. But still . . . I know you journalists. I think you all ought to be given special international passports, so that you can travel wherever you want. That is the only solution. You may enter Bulgaria.'

6

Portrait of Bulgaria

BULGARIA, deceptively, seems a country full of air and space. There are broad sweeping valleys, massed mountains, long hillsides of pine forests or oak woods, great clear deep skies. It does not feel like a tiny overcrowded country. It is a long way between villages. There are great stretches of bare untilled land. It is hard to realise that nearly every scrap of soil on which things can be grown has been painfully tilled and tended, that the rest of the countryside is unfertile, that the peasants are huddled together toiling on too few, too tiny strips of earth, that they are pitifully poor by average European standards. On an average, there are 116 people living on every square kilometre of cultivatable land in Bulgaria.

A village street in south Bulgaria in September does not look poor. Under the broad overhanging wooden eaves of the rough red brick or grey stone houses, long deep gold tobacco leaves are hanging to dry in the rich autumn sun. Outside other houses there are hanging clusters of orange corn-cobs, or shiny red peppers. Red apples and bulging yellow pumpkins are lying in the open store-rooms on the upper floor.

In the deep sandy dust of the village street dozens of scrawny hens, ducks and little pigs are rootling about. The street is almost blocked by a big wooden cart drawn by creamy oxen with broad, smoothly curving horns. There are plenty of sturdy muscular village children, often enough yellow-haired and fair-skinned, although by the time they are grown-up almost all Bulgarians are dark and brown-skinned. The children may be eating, whole and off the stalk, purply-brown grapes, left-overs of the wine-grapes. There is one small flyblown café. At best, it has little three-legged rusty iron tables. Since the war there is thick, gritty, syrupy stuff to drink instead of real Turkish coffee. There is an inn with bare wooden tables, benches and floor, a little squalid. Here there is plenty of slivova—harsh, slightly musty-tasting plum spirit—and rather sour wine to drink, but usually little to eat for strangers, though there may be a rich reddish stew with plenty of onions and peppers but little meat in it. There are big hunks of coarse, salty, brownish bread, but, for strangers, no cheese now, although a year or two ago goat's milk and sheep's milk cheeses and sour milk used to be very common.

The village houses, inside, are neither flyblown nor squalid, but look cared for and scrubbed, if bare and simple. There is enough food, though that too is mostly bare and simple.

The village may look across to the great long line of the Rila mountains, shadowy with pine forests, topped by bare rock; or to the Pirin, a higher and steeper range, with crests of bluish-white snow glistening in the September sun.

In the rolling hills north-east of Sofia are oakwoods and beechwoods, just beginning to go yellow at the end of September. By November, boughs of oak, covered with dry brown leaves, have been stripped from the trees and stacked ingeniously on great wooden frames, to be used instead of fodder for the farm animals during the winter. The stripped lanky oak trees look scrawny and miserable.

In a village in this district, a wedding was to be held one autumn Sunday. It was to be in a small peasant house. There was no ground floor, properly speaking: the space was used for stacking firewood and logs and for housing some of the animals. You climbed up steep wooden steps to the upper floor. There was a little wooden balcony, with some of the usual vegetables drying. Inside there were bare, whitish wooden floors and walls, beautifully scrubbed, a plain wooden table and plain wooden stools as chairs. The beds were a few coverlets laid on a narrow wooden platform raised about a foot above the rest of the floor; over the coverlets were laid tidily deep crimson wool rugs, woven in the country. In the corner was a small ikon with a tiny oil lamp burning in front of it. An old grandmother, bent, toothless and wrinkled, but grinning and amiable, was making a stew in a little cauldron over an open fire. The girl who was to be bride, pretty and fair-haired, seemed calm, unembarrassed and gay. She was wearing a white linen embroidered blouse and a long, full, red wool skirt and showed off the tinsly crown with long ribbons she would wear at the wedding.

None of the family seemed at all shy or surprised at sudden foreign guests. The father, who had a long curling moustache, powerful shoulders and a portly belly bound round by a long dark red woollen cummerbund, poured out more and more home-brewed slivova. He had dignity and a look of strength; he did not say very much, but talked as an equal to equals.

Further, beyond the wooded hills, come the bare rocky mountains around Vrattsa, where Christo Botev, the national poet of the last century, fought against the Turks. Some of these mountains are tipped with jagged edges of bright brown rock. In between the mountains, the valleys are narrow and twisting, as rough sharp shoulders of rock jut out into them from the slopes.

North-east again come the plains, and then the Danube, Bulgaria's northern frontier. In the far north-east corner there is the rich land of the Dobrudja—part of it regained from Rumania in 1940 with the blessings both of Hitler and the British government—a land curious for its storks, its minarets, and the trousered women of the Turkish minority. In the east of Bulgaria are the wheat-growing flat lands, and beyond them lies Bulgaria's only sea-coast, on the Black Sea, cut off from the Mediterranean by the Turkish-held Straits. In the south, Bulgaria once had a coast on the Aegean, and so had free access to the open waters of the Mediterranean; but she lost this through the Treaty of Neuilly after the first world war and failed to win it back at the Paris Peace Conference of 1946.

Deceptively, Bulgaria seems a country of space and variety. In reality, it suffers from acute agricultural over-population and under-employment, even with its present population of around seven millions. Yet Georgi Dimitrov in June, 1946, speaking to the new Fatherland Front 'Union of Those with Many Children', said: 'The task of the whole nation must be to bring it about that in the near future our people numbers at the very least ten million souls.'

Deceptively, Sofia seems a spacious city. But in the autumn of 1945 it was officially reckoned that 37,000 families were living there without housing-space, and that 50,000 people were living there 'illegally'—that is, they had been ordered to leave the badly overcrowded capital, but had stayed. There were two reasons for this overcrowding: British-American bombing during the war had destroyed or damaged one out of every four houses in Sofia; and when the Fatherland Front seized power, a flood both of those who were ambitious and of those who feared disorders in the provinces swept into Sofia from the country.

All this does not show much. Sofia seems a city of trees and air. If you look down from its neighbouring mountain, Vitosha, it seems as though about one quarter of the whole city were tree-covered green space. That is mostly the big unkempt Boris Park, now called by another, un-royalist name. The big Russian-style Orthodox cathedral, with its green domes and golden crosses, is the most imposing building in Sofia, set on high ground in a big open space. The main streets are broad, sometimes laid out in avenues, rather in South German style. In the Boulevard of the Tsar Liberator, which is paved with brownish-orange tiles, there are two double rows of chestnut trees, shading broad walks on each side of the main roadway. Sometimes in September, when the conkers are already getting ripe in their spiky jackets, the trees suddenly burst for a second time into rather shrivelled but startling white flowers. Perhaps the chestnut trees, like the Bulgarian themselves, have too much vitality. They do not know what to do with it.

The Boulevard was the great street for people to stroll up and down, every evening of the week and every Sunday morning, staring, talking, humming, bowing to acquaintances, stopping to chat with friends and relations. To stroll down the Boulevard, all the men were decently, and all the girls were prettily, dressed. At the lower end, where the Boulevard narrowed between the Palace garden and the main hotel, the throng would get really dense. People would mill slowly up and down here for perhaps one hour before and one hour after dusk. There was the curious noise of the slither and pad of hundreds of leisurely footfalls, the vibrant almost rhythmic hum of hundreds of gossiping voices, as the light faded and darkness fell.

At its thickest, it was a crowd you had to force your way through. One summer evening in 1946, just after the Fatherland Front government had taken over the Palace as their cabinet offices, three important non-Communist members of the government strolled slowly through the crowd, smiling and chatting, on their way home from work. They were the Prime Minister, Kimon Georgiev, his close friend the War Minister, Damian Velchev, and the Minister of Information, Dimo Kazasov. Bulgarians noticed them without surprise. They expected their public men, even their Kings, to walk along the street and mix with ordinary people. Class distinctions had always been very slight. Bulgarians practised equality in their way of life. A prime minister was just an ordinary man, perhaps rather luckier than others.

What was curious and annoying to Bulgarians was that the Communist leaders, since they came to power, did not behave just like ordinary men. The really important ones always drove everywhere in big cars, well guarded. They seldom mixed with the crowd.

Georgi Dimitrov, when he drove anywhere, would be followed or preceded by a guard car. He himself was accompanied everywhere by a bodyguard. When he went to Parliament, in the days before he became Prime Minister, he would take his place, democratically enough, in the Communist block. His bodyguard, a bullet-headed wiry little man with unblinking eyes, took his place behind him, in a corner of the press box. His right hand was always tucked into the left side of his jacket, watchfully. Yet everybody who entered the parliament building had been searched for arms at the door. People thought the bodyguard was a Russian, but no one dared ask him.

When Dimitrov came home, he took a house in a quiet tree-shaded street in the smart quarter of Sofia. It was quite a small and modest house by Western standards, but definitely elegant. The average Cabinet Minister lived in a small flat in a less distinguished part of the town. Dimitrov's house annoyed people because they thought that, being a Communist, he should have taken particular care to live modestly. He annoyed them still more by having a twelve-foot fence put up on top of the wall round the house; and the story was that he also forced people living in the surrounding houses to block up any windows overlooking his house. At night floodlights at the top corners of the fence were switched on—presumably to protect the house, but it looked like a miniature prison.

The disgruntled Bulgarian thought the fence was undemocratic. A leading Social Democrat said: 'I have been a convinced republican all my life, but I must say that King Boris never behaved the way Georgi

Dimitrov does. Boris walked around the streets and talked to people, simple people. I am all for abolishing the monarchy, but not if Dimitrov is going to set himself up as Emperor.' A young Bulgarian woman said: 'I remember King Boris stopping his car once, so that he could get out and buy some coloured balloons for his two children. He stopped and chatted with the old woman who was selling the balloons. Can you see Georgi Dimitrov doing that?'

One hot summer morning in 1946 there was a national congress of co-operatives in Sofia. The Prime Minister and most of his Cabinet, including the lesser Communists, stood sweating and slowly grilling in the midday sun for an hour or more, smiling and waving as the co-operators marched past them. The co-operators carried banner after banner of greeting to Georgi Dimitrov, and to no one else. But he was not there. There was only a three-times-life-size poster portrait of him, propped up among the Cabinet Ministers to take his place.

Practice of equality is inborn in Bulgarians. They are equalitarian, not in theory, but in their lives. No trace of the feudalism or aristocratic system which must have existed in Bulgaria in the Middle Ages seems to have survived the levelling centuries of Turkish rule. The kings whom they have had in the last seventy years have been German kings, who have not married with Bulgarians and who have created very little snobbery among the people. Bulgarians are a real peasant people, even if Bulgaria has never yet been a real peasant State.

Although there is antagonism and mistrust between town and country, this is caused by conflict of material interests, not by any deep social or psychological cleavage. The townspeople all have close relatives in the country and are themselves peasants by origin. The man of the town middle-class has a sound respect for the peasant and his wisdom and good sense. The peasant talks to the townsman as to an equal, not a superior.

That is why it has been important for anyone who wished to rule Bulgaria to take care at least to put on a show of being democratic and equalitarian. King Boris, in spite of his many grave mistakes, realised this clearly and acted accordingly. In return a good many Bulgarians, who had a kind of primitive instinctive need for a king as symbolic father of the people, stayed loyal to the monarchy even when it had for the second time led Bulgaria to defeat in 1944. But few Bulgarians would have the same feeling of loyalty for an un-royal dictator or 'big man'. The Stalin legend or the Tito legend would not in normal circumstances catch on easily in Bulgaria. The natural reaction would be resentment and mistrust for any man who claimed to be something apart from his fellow-men. The response to the man who 'puts himself forward' is to say rather spiteful things about him, to tell funny, malicious stories about him showing him in a mean or ridiculous light.

Yet this quality of equalitarianism is not unmixed. In a fair number of Bulgarians there is a strong strain of opportunism, even in extreme cases of servility, partly, probably, a relic of Turkish oppression, partly a symptom of general economic insecurity. For this reason, in any election, whether or not terror were used, there would always be a fair percentage of Bulgarians who would vote for 'the government', whatever it might be, although they hated it.

The Bulgarian is a fierce individualist, just like any Balkan peasant who owns his very small plot of land, or any Balkan townsman who has managed to scrape together his very small savings. But his individualism is mixed with a sense of social discipline and group loyalty which hardly exists among the non-Slav peoples of the Balkans—the Rumanians and the Greeks. The Bulgarian's loyalty goes more easily to a small group than a large group, to the local branch of his party than the party head office, to his party rather than the government. His biggest loyalty is usually a rather narrow national feeling. The negative side of his loyalties is a feeling of suspicion and enmity towards rival groups. He has none of the easy-going almost flaccid tolerance of the Rumanians. But along with his loyalty he expects his group to be the protector of his individual independence and his small individual possessions. Though he gives his loyalty to the group, he keeps his right to his own views, and it is hard to get him to make material sacrifices for the group.

The growth of the Bulgarian co-operative movement has shown this. In Sofia, for instance, most blocks of flats are 'co-operatives': you buy permanent ownership of your flat, and then help to run the common affairs of your 'co-operative' through a committee of flat-owners. There have for some years past been co-operative banks, particularly to provide loans to peasants, consumers' co-operatives, and to a smaller extent co-operatives for the marketing of agricultural produce. This movement steadily gained strength among the peasants, because it made their difficult lives slightly easier and more secure. But the peasant did not want to give anything away: he wanted to keep what was his own and gain something more through the group—cheaper loans, cheaper manufactured goods, better prices for his crops. Although the co-operatives were essentially group enterprises, they had to safeguard the individual and his property.

The first breath of suspicion that the Fatherland Front might make use of the co-operative movement to bring in collectivisation brought a strong reaction among the peasants, and the Front had to slow down its modest plans.

One side of the Bulgarian's individualism and independence is his sense of his right and duty to say what he thinks on all occasions. This is slightly different from telling the truth. The average Bulgarian is not sufficiently critical to judge finely between truth and fantasy or exaggeration. And in their international dealings Bulgaria's rulers have won a reputation for deliberate falsehood which is perhaps only partly deserved. But in everyday life, it seems almost a physical need for the ordinary Bulgarian to pour out his views and feelings, even if it is tactless, awkward, risky, or downright dangerous.

Bulgarians would come up to a stranger, known to be a foreigner, in the street, and burst out into little speeches. Usually the theme was: 'Do you call this liberty, do you call this democracy, what we have here?' In the Sofia post office, if a foreign journalist took in a press telegram, the clerk on duty would often start a political harangue—for the Fatherland Front if he were on that side, for the Opposition if he were on the other. The mere sight of the words 'Nikola Petkov' in a long telegram would be enough to produce smiles in one clerk and sharp hissing noises from another.

Once a small group of about six men and women post office clerks, all in varying degrees pro-government, gathered round one journalist and shot criticisms. 'Why do you not tell the truth about Bulgaria?' 'Why do you hate us? Is it because you love the Greeks or don't you want us to have a peace treaty?' 'No, it is not that you do not mean to tell the truth, but you are badly informed, so you tell lies by mistake.' 'No, that is what is called objectivity, these foreign journalists do not wish to take sides.' In the end they turned on each other and left the journalist to slink away.

A poor man, a worker, who was arrested by the Militia in connection with the case against the Agrarian Dimitrov, was held for several months for interrogation, and was beaten up. He was finally released. A few months later, when the trial against G. M. Dimitrov was coming on, one of the lawyers for the defence wanted to call this man as a defence witness. The man came to the lawyer and said almost weeping: 'I beg you, please, do not ask me to be a witness. However much I want to play safe, I know that the moment I appear in Court, I shall find myself telling the truth and saying what I think. Then they will arrest me again and start beating me again, and this foot of mine is not yet healed from the last time. I cannot work properly yet, so I cannot afford, for my family's sake, to be beaten again. But I should not be able to help myself. Please do not call me.'

In the two big political trials held in Sofia in June, 1946, it was startling how much free and even violent speaking there was by the defendants and the defending lawyers. Some of the defendants claimed to have been tortured during their months in prison before the trial, and all faced at best long sentences of imprisonment. There were Communists as prosecutors and judges. Armed militiamen were standing on guard in the courtroom, sometimes the public in court was hostile to the defence. It made no difference. The defendants had to say their say, even if it meant going over to the counter-attack against the prosecution, the Communist Party, the Fatherland Front and the government.

One of the trials was of Krustyu Pastuhov, a seventy-two-year-old Social Democrat, one of the leaders of the Opposition wing of the party. He was accused of writing articles in the Social Democrat newspaper, *Svoboden Narod*, 'with the aim of impairing the military efficiency and fighting spirit of the Bulgarian Army'. What had really caused displeasure was that he had criticised the Communist leader, Georgi Dimitrov, for interfering in the Army, had warned against the appointment of Communists as political commissars, or 'assistant commanders' and had attacked the whole Communist Party attempt to get control of the Army.

During his four months in prison before the trial, Pastuhov had been ill. But he stood the long wearing twenty days in the small hot overcrowded courtroom without wilting. A short, broad-shouldered old man with flushed cheeks and a deep powerful rather harsh voice, he would rise to his feet and cut sharply into the eloquent flow of the young Communist prosecutor with a biting question, retort or protest.

The prosecution accused him of being an enemy of the workers and the peasants, and life-long opponent of Communism and Soviet Russia, a stooge of the Bulgarian monarchy and a reactionary, throughout his long career as a Social Democrat.

This career had clearly had its ups and downs, even its deviations from the narrow Socialist path. But Pastuhov defended himself with a kind of harsh melancholy anger; he was probably certain he was going to be condemned but he was unmistakably certain he was in the right. Though sometimes in the stifling afternoons his eyelids drooped and his head nodded, he would always leap up the moment he felt his political honour too grossly assaulted or saw a chance of a sharp counter-thrust.

He was not alone. Usually the two or three hundred people crowding the courtroom were with him. Although the judge strictly prevented applause and groans, the sympathy of the young Social Democratic students or workers or old friends in the court could be guessed from their faces or an occasional irrepressible murmur. Pastuhov's wife was there too. A grey-haired old woman with a strained sunken face, she sat quietly but looked anxiously at her husband from time to time.

Pastuhov had a big team of defending lawyers. They were nearly all old-time Social Democrats, but there was one lawyer each from the Opposition Agrarian and Democratic parties, to show political solidarity. Between them they laid down a powerful barrage of political argument, historical anecdote and personal appeal. They were all more experienced and distinguished men than the two young Communist prosecutors, who, however, poured out a tireless flow of smooth ideological oratory.

One of the defending lawyers, Ivan Kolarov, an elderly Social

Democrat with a parchment-white haggard face and a muffled voice, made a final plea lasting nearly two days. In substance, he put the whole case for 'reformist' Social Democracy against revolutionary Socialism or Communism. He ranged the Second International against the Third International; he attacked the Molotov-Ribbentrop Pact of 1939 and Communist collaboration with the Germans in the first twenty-one months of the war. He seemed to feel that if he could vindicate Social Democracy he could vindicate his old friend Krustyu Pastuhov.

Others also came to Pastuhov's help, from the side of the Fatherland Front. Petko Stainov, who had been Foreign Minister only three months before and was still a member of the Front, appeared as witness for the defence and said: 'In my view Pastuhov was a Russophil. He did not like the Communists. And they quarrelled with him. But as regards foreign policy he was always a friend of Russia.'

Tsvetko Boboshevski, one of the three Fatherland Front Regents—Bulgaria had not yet become a republic—also bore witness for an old friend: 'Pastuhov was a determined adversary of Hitlerist policy.'

Damian Velchev, the War Minister, gave evidence. Asked about the effect of Pastuhov's articles on the Army, he said: 'In my view Pastuhov has always been a good Bulgarian, and I believe he has always wanted a strong People's Army.'

No one, however, could clear Pastuhov of the real charge against him—of disliking the Communist Party and proclaiming his dislike.

Both the lawyers and the leading witnesses for the Defence were attacked in the Communist press. Against Damian Velchev, it was the beginning of a campaign which, inspired by Communist fear of an anti-Communist coup by the Army, ended in his retirement from the War Ministry and from the government and from public life. But inside the court, there could not have been greater freedom of speech, more freely exercised. The judges, whatever their own convictions, allowed the defence to drag in political and historical arguments which had only the remotest bearing on the formal charges against the accused, in spite of regular protests from the prosecution—who were themselves employing equally remote arguments. Only when Pastuhov himself was making his final three-hour plea, looking ill but still speaking powerfully in his harsh voice, did the judge nervously ask him to hurry up and get done.

Nevertheless, Pastuhov ended, unchecked, with a passionate defence of the Opposition movement in Bulgaria. 'I declare that the Bulgarian Opposition is not the enemy of Bulgaria,' he said. 'Several times it has been ready to make concessions in order to reach agreement for participation in the government. It has acted for the sake of Bulgaria and for the sake of the Bulgarian cause. We want free elections, freely expressing the will of the Bulgarian people. On this basis we will participate in the government. We are ready for sacrifice. I am willing to be the sacrificial beast.

'You may take my body, but my spirit will remain, because it is the expression of the soul of the Bulgarian people.'

The Court adjourned to consider its verdict. The sentence was announced five days later. Pastuhov got five years' imprisonment. His close friend Kosta Lulchev said: 'He is a sick man. He has heart trouble and other maladies. Prison life may well be fatal for him. The real reason why they hate him is to be found in the forty years' struggle of ideas between the Communists and the Social Democrats, in which life itself has vindicated Social Democracy.'

The other big trial of June, 1946, which was really a trial of the Opposition Agrarian movement, was less stirring because the chief defendant, G. M. Dimitrov, was not in Bulgaria. Of the fifteen other accused, most were young men of the Agrarian party, charged with helping G. M. Dimitrov escape from house arrest, with conducting defeatist propaganda during Bulgaria's war against the Germans, with maintaining links with Drazha Mihailovitch (who at that moment was being tried for treason in Belgrade), or with 'forecasting the entry into Bulgaria of foreign troops' (that is, Anglo-Americans).

The most outstanding of these was a young man called Eftimi Arsov, a leading member of the Agrarian Youth organisation. He was said to be a consumptive. He coughed often. He was very dark, with a tense but alert face and very big black watchful but lively eyes. He, like most of the other accused, retracted in court statements he had made in prison to the Militia. He said he had been kept three days in water and subjected to 'physical and moral torture' for twenty days to force him to make incriminating statements.

A Militia officer formally denied that any of the accused had been tortured in prison, but the general public did not take this very seriously. The Bulgarian police in the past had usually mishandled political prisoners. Why should the Communist Militia change? One of the lawyers for the defence, when he was asked privately whether he thought the Militia were any different from the old Police, answered: 'No, on the whole they are just the same, except that they take less trouble. In the old days, the police held the prisoners until the prison doctors had managed to heal up the scars so that they didn't show much. Now the Militia turn them out without bothering about that sort of thing.'

The young man Eftimi Arsov denied all the charges against him. He next made a long, lucid and eloquent speech explaining and defending the aims of the Opposition Agrarian movement. The Agrarians, he said, had always wanted to work loyally, on equal terms, with the Communists. But the Communists had made it impossible. They were always trying to interfere and domineer. They wanted to be masters; they would not be equals.

Nikola Petkov and Boris Bumbarov came into court as witnesses for

G

the defence to back up these arguments. For the prosecution, the Communist, Tsola Dragoicheva, made a bitter personal speech against G. M. Dimitrov, accusing him of disloyalty to the Fatherland Front and anti-Russian intrigues. Alexander Obbov, leader of the pro-government fraction of the Agrarians, joined in the fray.

Damian Velchev once again, although a Fatherland Front Minister, gave evidence for the defence. The court adjourned to a blue-carpeted conference room in the War Ministry. Velchev, in general's uniform and wearing all his medals, stood to answer the questions of the court. He said that G. M. Dimitrov, his old friend, had always supported the Fatherland Front and never had opposed the Soviet Union. Velchev himself knew nothing of defeatist propaganda in the Army. He was asked what had been the attitude of Nikola Petkov and the other Agrarian leaders towards the Fatherland Front before they resigned from it in 1945. He answered: 'Excellent'.*

Nevertheless, the court sentenced G. M. Dimitrov to death in absence and most of the other accused Agrarians to heavy sentences of imprisonment. The course of this trial, like that of Pastuhov's, seemed to bear little relation to the verdict. Many people felt that the verdicts had been fixed before the accused had been arrested.

The Bulgarian passion for free and sometimes violent speech could have very disagreeable consequences. There was a well-known writer called Trifon Kunev. He had been president of the Bulgarian Writers' Association. He was a tall powerfully built old man with a biblical white beard and a charming smile, who now wrote satirical political commentaries for the Opposition Agrarian newspaper, *Narodo Zemedelsko Zname*.

In the summer of 1946 he was usually sitting quietly at a small rough wooden table in the tiny overcrowded noisy office—which was more like a work-shed—of the Opposition newspaper, benevolently watching the young people rushing about, while he thought up his next stinging crack at the Fatherland Front régime.

That summer, the official Fatherland Front trade union organisation, O.R.P.S., was carrying on a particularly violent campaign to get the newspaper closed down permanently. O.R.P.S. delegates one day burst into the office and harangued the printing workers, warning them against the dreadful consequences of working for such an 'anti-people's' rag. But the newspaper had already had trouble in the past with its printing workers; now they were nearly all non-union workers, mostly anarchists. The workers stood firm, though they got nervous. But a few

---

* It was surprising that Velchev was not accused in the 'Neutral Officer' trial of the winter of 1946-47, nor in the trial of Nikola Petkov in August, 1947. In both, the charges were of military conspiracy involving senior Army officers, against the Fatherland Front.

days later, on June 7th, the O.R.P.S. delegates came back in force, with a strong Militia guard, entered the office and chucked out the editorial staff and the printers.

Next day Trifon Kunev thought he would find out whether he would be allowed into the office or not. He got there early. An O.R.P.S. picket at the gate let him through. As he was walking up the rickety wooden stairs to the office, a band of 'unknown persons' fell on him and beat him over the face and head. Badly hurt and bleeding, he got to Nikola Petkov's house and told him what had happened. Petkov decided he must suspend his newspaper until he could guarantee the bodily safety of his staff.

That was not the end. The attackers were not identified or arrested. A fortnight later Trifon Kunev was arrested, for speaking in one of his articles of the Bulgarian 'resistance movement'.

This article had been a reply to a speech made by Georgi Dimitrov, in which the Communist leader had sharply attacked a foreword which Kunev had written to a reprint of his satirical commentaries in booklet form.

In this foreword, Kunev had spoken of the 'rugged individualism and originality' of the Bulgarian and his unfittedness for herd life. 'On these qualities of the Bulgarian character is based the strength of our resistance and our resolute refusal to become putty in the hands of political and economic fantasists who wish to change the historic form of our people,' he said. 'This book is a contribution to the Bulgarian people's struggle for freedom and a document of the resistance movement in Bulgaria to-day.'

These were the words that had provoked Georgi Dimitrov to attack Kunev as an enemy of the Fatherland Front. Kunev, replying to Dimitrov, wrote: 'Georgi Dimitrov is to-day all-powerful in Bulgaria and I am only a member of the Opposition. But in our camp force counts for nothing—just as when in the past, at the Leipzig trial, Dimitrov found winged words to launch against the all-powerful Goering.'

On November 14th, 1947, Trifon Kunev was sentenced to five years' solitary confinement, 'in consideration of his advanced age'.

The 'rugged individualism' of the Bulgarian, although an admirable human quality which particularly arouses Western sympathies, had another aspect. From another point of view, it was a natural stubborn conservatism resisting a necessary process of economic and social development, which would inevitably curtail individual rights in order to bring about the progress of the whole group or society. From this point of view it was as irritating as the endless American slogans about 'free enterprise' or Lord Beaverbrook's hackneyed and hollow phrases about 'the rights of the small man'.

For instance, an intelligent Bulgarian constructional engineer, who employed about twenty workmen, refused to see that there could be any justification for the organisation of labour. 'My workers have no need of a union at all,' he said. 'I pay them wages that are better than union rates. I look after them when they are sick or their families are in trouble. They are much better off if they trust in me than if they are always running off to get some union to protect their rights. Things will not go nearly so well if a union organiser comes interfering between me and them. You may say that other employers do not behave as generously as I do, but I still do not see that unions are anything but harmful. I believe that each employer must always have his own rights and responsibilities, as a human individual.'

Many peasants so mistrusted any pooling of land or agricultural implements, for fear that they might be done out of some fraction of their individual share of profit, that they would rather carry on with mediæval methods of agriculture than experiment with modern methods. The average middle-class townsman was so afraid of losing any part of his small savings that he would be loth to invest them in any big scheme of industrialisation.

Given these attitudes, there were obvious arguments in favour of a certain amount of State compulsion in order to speed economic and social progress.

Suppose the usual argument between a 'Liberal' and a 'Progressive' applied to Bulgaria:—

Progressive: Of course the Bulgarian people have the traditional peasant virtue of stubborn individualism. But that is not enough. Bulgaria is still pitifully poor and economically weak by European standards. Like the other Balkan countries, she needs to modernise her agriculture rapidly and she needs rapid industrialisation. Unless these things are to take many years, she needs a clear-cut and firmly enforced economic plan, carried through with drive and even ruthlessness. It is only the Communists who are trying to provide this plan.

Liberal: If the Communists are as ruthless, or even as tactless, as they seem to be, they will arouse such opposition that they will perhaps wreck the plan. Anyhow, do the Communists want to execute the plan in order to consolidate their own political power, or do they want political power in order to execute the plan?

Progressive: Does that matter? It probably depends on the temperament of the individual Communist. What is important is that they have the plan and mean to carry it through quickly.

Liberal: All right. But to carry the plan through smoothly and effectively, they would have to take into account the human beings, with all their feelings and prejudices, who have to do most of the actual work. At least in the first two and a half years of their dominion, the Bulgarian Communists seem to have handled human beings clumsily and stupidly, and so built up a lot of unnecessary resistance to the plan.

They have behaved as though demagogy could replace real understanding. They have made the bad mistake of letting it appear that they
were really only interested in the struggle for power, that talk of
economic and social progress was only window-dressing.

Progressive: This is only a transitional stage. You cannot yet judge.
If the plan turns out a good one and works, its final success would
outweigh the early errors and brutalities, the suspension or destruction
of some of the old human liberties. Until Bulgaria has something like
an average European standard of living, how can Bulgarians live as true
human beings?

Liberal: If you destroy or suspend a liberty do you ever get it back?
Anyhow, this argument is all in the air. We can only wait to see if the
plan works.

7

Economic Plan for Bulgaria and Rumania

ANY economic plan for Bulgaria and Rumania—or for the other Balkan countries—had to meet the following needs:
It must raise the productivity of the peasants, and so raise their living standards.

It must find work for those peasants who were permanently under-employed or unemployed, because there was no room for them on the land.

It must develop both agricultural and other industries, so as to strengthen the country's economy, help provide cheap manufactured goods needed by the peasants, and find an outlet for the peasants who were unwanted on the land.

There was no serious difference between the Agrarian parties and the Communist parties over these needs. For years before the war the more intelligent members of the Agrarian parties had recognised them and been discussing them, though they had not been able to do much about it. When the Communists became powerful after the war, they accepted and took over many of the old ideas of the Agrarian parties. But differences were inevitable over methods, pace of action, and emphasis.

The first point on the Communist programme for all Eastern European countries, including Bulgaria and Rumania, was land reform. In some cases it even took precedence over recovery from war conditions and reconstruction of war damage. It was dogmatic of the Communists to make this a first requirement in all cases.

In Hungary and even Poland, land reform was the basic and most urgent economic and social problem, and unless it was carried out quickly, the disorganisation and chaos caused by the war would only increase and reconstruction and recovery would be delayed. But the Balkan countries had already had earlier land reforms, particularly after the first world war. In Rumania there were still a few biggish estates, in Bulgaria none. A certain carefully planned redistribution of land might prove economically useful in these countries, but land reform as such was not urgent and might only cause disorganisation. It could not solve their basic economic needs. Nevertheless, because it was part of the general plan of the Communist parties, it was made a priority.

In Rumania, the new land reform had a wider scope and rather more justification than in Bulgaria, where it was almost meaningless. In both countries, there was grave overcrowding of the land. In Bulgaria the official figure was 116 persons to one square kilometre of cultivatable land; in Rumania the proportion was nearly as bad. In Bulgaria the land had usually remained in the hands of the peasant families that had owned it since the earlier land reform, or long before, though it had to be subdivided. In Rumania, in the years after the first world war, owing to constant subdivision of family plots and to the steady impoverishment of the peasants, who lacked credit or equipment to develop the land they had been given, peasants in a number of cases had to sell their land, and were left as landless labourers. Their land passed to richer farmers or absentee landlords living in the town, even to the old landowners.

Changes were needed to restore land to the peasants. Then again, when the Hungarians took Northern Transylvania from Rumania in August, 1940, they reversed the earlier land reform and in some cases restored the old Hungarian landowners who had held estates in Transylvania before 1918. Finally, a number of the richer or more compromised members of the big German minority in Rumania fled with the German Army in the autumn of 1944, leaving land empty.

In the chaos left by the months of fighting between the Germans and Russians in Rumania, it was natural that the Rumanian peasants, especially in remoter parts, should tend to take things into their own hands and seize land where they could. But in the spring of 1945 this trend was deliberately stimulated, for political reasons, by the National Democratic Front, the bloc of Left-wing parties in which the Communists held chief power. The Front at that moment was represented in the Rumanian government but was not in control; the Prime Minister, General Radescu, was conservative-minded, stubborn and rapidly becoming anti-Communist. The Communists thought the time had come to get rid of him, so the Front used agitation for immediate land reform as a political weapon against him.

General Radescu took the attitude that any land reform must be carefully planned, not improvised, and above all that the government must wait until all Rumanian soldiers had come home from the front, so that they could be sure of getting their fair share of the land. In this attitude he was advised by Iuliu Maniu, the leader of the National Peasant Party, who was already out of the government, and, like Radescu, rapidly becoming anti-Communist. In theory it was a wise and noble attitude; in practice it was ostrich-like and unrealistic, since in many parts of the country, particularly Transylvania, the peasants were already grabbing what they could get. The government had to step in.

At bottom, Radescu probably thought the politicians of the Front a lot of whippersnappers and upstarts, in whom it was sheer impertinence to purloin the slogans of land reform, and who needed putting in their places. But he gave them a fine excuse to call him undemocratic and reactionary and to say he was robbing the peasants of their rights.

In March, 1945, Radescu was winkled out and a National Democratic Front government took power. On March 22nd, as one of their first acts, they promulgated a land reform law. In part this merely gave legal blessing to what the peasants had already done. In part it extended expropriation of medium and large estates to the rest of the country. Landowners were allowed to keep land up to 50 hectares. All land over this amount was expropriated without compensation. Model farms were allowed to keep up to 150 hectares, and Church property and State institutions were exempted.

The man directly responsible for carrying through the reform was Romulus Zaroni, Minister of Agriculture in the National Democratic Front government. He was not himself a Communist. He belonged to the small pro-Communist peasant party, the 'Ploughman's Front'. He was a big broad man with the high cheekbones and narrow, watchful, shrewd eyes of the peasant. He wore his heavy coarse linen shirt flowing nearly to his knees. Like nearly all peasant politicians in Rumania, of whatever colour, he had presumably taken to heart the saying that a Rumanian ceases to be honest when he tucks his shirt inside his trousers. The Opposition passed round a number of funny stories about his supposed dumbness and ignorance. But in reality he seemed sensible enough.

A year after the promulgation of the land reform law, he explained that it had taken 1,400,000 hectares of land away from the former owners. This was a smaller amount than had been expropriated in either of Rumania's two earlier land reforms. In 1864, 1,800,000 hectares had been expropriated in the old, smaller Rumania; in 1921, after the first world war, over 3,000,000 hectares had been expropriated in greater Rumania.

This time, Zaroni said, the peasants who had a right to claim land, either because they were landless or because their plots were too small to yield them a living, numbered 800,000 to 900,000. Fewer than 500,000 peasants, he said, actually received land under the reform. They got between half a hectare and five hectares, or an average of three hectares each.

(According to fresh Rumanian figures issued over a year later, in the spring of 1947, the 1,400,000 hectares of land confiscated were distributed among as many as 822,170 peasants, or over 300,000 more than the figure given by Zaroni. If the higher figure is right, each would have got an average of about one and three-quarter hectares. This would probably mean that many would still be left with too little land for livelihood, even if they had received land under the reform.)

The land reform could not fully satisfy land hunger. Many peasants were left discontented and turned their discontent against Rumania's new pro-Soviet government. There were other grumbles too. The reform had been carried out, or sanctioned, by land committees in the villages. Often enough the committees paid off personal grudges or satisfied personal greeds. Rumanian soldiers, when they came home from fighting alongside the Red Army, often complained that there was no land left for them. Hungarian minority peasants in Transylvania said that they were unfairly treated.

These were minor evils. On an overall picture, the reform had probably contributed to social justice among the peasants. But it had not brought about any deep change in the social structure. The old Rumanian aristocracy had already lost most of its power twenty-five years earlier; such as it kept was no longer based on ownership of land. Nor did the reform increase agricultural productivity nor solve the basic problem of overcrowding of the land.

Zaroni said the government had a number of small-scale schemes to absorb the remaining surplus agricultural population.

They planned to direct some peasants to forestry work or forest industries. Others again might be sent to work on the reclaiming of flood land near the Danube, Siret and other rivers, on schemes which might eventually make 2,000,000 hectares of fresh land available for agriculture. Finally, the government might at some time be able to use between 60,000 and 80,000 peasants in the agricultural machine centres which it planned to set up all over the country.

Even these schemes seemed unlikely to absorb all the surplus peasants. And within a generation, unless new industries were developed, the overcrowding problem would grow even more acute. The Rumanians have a high birth rate, and new peasants' sons would grow up to demand their share of the three or five hectares belonging to the father, because there was nothing else they could do.

The other task of the National Democratic Front government was to increase the productivity of the land. About this, Zaroni seemed to have certain rather vague ideas, but not a connected programme. He said that the government was helping needy peasants by letting them have seed and the use of tractors and other machines on credit. They were also thinking of setting up a new Credit Institute for Smallholdings in addition to the National Co-operative Institute and Rural Credit Institute which already existed. But the government was very definitely not going to experiment with collectivisation or the kolkhoz system, even if this would increase production.

'Land ownership is one of the deepest instincts of the Rumanian peasant, and the government has no intention of going against it,' Zaroni said.

He did not accept the view of certain foreign experts, that the latest land reform had definitely decreased Rumania's wheat production and finally ruined her chances of remaining a big wheat exporter. He did not agree that wheat could not be grown on an economic basis on smallholdings, only on larger-size estates or on kolkhozes. He believed

Rumania could get back to her pre-war average export figure of half a million tons of wheat and barley a year.

Ion Mihalache, agricultural expert of Maniu's Opposition National Peasant Party, took a different view. On the one hand, he thought that Rumania should continue to grow enough wheat for greatly expanded home consumption of wheat flour. The ordinary peasant has so far lived mostly on mamaliga, a kind of porridge made out of maize flour, which alone is not nutritious enough to maintain good health. The peasant, Mihalache said, must learn to eat wheaten bread as well as maize, so that he could get the right vitamins.

But in general the Rumanians, as a people of smallholders, should switch over more and more to other forms of agriculture. They should grow more fruit, vegetables and vines, and more fodder so that they could keep more animals. From these they could make bigger profits than from wheat, and so improve their standard of living. Then they would be able to learn to eat not only wheaten bread, but also milk, meat and eggs. So far the richer peasants had produced these things, but had preferred to sell them rather than eat them.

At the same time, Mihalache said, there must be a State-guided scheme for the education of the peasants in more scientific methods of agriculture. There must be State-guided development of producers' and consumers' co-operatives, to be controlled and run by the peasants themselves.

Even these things, he added, would not solve overcrowding of the land. So there must simultaneously be a big programme of industrialisation. This should start with extensive public works on roads, irrigation and similar projects, on which peasants could be employed. It should go on to the development of agricultural industries, to which again peasants could easily adapt themselves. Then it should pass to the expansion of heavy industry.

Mihalache was attacked by the government press as one of the most reactionary, anti-Communist and undemocratic of the politicians of the Rumanian Opposition. His economic ideas, however, were of the kind that any Communist could reasonably accept. The only difference was that he had worked them out fairly carefully, experimenting in his own village, near Campulung, north-west of Bucharest. Here a number of peasant industries had been started in the years before the war, and it had become famous in its way as a prosperous model village.

Few if any of the Communists or their colleagues had such practical experience. Perhaps that was why there was a rather academic flavour about their schemes for development of agriculture.

The Bulgarian Fatherland Front, very sensibly, was in much less of a hurry with its land reform than the Rumanian National Democratic Front. There was, in fact, little land to distribute, except in the part of the Dobrudja which Bulgaria had regained from Rumania in 1940. Here the holdings were rather larger than the Bulgarian average. But there were no German or other minorities from whom land could be taken, and no large Bulgarian landowners at all. On the other hand, land overcrowding was so bad that, according to Fatherland Front figures for 'hidden unemployment' in the villages, the labour of about 1,300,000 adults was not being utilised.

The Bulgarian land reform law was not brought in until the spring of 1946, and even after that it was applied gradually. Mihail Genovski, a youngish pro-government Agrarian of the Obbov group, was regarded as the man mainly responsible for drafting it. He himself said that the new scheme was mainly based on the ideas of the Agrarian Party, dating back to the Stamboliski government of 1921.

According to him there were 1,117,077 peasant families in Bulgaria. When the Fatherland Front took over in 1944, 34 per cent. of these families owned plots of less than one hectare. There were around 80,000 completely landless peasants. About 10,000 families owned over 20 hectares.

In order to provide every family with a plot of from 3 to 5 hectares, it would be necessary to find 1,100,000 hectares of land, Genovski said. The new reform could at very most provide only 450,000 hectares. (According to later figures the final total was only about one-third of this figure.) It could not solve the basic problem of overcrowding on the 40 per cent. of Bulgaria's total surface which has so far been regarded as cultivatable.

The principle of the new reform was that no holding should exceed 20 hectares, and that there should be no absentee owners. An exception was made for the Dobrudja, where holdings of 30 hectares were permitted. But only 'working peasants' had the right to retain land. Absentee owners were given six months in which to start tilling the land themselves; otherwise they lost it. (Soon after the law, you could see a portly banker, stripped to the waist, virtuously scything the hay on a Sunday afternoon in the small field belonging to his week-end cottage outside Sofia. This was to prove he was a 'working peasant'). Those expropriated were, however, to be compensated by the State. The Orthodox Church was to be allowed to keep about one-half of its land property, mostly attached to monasteries. There was a sliding scale for the amount of land to be retained according to the number of monks per monastery.

Genovski, explaining that the new law followed closely the law passed under the Agrarian government of Alexander Stamboliski twenty-five years earlier, said the chief difference was that then the maximum holding permitted was 30 hectares; this had now been reduced to 20 hectares. In an aside, he added that the pro-government fraction of the Agrarians had wanted to reduce it to 10 hectares, but the Communists had stood out for 20. In this as in other ways, the Communists obviously had not wished the Fatherland Front to be bathed in too revolutionary a light.

Given the figure of 20 hectares for the maximum holding, there would only be enough land available for redistribution to satisfy 35 per cent. of the needy peasants. The other two-thirds would still be land-hungry. There would still be 400,000 peasant families owning less than 3 hectares of land, Genovski said. These could only be helped by industrialisation.

He agreed that the aim of the new reform was not to increase the productivity of the land. Its purpose was 'social-ethical', to give greater justice to the peasants.

To increase productivity, both the Rumanian and Bulgarian governments set great store by big programmes for introducing tractors. To the Communists, the tractor was the symbol of progress. They worshipped it rather blindly: although it was true that tractors would be very useful in the wheat-growing plains of Rumania, and to a lesser extent in the flat lands of Bulgaria, they would be of much less value in districts where peasants cultivated tiny plots of tobacco, vegetables, sunflower or fruit. Also, from the short-term point of view, tractors—according to some foreign experts—could only increase peasant unemployment, since far fewer people would be needed to till the land. The tractor was not a universal panacea for all ills, however big its propaganda appeal.

In Rumania the plan in 1946 was to set up 320 agricultural machine centres throughout the country. It was not stated how many were already in existence. In Bulgaria the plan, more modestly, was to set up fifty tractor centres, but in the summer of 1946 only twenty-seven had been started. The great difficulty was to get the tractors and keep them in repair. In Rumania, Zaroni said there were in 1946 about 10,000 out of the 25,000 tractors which the country needed, and only 60 per cent. of the 10,000 were in working order. In Bulgaria there were 4,900 tractors, of which only 1,711 were fit for use. Both countries had hopes of getting tractors from Russia, but they did not know when they would arrive. Meanwhile, the Rumanian government had ordered 5,000 tractors from Rumanian factories which had earlier been engaged on aircraft production, but owing to lack of materials production would probably be delayed.

Both governments also had big schemes for training 'agronomes' to teach the peasants to work the land more intensively and more profitably. This was not a new idea. A certain number of agronomes already existed and were working in the villages, though as their sympathies were usually with the Agrarian movement they tended to belong to the Opposition. But the new government-trained agronomes were intended to work in and through the agricultural machine centres, in Rumania, or the government-sponsored co-operatives, in Bulgaria. They might thus be expected to be politically orthodox and to influence the peasants in favour of the new governments.

The most important part of the Bulgarian government's agricultural schemes was rapid development of the co-operative movement, which already before the war was much stronger in Bulgaria than in Rumania. Co-operative banks and agricultural credit institutes and consumers' co-operatives were already firmly established in Bulgaria. The aim of the Fatherland Front was to extend co-operative farming, on a village basis, over the country.

They soon found that they would have to go slowly, otherwise they would panic the peasants into passive resistance through fear that they would lose their land and be collectivised.

The government had, however, a firm basis to work on. The idea of co-operative farming had first been born in 1921 under the Agrarian government of Stamboliski. It first began to be worked out in practice, under the influence of the Agrarian movement, about ten or twelve years later. In 1935 the first land co-operatives began working. By the time the Fatherland Front took power there were farming co-operatives in about fifteen villages. All these had been formed voluntarily, not under government control. In May, 1945, the Fatherland Front government passed a law for the extension of co-operative farming. A year later there were 'co-operative land organisations' in 432 villages. In February, 1947, there was a total of 438 land co-operatives, in which 44,188 peasants had joined, owning altogether 186,781 hectares of land.

The professed principle of the Fatherland Front was that each individual peasant, when entering the co-operative, kept ownership of his land. He entered voluntarily, placing his land in the common pool, but keeping the right to withdraw from the co-operative whenever he wished. That was where the snag came in. If his original strip or strips of land lay in the middle of the area worked by the co-operative, he could not claim the identical strip or strips back again, but was to be compensated with 'equivalent land' outside the area worked by the co-operative.

This provision at once made the more suspicious peasants feel that they ran the risk of being done down if they entered the co-operative: they might lose good strips close to the village and only get back bad strips of land, far from the village, in exchange if they wanted to quit the co-operative.

The profits of each co-operative were to be distributed on the basis of a rather complicated reckoning. Each peasant was to receive his share in proportion first, to the amount and value of the land he had put into the pool, second, to the number of days he had worked on the co-operative's land. The relative amounts of the 'capital dividend' and the 'labour dividend' were to be decided by the members of each co-operative: the usual figure was 30 to 40 per cent. 'capital dividend' and 70 to 60 per cent. 'labour dividend'. On this reckoning hard work could increase the individual peasant's share of the profits.

This method of sharing profits, Genovski said, distinguished the co-operatives from the Soviet kolkhoz system. In Russia the land belonged to the State, and if a peasant left a kolkhoz he could not claim back land for himself. In Russia, also, the kolkhoz handed over a percentage of its produce to the State; under the Bulgarian scheme the co-operative paid taxes in money in the normal way. Finally, in Russia there was no such thing as the Bulgarian 'capital dividend' but only a 'labour dividend'.

Although the Fatherland Front's scheme was modest and reasonable enough, many peasants panicked and the application of the law had to be slowed down to stop the growth of peasant passive resistance to the government. The panic had two causes. The peasants had a traditional belief that the Communists wanted to take away their land from them; there were Communists in the Fatherland Front government; so they reasoned that the government must be trying to take away their land. Then the local Communists in the villages were tactless, pushing and domineering. Although co-operation was supposed to be voluntary, all kinds of compulsion were used in the early months to get hesitant or reluctant peasants into co-operatives.

One provision of the law in particular frightened the peasants: if most of the peasants of a village wanted to form a co-operative, but two or three peasants owning strips in the middle of the area to be worked by the co-operative refused to join in, then these two or three peasants could be compelled to exchange their strips for other strips outside the co-operative area. The peasants, of course, always believed that the new strips would be much worse land than the old. In general, they leapt to the conclusion that the Fatherland Front law was really compulsory, although it pretended to be voluntary, and that it was a concealed form of collectivisation.

Peasant mistrust and opposition grew so much that in the later months of 1945 the government fraction of the Agrarians, led by Alexander Obbov, had to intercede with the Communists to get them to restrain their local enthusiasts and slow down the whole process. In the summer of 1946, according to Genovski, although there were 432 'co-operative land organisations', there was not a single case in which an entire village had gone into a co-operative; and he solemnly declared that in a village where no one wanted a co-operative, no kind of pressure was now exerted. He also declared that only one-fifth of those peasants who had been compelled to exchange strips lying inside the area of a co-operative for strips outside it had complained to the authorities of injustice in the exchange.

The Opposition, of course, told a different story.

The 1946 land reform law added a new element of compulsion to co-operative farming, but not a very serious one. If there were one hundred peasants in a village, and if the land confiscated under the reform were not enough to provide one hectare each for all the claimants, then the government was to form a co-operative of the confiscated land. Land claimants had the right to enter the co-operative, but they must also throw such land as they already possessed individually into the pool. This was, of course, government-compelled formation of co-operatives. But Genovski claimed that it would only apply in a small number of villages.

He agreed that the Government's attempt to spread co-operatives had so far had a rough passage. The Fatherland Front's power to create faith in it would depend on how far the Front could send tractors and agronomes to the co-operatives. These he believed—perhaps optimistically—would have a big psychological effect, because they would convince the peasants of the material advantages of co-operation.

The Opposition, however, believed that it would take far more than tractors to overcome the peasants' blind mistrust of the Communists.

In Rumania, the National Democratic Front government were so afraid of creating a collectivisation panic among the peasants that in 1946 they did little about encouragement of co-operative farming. Their chief idea was to establish State-controlled co-operative shops in the village. In theory this scheme was excellent, since it would provide paraffin, salt and manufactured goods to the peasants at low government-controlled prices, instead of leaving them to buy in the towns at fantastic black market prices. Many of the peasants, however, did not see it in this light. They could do very well on the black market by bartering their produce. But if they were forced to buy in government co-operative shops, this would give the government a stranglehold: if the peasants refused to give up their crops to the authorities at unprofitable government-controlled prices, then the government could in theory withhold essential goods from the co-operative shops, and starve out the peasants. They also felt that the government was much too incompetent to supply the essential goods they wanted.

In practice, of course, the scheme was not nearly so sinister. No Rumanian government, of whatever colour, was capable of stopping black marketing or of forcing the peasants to sell at controlled prices. But the scheme added to the general mistrust of the National Democratic Front.

That was the whole difficulty with all the schemes for helping the peasants propounded by the new governments in Rumania and Bulgaria. In theory, the schemes were in many respects excellent, except that perhaps they were apt to be piecemeal and haphazard. There was little in them which the Opposition peasant parties could criticise. The land reforms, even if they solved no basic economic problems and caused some temporary disorganisation, would in the long run contribute to social justice. But so long as the peasants in general mistrusted the governments and read sinister political motives into all their words and works, the schemes were bound to be held up by passive resistance and non-co-operation. Either the new governments would have to employ wholesale force against recalcitrant peasants, or they would somehow have to create faith and trust. Up till the end of 1946 it seemed that they had not made up their minds and were dithering between the two courses.

In one sense it was a handicap that neither the Bulgarian nor the Rumanian government had the chance of proving its worth quickly through rapid and efficient schemes of reconstruction of war damage. Yugoslavia and Poland had suffered great damage in the fighting; their new governments did wonders, which non-Communistic governments could probably never have achieved, in the way of reconstruction, and so convinced many of their opponents of their drive and competence. But in Bulgaria there was very little war devastation, except for bomb damage in Sofia. In Rumania, although the country had been fought over, the campaign had moved fast except in Moldavia, and, in general, damage was superficial. So there was no need for big reconstruction schemes through which the new governments might have won laurels and created public confidence—as the Bulgarian government almost certainly would have done, although the Rumanian government probably would not.

Instead, the main job for both governments, as the fighting ended, was to maintain financial stability and a reasonably steady currency and to restart industry. Both countries faced economic crisis. Large-scale occupation and requisitioning by the Russian Army meant a heavy strain. The defeat of Germany meant that both countries were suddenly cut off from their old sources of supply of manufactured goods and certain raw materials, and had lost their old market for their agricultural produce. Both Rumanian and Bulgarian armies were heavily engaged in the last months of the war, which meant a serious drain on finances. At the end of the war, industrial production in both countries dropped to less than half. There was grave danger of runaway inflation.

Bulgaria somehow miraculously escaped inflation. An extremely intelligent and sober economist, a youngish Communist called Ivan Stefanov, formerly teacher of economics at Svishtov, a Bulgarian provincial town, was first Director of the National Bank and then Minister of Finance under the Fatherland Front régime. He was the brain behind financial, economic and trade policy. Somehow he managed to keep the leva steady, to prevent prices from soaring, even to balance Bulgaria's tiny budget.

In effect, rigid economy and a more than usually frugal life was imposed on Bulgarians. There was rationing of basic foodstuffs and essential clothing, which was moderately effective in the towns, and rationed goods were sold at low controlled prices. There was, of course, a black market in food and clothing, but it was relatively smaller than in most European countries. The ordinary middle-class Bulgarian was too poor to buy on the black market. The richer Bulgarian did buy butter and silk stockings on it, but was circumspect and thought twice before plunging: the government was always issuing fierce warnings against black market dealings.

At the same time the government pegged wages and salaries at a low level. In 1945, 25,000 leva a month, or about £16, was fixed as the maximum for any State official, including heads of departments, and for other salaried workers. State expenditure, which rose in 1945 to cover Bulgaria's military effort in the early months of the year, was reduced again in 1946 to just below the 1944 level. A serious effort was made to collect direct taxes, though these were and remained very low; the annual income tax was under 2,000 leva per head of the population, or just over thirty shillings.

All in all, Stefanov managed to maintain financial stability during the opening years of the rule of the Fatherland Front. The same could not be said of the Rumanian government. Rumania was a relatively much richer country than Bulgaria. It had a gold reserve of 239,480 kilograms of gold, which was not touched by the Russians when they arrived in Bucharest, although the Rumanians had been in such a panic lest it should be looted by the Red Army that they had seriously thought of distributing the gold among the Rumanian population at a few ounces per person. On the other hand, the Red Army requisitioned much more heavily in Rumania than Bulgaria; industrial equipment was removed, in compensation for Russian property looted by the Rumanians, in large quantities during the early months; and Rumania had to start paying almost at once her reparations to Russia, finally fixed at 300,000,000 dollars payable over eight years starting from September 12th, 1944. Bulgaria was let off reparations to Russia, and it was only in the peace treaty that it was finally determined that she should pay 45,000,000 dollars to Greece and 25,000,000 to Yugoslavia in manufactured and agricultural products.

The bad harvest of 1944 and the droughts of the next two years created a shortage of foodstuffs in Rumania; the sharp fall in industrial production in 1944-45 and the loss of supplies from Germany created a shortage in manufactured goods. These shortages turned Rumania into one vast black market with the price of goods steadily shooting upwards. The National Democratic Front government was unable to check the trend. Also, the more the public lost political confidence after King Michael's breach with the government in August, 1945, the more rapidly they lost economic confidence.

The British Mission's rate for the lei, which was based on the current cost of living estimate drawn up by one of the main oil companies for its staff, was 32,000 to the £ in December, 1945. Little over a year later, it had reached 500,000 to the £, and quickly shot to 1,000,000 and beyond. Meanwhile the salaries of State employees and office workers and the wages of the workers did not even begin to keep pace with this inflation. During the year 1945, on official reckoning, the lei lost one-fifth of its value and the cost of living increased over twelve times. But

H

salaries and wages remained fixed throughout the year. After that there were slight increases, but never even remotely in proportion to the rise in the cost of living.*

In the spring of 1946, a fairly high-grade civil servant got 100,000 lei a month, an Under-Secretary of State got 180,000 lei a month, a university teacher 80,000 lei, an industrial worker 200,000 lei. At that moment one kilogram of meat cost 15,000 lei, a kilogram of sugar 30,000 lei, a pullover 160,000 lei, an egg 500 lei, a meal in a first-class restaurant 45,000 lei. As time went on the disproportion between earnings and prices got even greater. Basic wages and salaries were still about the same a year later, but sugar had risen to 150,000 lei per kilogram, and an egg had reached 8,000 lei.

On the basis of such figures it was, of course, impossible to see how any man ever lived on his salary or wages. The answer was that he very seldom did. Many dealt on the black market themselves to make something extra; it was a situation which encouraged the still further growth of bribery and corruption of all kinds.

The government themselves did not set a good example in every respect. It was commonly known in Bucharest that a rich Rumanian, if he paid enough, could buy an exit permit. He had to go to a certain high Communist functionary in the cabinet offices. The cost depended roughly on the wealth of the applicant; 30,000,000 lei was one price fixed in the winter of 1945-46. The rate presumably increased later with the inflation. From one point of view this might be called a justifiable capital levy on the idle rich. The Fatherland Front did things more elegantly by introducing a retroactive law early in 1946 for the confiscation of 'all property acquired illegally through speculation'. This seemed a better form of capital levy under a progressive régime, even if it was so framed that it could be turned particularly against the régime's political opponents.

In general, the main concern of the Rumanian and Bulgarian governments during the first two post-war years was just to keep things going somehow without introducing great changes. The Bulgarian government succeeded, the Rumanian government kept only a very loose grip on the reins. In both countries there was little direct interference with private property and private enterprise, except through State organisation and control of labour.

The creation of one single nation-wide trade union and professional organisation was the first step of the Communists in both countries when they came to share power. This organisation swallowed up all old unions, and it was practically compulsory for every worker to belong. Since it had the backing of the government, and so of the State, and

* It was not until the late summer of 1947 that the government, on Communist initiative, made its first serious effort to stop inflation and stabilise the currency.

since it was highly organised by energetic and forceful Communists, it was very powerful. The employers were left in a very weak position; in Rumania there were some few owners of large-scale factories or industrial combines, but in Bulgaria most 'industrialists' were owner-managers of tiny factories that were more like big workshops, employing at most a few hundred men. They could not bargain with a nation-wide union organisation with the power of the State behind it.

So both in Rumania and Bulgaria the employers had to raise industrial wages to a level higher than that of the highly-trained professional man. They had to allow the workers the right to hold meetings in the factory in working-hours. And they had to provide the workers with certain material advantages. In Rumania these took the form of canteens, where the employers had to provide food, bought by themselves at high prices on the black market, to the worker at low government-controlled prices. There were also 'economats', or factory shops, where workers could buy foodstuffs, clothing and other household goods, purchased dearly by the employers, at the same low prices. Employers would have to send out lorries on scouting expeditions to scour the countryside and to find food and other supplies for the canteens and economats. All this meant a lot of extra expenditure for the employers, who soon complained that their costs were becoming enormous and they would soon be bankrupt. In fact, they saw it all as part of a plot on the part of the government—or the Russians—to ruin them and expropriate them as quickly as possible.

In the first two years, at least, there was practically no expropriation or nationalisation. One of the few exceptions was the Petroșani coal mines, Rumania's main source of coal. Here production dropped steeply in 1945 and could not be raised again. The workers, or their union leaders, fell out badly with the owners. The National Democratic Front government blamed the owners and placed Petroșani under direct State control to appease the workers and increase production. The government said that more coal was a vital national need, since at that time so much of Rumania's oil—usually her chief fuel—was being exported to Russia as reparations that coal was needed to replace oil for home consumption. Early in 1946 official figures were published showing a startling rise in coal production. These were quoted to show that the owners' 'reactionary attitude' to the workers had been all that was wrong.

The Bank of Rumania was also nationalised at the end of 1946. This change had political rather than economic importance. The Bank had always been very closely linked with the State. It had in the past been controlled largely by the powerful banking family of the Bratianus who, through the National Liberal Party which was also identified with the Bratianus, had often also ruled Rumania politically. But since the National Democratic Front came to power, the National Liberal Party, or at least that wing of it which was ruled by the Bratianus, had gone into strong opposition to the government. Although after that the family retained little practical control of the Bank, the Front presumably thought it safest that the State, that is, the Front, should take over the Bank formally as well as in practice.

In Bulgaria the National Bank was already in the hands of the State when the Fatherland Front took power. So too were most of the main economic concerns of national importance, in particular the Pernik State mine, Bulgaria's chief source of coal. Nevertheless, although the Communist Party was strong among the Pernik miners, there was a serious drop in coal production in 1945, though not as sharp as at Petroşani. The Fatherland Front had to conduct intensive propaganda to remedy this drop, which was not only causing hardship to the ordinary householder in the towns but was also threatening to paralyse the railway system. This propaganda was partly successful. The situation was saved.

The policy of leaving the old owners at least in nominal control of most industries in Bulgaria and Rumania was not a satisfactory compromise. In most cases the smaller industrialists, who were intensely conservative and individualistic, felt that they were hamstrung by labour legislation and agitation, by the power of the local Communists, and by State interference. They made up their minds that they would no longer be able to make profits, that sooner or later they would go bankrupt, and that they were slowly but deliberately being forced out of business by the new governments.

They were also, in some industries, cast into gloom by being cut off from their old contacts with Germany or Western Europe. They felt that the new situation, in which they could for the time being trade only with Eastern Europe and Russia, was hopeless. The Bulgarian textile factory owners of Gabrovo, very grandiosely called the 'Bulgarian Manchester', grumbled bitterly because they could now get replacements of machinery neither from Germany nor England: their older machines were English and their newer machines were German. Nor could they get the types of wool and cotton to which they were used. They said they disliked the cotton they got from Russia because it was of uneven quality and unsuited to their machines.

With this gloom and disbelief among the industrialists, the new governments could not very well hope to launch out successfully on big ambitious schemes for steep increases in industrial production, on the Soviet model. On the other hand, many of the smaller factory owners were not just remote absentee profit-takers. They were working managers of their concern, who had technical knowledge of the process of manufacture from bottom to top. To throw such men overboard would be to lose valuable experience which it would take time to replace. It was a dilemma. But during 1946 it became clearer and clearer that the State would have to interfere more and more heavily in industry if big economic plans were to be launched.

One symptom of this trend was the Rumanian government's plan, announced early in 1947, for setting up 'industrial boards' to control allocation of raw materials and machinery, types of goods produced, sale and collection of payment for all goods produced. The directors of each board were to be appointed by the Minister of National Economy. Owners and managers who did not obey the orders of their board were liable to one to five years' imprisonment. This plan, if carried out more logically and thoroughly than things usually were in Rumania, was likely to leave the industrialists bound hand and foot. But in practice compromise and confusion were likely to last some time longer.

Another very important development which made it unlikely that Rumanian industry could last on a basis of private ownership, was the creation of a number of 'Sovrom' enterprises, based on joint Rumanian-Soviet State ownership. These came into being fairly soon after the Russian occupation. They were joint combines to control and run certain industries and undertakings in Rumania, with at least theoretical fifty-fifty participation by each side. (According to Opposition rumours, the Russians always had the casting vote.) This meant in practice that the Rumanian State, not the individual owner, became the partner of the Soviet State in certain key undertakings. There was Sovrom petrol, for the oil industry, another Sovrom combine for Danube shipping, and yet another for all civil aviation.

The creation of these Sovrom concerns, together with endless rumours that the Russians were buying up shares in private Rumanian industries, made it easy for the Opposition to declare that Russia was turning Rumania into a Soviet economic colony. This, of course, conflicted with the other favourite Opposition assertion that Russia was deliberately trying to ruin Rumania's economy, so that the way would be open for full-blooded Communism. But no one seemed to notice the contradiction, and it was true that there often seemed to be curious confusion and conflict in Russia's economic policies.

In theory the Sovrom oil combine should have been the most important, since oil was Rumania's chief traditional source of wealth. In practice the Soviet share in Rumanian oil remained small. According to authoritative Rumanian figures for the first six months of 1946, the 'Anglo-French' group of oil companies—Astra Romana, Steaua Romana, Unirea and Dacia Romana—was responsible for 51.13 per cent. of Rumania's total production, compared with a corresponding figure of 42.95 per cent. in 1939. The American company, Romana Americana, was responsible for 11.16 per cent., compared with 12.50 per cent. in 1939. The Sovrom group, consisting of about a dozen small companies, was responsible for 28.20 per cent. In 1939, the same companies had jointly been responsible for 31.05 per cent. Various small companies were responsible for the remaining 9.51 per cent.

So it was impossible to say that the formation of Sovrom petrol had given Russia a controlling interest in Rumania's oil industry. The British and American companies still had the great part of the industry in their hands. But it was questionable whether the British and Americans would find it worth while, on purely economic grounds, to keep their old-established share in Rumanian oil. Their oil men complained that the industry was no longer profitable and had no future. All oil now had to be sold to the Rumanian State, at unprofitable prices fixed by the State, to go to Russia as reparations under the armistice. Labour agitation and labour legislation meant repeated concessions to the workers. Shortage of equipment and a much slower rate of work held up fresh drilling. Above all, from the long-term point of view, it was a great handicap that the Rumanian State was now, through Sovrom Petrol, a direct competitor in the oil industry. The State could obviously hamstring its foreign rivals with legislative restrictions and red tape. In particular, fresh prospecting in new fields, urgently needed if the production level was to be maintained or raised since the old oil fields in the Ploesti-Campina district could not last for ever, was pretty well out of the question for foreign companies.

Prospects, therefore, seemed poor. The overall production of the Rumanian oil industry showed a downward trend. Total production for the eleven months ending December, 1946, was 3,868,285 tons, compared with 4,261,723 tons for the corresponding period of 1945. During Rumania's peak pre-war year, the annual production had been 8,000,000 tons.

In these rather depressing circumstances, it seemed dubious whether the British and American companies would be able or willing to stay in business permanently. If, in the end, they should decide to get out, then the Rumanian State, probably in partnership with the Soviet State, could be expected to get the whole oil industry in its hands. Since oil was Rumania's key industry, this development would strengthen the trend towards bringing all Rumanian industry under direct State ownership.

In Bulgaria, the trend could be judged from the stormy debate which rose at the end of 1946 in the parliamentary committee for drafting the new republican constitution, over the clauses about private property.

The original draft presented to the committee said: 'Private property and private economic initiative shall be recognised. . . . No one may exercise his right of private property in a manner contrary to public interests, or in a way prejudicial to the security, freedom and existence of others.' After debate in the committee, in which a sixth of the members belonged to the Opposition, this was toned down a little. The words 'or in a way prejudicial to the security, freedom and existence of others' were cut out. Both the original and the final draft forbade private monopolies, cartels and trusts, but declared that private property 'acquired through labour and savings' should enjoy 'special protection and encouragement'. Both declared: 'private property may be expropriated but only in public and State interest and against equitable compensation.'

These draft clauses, though most Bulgarians would probably have accepted them calmly in stable and normal conditions, aroused alarm and despondency in Bulgaria's atmosphere of change and transition. So far the more wily factory owners felt that they could wangle survival by hook or by crook. One nervous young industrialist had, from the very start of the Fatherland Front régime, paid large subscriptions of varying size to all political parties, both of the Fatherland Front and the Opposition. The biggest went to the Communist Party, as the most powerful. The next biggest went to Nikola Petkov's Agrarian Party, because the young man had a sentimental streak. Under the new constitution, it seemed that this ingenious system of insurance and reinsurance could not last. The day of uncontrolled private enterprise, on the nineteenth century liberal model, was passing fast.

The fate of private enterprise and industry, both in Rumania and Bulgaria, was still at least theoretically unsettled and things were still in a muddled state of compromise, when the moment came for the new governments to launch a big economic plan. Throughout Eastern Europe, the season was judged ripe for planning in the spring of 1947.

Rumania lagged behind all the other governments of the Soviet sphere. The spring passed and still she had no plan. Perhaps the internal chaos was too great. But Bulgaria, just at the time when her peace treaty was signed, at last launched her first general plan.

It was a Two-Year Plan, on the general Soviet model, but particularly closely linked with the Czechoslovak Two-Year Plan. It was modest and sober, compared with Yugoslavia's much more ambitious Five-Year Plan; but it was ambitious enough. Its aim was radical improvement of the living standards of the country by industrialisation, by mechanisation and rationalisation of agriculture and by 'giving an impetus to all branches of the national economy'.

The first task was to reach the levels of production of 1939: the next was to surpass them before April 1st, 1949. By then, industrial production was to exceed them by 67 per cent., agricultural production by 34 per cent. At the same time, as part of a big electrification scheme, dams and power stations were to be built. Communications were to be improved, and new factories erected.

For agriculture there were to be tractor centres, supplies of agricultural machinery, and encouragement and aid for co-operatives. The establishment of a State tobacco monopoly—tobacco is Bulgaria's chief export—to organise production and marketing of tobacco, coincided with the announcement of the Plan.

The Plan was to be financed largely by credits from the State and co-operative banks, and to a much smaller extent by the State Budget. Foreign loans were not specified as an essential means of financing the Plan, which was in fact usually presented by the Communists as a way of making Bulgaria free and independent of 'foreign exploitation'.

On the industrial side the most revolutionary element of the Plan was the ambitious electrification scheme, which had already been announced in part in 1946. It started fairly modestly as a scheme estimated to cost 2,100,000,000 leva, or somewhere in the neighbourhood of £1,400,000. Within a few months the estimate had risen to 5,000,000,000 leva. It looked as though it might well expand more. The backbone of the scheme, which aimed to provide electric power for existing and future industries all over the country, and also to bring electricity to the villages, was the building of several big dams—Rositsa, Topolnitsa, Tash Boaz, a big Rila-Rhodope 'combine'—to harness water power.

The Rositsa dam, hopefully called the Bulgarian Dneprostroi, was to provide water power for two hydro-electric stations with an annual capacity of 35,000,000 kilowatts, or enough to provide electricity for the 'larger part of Northern Bulgaria'. This dam was also to provide water to irrigate 28,000 hectares of land belonging to twenty-five villages.

Labour for work on the Rositsa dam was, at least for the first year of the Fatherland Front government, provided mainly by political suspects from a neighbouring concentration camp or 'labour educational camp'. So labour costs were cheap.

In March, 1947, it was announced that work had started on a new dam, 'Koprinka', which, it was said, would be the first great enterprise undertaken in accordance with the Two-Year Plan. Here Youth Brigades were to do the building work, so once again labour would be cheap.

The whole electrification scheme was linked with a big plan to utilise Bulgaria's rivers and underground waters to irrigate large areas: it was prophesied that fresh land could be won for agriculture totalling about 60 per cent. of the existing area of arable land. Electrification was also linked with a scheme for increasing coal production, especially through the exploration of new coal fields, to supplement the Pernik State Mine which had so far produced 80 per cent. of the coal consumed in Bulgaria.

One obvious problem was: where could Bulgaria, who had practically no foreign currency, get the electrical machinery—turbines, power plants and so on—needed to put this vast scheme into action?

In June, 1946, a burly youngish man, Traicho Kostov, who after being secretary of the Communist Party had become Minister of Electrification, went to Moscow to see what Russia could give. The main thing he got was a promise of a 12,000 kilowatt power-station consisting of two 6,000-kilowatt generators. It was to be set up under the direction of Soviet technicians near the Sofia main station, to electrify the station quarter of the city, where there were several factories. There was also agreement 'in principle' that Russia should supply further machinery, but quantity and date of delivery were left unpublished.

The 12,000 kilowatt power-station arrived very quickly, a few days after Traicho Kostov had come back in triumph. Sceptics were soon putting around the story that it was of American make, not of Soviet manufacture.

More certain help for Bulgaria's electrification scheme came in the spring of 1947, when an important four-year trade agreement with Czechoslovakia was signed. Spokesmen of both countries said that one of its particular aims was to speed Bulgaria's electrification. Czechoslovakia promised, among other things, machinery for dam-building, power stations, electrical goods and—for the coal production scheme—mining equipment. All that remained to be seen was whether Czechoslovakia could supply these things on a large enough scale to make sure that the scheme went through quickly, and at cheap enough prices for Bulgaria to be able to pay her back with tobacco, oil seeds and other agricultural products. For Czechoslovakia, Bulgaria could never be an important market, but would be a stable and lasting one even in the face of foreign competition. For Bulgaria, Czechoslovakia was important because she was ready to trade on a barter basis without demanding foreign currency. Bulgaria would not have to go begging for a foreign loan.

Both for Bulgaria and for other Balkan countries with very weak financial resources, there were two particular problems in the way of carrying out any quick plan of economic development. These were: how to pay the labour needed for the big public works, the building of railways, roads and dams, and so on; and how to pay for the machinery, material and equipment which at least in the early stages would have to be bought abroad.

Bulgaria had found, long before the Fatherland Front came to power, that compulsory or voluntary labour in some form—as distinct from normal paid labour—was the only form of cheap labour. After the first world war, when Bulgaria was placed under disarmament restrictions and was forbidden a conscript army, 'labour service' under more or less military conditions was instituted to replace military service. The young men of the labour service battalions built or kept in repair many of Bulgaria's roads which, by Balkan standards, were relatively good. During the second world war, when concentration camps for Jews and political suspects were started on a large scale, the pro-German governments found a new source of cheap labour. The Fatherland Front took over the idea.

To mark its first anniversary, the Fatherland Front government opened with great ceremony the new almost-completed railway down the Struma valley, running to within a few kilometres of the Greek frontier. As the governmental train passed, at every station men of the new labour service battalions were drawn up under Fatherland Front banners, wearing semi-military uniform and with their picks or shovels over their shoulders, to cheer the Fatherland Front leaders. When the train reached its goal, the Exarch Stefan, head of the Bulgarian Orthodox Church, broiling gently in his heavy rich embroidered robes in the midday southern sun, smiled benevolently over his long curling beard as his fellow priests chanted a religious ceremony and the white ribbon was cut which barred the triumphal arch of green branches marking the last lap of the new railway.

Special trains overflowing with Fatherland Front followers steamed slowly up just as the ceremony started. The engines were hung about with wreathes of pine and green boughs and flowers. The most faithful young men and boys had also draped themselves on the front of the engines among the boughs, clinging on with one hand and waving flags with the other. The festival of the new railway was the festival of Fatherland Front progress.

Afterwards a young middle-class Jew said: 'Of course it was really I—and people like me—who built most of that railway, during the war. As a Jew I was in a concentration camp at Dupnitsa. We worked very long hours on excavating and building the track. It was very hard work for many of us because we were not used to manual labour. We lived in very primitive conditions. The guards were seldom physically brutal, though of course if you disobeyed an order you got beaten. Anyhow, it was we who did most of the work. The Fatherland Front just carried on and finished it off.'

The Fatherland Front inherited the concentration camps from the pro-German governments. The Jews and Communists went out. The camps were filled with men suspected of 'fascism', of political hostility towards the Front, or at least of unreliability. They could be detained without trial on the recommendation of the Militia. The camps were rechristened 'labour educational camps'. There was little education or even political propaganda, only hard work in hard conditions. But the Front had a source of cheap labour for public works schemes.

An elderly intellectual, whose somewhat perverse sense of humour had taken an anti-Communist twist during the war, and who found himself in a concentration camp soon after the Fatherland Front came in, naturally found life in a 'labour educational camp' extremely unpleasant. For him, food was dreary; there was very little meat; there was no medical attention except from fellow-prisoners. You had to try to sleep on dirty straw in overcrowded three-tier bunks with several in each bunk. If you worked badly you might be beaten up. The senior Militia guards were 'neurasthenic cases', but the younger ones were often peasant boys, and quite kindly. Punishment was being hit on the face or confined in a waterlogged underground cellar. Hours of work were very long, but he could remember no deaths through illness, exhaustion or epidemics. You could only see visiting relatives under the eye and in the hearing of the Militia guards. Your letters were rationed and censored. There seemed no rhyme or reason in the release of prisoners. Those released were told warningly to go and vote for the Fatherland Front in the next election.

Some men got their release through the intervention of a member of the government. When a non-Communist Minister, even the Prime Minister, wanted to get a prisoner freed, he would send along a special plea for the individual to Militia Headquarters in Sofia, to General Russi Christozov, a young Communist. Sometimes, after a few weeks, the plea would be granted—which was regarded as a triumph for the Minister who made it—sometimes not.

The 'labour educational camps', though a useful source of cheap labour, probably only provided a few thousand workers. This was not enough. The Opposition were afraid the government would start some form of general labour conscription which could be used particularly against political opponents. Meanwhile there were the Labour Brigades and the Volunteer Youth Brigades.

The Labour Brigades were mostly townsmen and townswomen, technicians and craftsmen, doctors and dentists, who were willing to spend their leisure time at week-ends or during holidays, doing voluntary work for the community. They would go to the country and do jobs for the peasants on the co-operative farms, using their own particular skills where needed. They would do rush emergency jobs: loading coal on to railway trucks at Pernik during a transport crisis, pulling down the garden wall of the Royal Palace in Sofia when the government decided to move their Cabinet offices into the Palace.

The Youth Brigades closely followed the Yugoslav model. Young Bulgarians went to help Yugoslav Youth to build the 'youth railway' in Bosnia. The same thing was started in Bulgaria. The 'brigadiers' were young men who were ready to work voluntarily on special jobs, usually in the intervals of their studies. They were able to do the rough manual work needed in building dams or railways, leaving the skilled labour to skilled workers.

In the opening years of the Fatherland Front government, cheap forced or volunteer labour still only existed on a comparatively small scale. It was clear that if the Two-Year Plan was to be tackled quickly, either one or the other or both would have to be greatly extended. That part of the Bulgarian people represented, accurately or inaccurately, by the 30 per cent. of Opposition votes in the 1946 elections were not very likely to provide volunteer labour for the Fatherland Front, in spite of the Front's appeals for Opposition co-operation in carrying out the Plan. It therefore looked as though there would have to be an extension of the system of compulsory labour. The other alternative—to pay full union rates to ordinary workers for big public works schemes—would be an unbearable strain on the State finances and would increase the danger of inflation—particularly if no foreign loans were given to Bulgaria.

Bulgaria was in a particularly bad position to get foreign loans or credits from the Western Powers. She had, by 1947, a Communist Prime Minister and a Communist majority in Parliament, so that there was every political reason against her getting a charity loan from the United States. Economically, the country was pitifully poor and small and had no important mineral resources (except possibly uranium, but that was still a very doubtful quantity). Any other Balkan country had more inducements to offer to foreign capital, if it wanted. All the Balkan countries were in need of money and materials from abroad. But by the spring of 1947 the pro-Soviet governments were taking up a defiant 'don't care' attitude about the whole question of help from the West.

They knew that American loans and imports of American machinery and materials would probably make the fulfilment of their economic plans both easier and quicker, and would lessen the physical and moral strain on their peoples. But politically they thought American aid too dangerous. The Communists had, of course, always mistrusted Anglo-American capital and Anglo-American capitalists: they only served Anglo-American imperialist ends. The pro-Soviet governments feared the Anglo-Americans would use any economic foothold for political penetration and influence, to undermine the new régimes.

On the other hand, the Americans seemed to them to be getting more and more truculent about giving loans, credits or relief to any country with a 'Communist-dominated' government in the Soviet sphere. President Truman, in his historic message to Congress in the spring of 1947, said openly that America's policy was to give aid to those governments or countries, such as Greece or Turkey, which were resisting Communism. The broader and less anti-Communist interpretation of the 'Truman doctrine' which George Marshall gave in his offer of American aid to Europe was regarded as mere camouflage and rejected.

So the pro-Soviet governments abandoned their idea of economic or financial help from the West, and turned more and more to other countries inside the Soviet sphere to help them in their reconstruction and industrialisation.

From the short-term point of view, prospects were not very encouraging. There was Russia herself; but she needed badly very much the same things as the Balkan countries wanted, for her own reconstruction. Later she might be able to help more fully. For the first crucial years, her help would inevitably be very limited.

Then there was Czechoslovakia, a highly organised and efficient manufacturing country, whose industries had been further developed by the Germans during the war. She could naturally replace Germany, in part, as the chief supplier of the agricultural Balkan countries. On the other hand, she was trying to maintain in her own country a much higher standard of living than the Balkans ever had, and to meet the increased labour and production costs that had resulted from the nationalisation of her industry. She therefore had an interest in extending her trade with the richer Western Powers, if this was possible. But the attempt might break down, particularly as she had a Communist Prime Minister. She also feared growing Western competition, and also the competition of a revived Germany, in world markets for industrial goods. She might therefore increasingly rely on the Balkans as a safe, if not very profitable, market for her industrial exports.

Austria, whose heavy industry had, like Czechoslovakia's, been highly developed by the Germans during the war, might also help the Balkans with their industrialisation plans. But this depended on whether or not Austria fell completely under Western influence, and whether or not Russia managed to keep at least an economic foothold there through possession of important Austrian factories, defined as German assets and acquired as reparations.

Italy—in 1947 regarded as a borderline country which might yet fall under Soviet influence—was another possibility as a supplier of certain types of equipment, for instance railway wagons, to the Balkans. But that again depended on dubious political factors.

Finally, Germany might recover industrially and might be able to send machinery to the Balkans on a barter basis. That also depended on political relations between the Western and Eastern Powers and on the remote chances of a German settlement.

These various possibilities were set about with question marks. It remained true that Western, or rather American, aid could alone have helped the pro-Soviet governments to put through their industrialisation plans quickly with the minimum of hardship. Further, if there were a run of bad harvests, the Balkan countries would not even be self-supporting agriculturally, in their food supplies. They might again need food from the West if they were to avoid hunger and even famine such as struck the Rumanian province of Moldavia in the spring of 1947.

But by 1947 the old political and strategic struggle between East and West over the Balkans had been extended to the economic field. From then on, two things were certain: that Russia would permit no American economic 'penetration', which would, she believed, be used for subversive political ends, in the Soviet sphere; and that America would do nothing which might bolster up the pro-Soviet governments or help them to execute the economic plans on which their prestige depended.

It was in these bleak conditions that the Bulgarian and Rumanian peoples were called on to make the biggest economic effort of their national histories.

8

Rumania's National Democratic Front

ON a bleak gusty day, March 6th, 1946, everything was set for the Rumanian National Democratic Front government to celebrate the first anniversary of taking power. In particular there was to be a gigantic outdoor demonstration in the vast 'Place of the Nation' in Bucharest, in the shadow of the pretentious parliament building.

This was fixed for the afternoon. By noon columns of a few hundred men were gathering and parading in Bucharest's main boulevard. Each column represented a trade union or a pro-government youth organisation or a factory. The men carried roughly scrawled banners saying 'Long Live the National Democratic Front' or 'Down with the Reactionaries' or 'Down with the Executioners of the workers'. Conducted by choir-leaders, they practised chanting 'Long live Grozea', 'Down with Maniu'; Grozea was the Prime Minister and Maniu the Opposition leader. The men looked neither enthusiastic nor particularly happy. On one or two faces was a ghost of the cynical grin typical of the town-bred Rumanian. Perhaps the gusts of wind and sudden flurries of rain depressed them. They had three hours to wait before they could march to meet other columns in the 'Place of the Nation'.

The bystanders looked at the columns with detachment or even distaste. On a few faces the cynical grin repeated itself more openly.

The afternoon came. The grey wet wastes of the Place of the Nation stayed deserted. There was no gigantic meeting to fête the National Democratic Front. Few Rumanians seemed much interested to find out why. Those who asked were told that the government had suddenly, at the very last moment, cancelled arrangements for an outdoor demonstration because of the bad weather.

Such a fiasco on such a solemn occasion could not have happened in a Slav country. Nor could it have happened in any other country where, as in Rumania, the Communists held chief power in the government. Rumania, as usual, drifted along her own private path.

Later that day in a warm dry cinema the Prime Minister Grozea made an anniversary speech. Recalling that Britain and the United States had just recognised the National Democratic Front government, he said: 'This confirms that ours is a democratic government based on the will of the people.'

It was true that according to certain modern meanings of the word, the Grozea government might be called democratic. But not even members of the government, talking privately, would have seriously maintained that it was based on the will of a majority of Rumanians.

That was the root of the whole problem of Rumania, for the Russians. Russia, not unnaturally, wanted a friendly and reliable government in Rumania, the only one of the Balkan states with which she actually shared a common frontier. A big majority of Rumanians was instinctively and traditionally mistrustful and resentful of Russia. Any government based on the will of the majority, even if its professed policy were devoted loyalty to Russia, would at heart be impelled by the same feelings of mistrust and resentment towards her. The Russians seem to have concluded that they must therefore have a government of the very narrow minority whom they could trust. But that in turn meant having a government without prestige or authority in the country, and driving the very few really able and competent and experienced administrators and politicians into opposition. It was a dilemma.

The modern national state of Rumania was founded on the idea that Rumania must be a bulwark of the West against Russia. That idea has been deeply rooted in the minds of the Rumanian educated classes for nearly one hundred years. It has even seeped through to the peasants who form three-quarters of the nation.

Grigore Gafencu, former Foreign Minister of Rumania, one of the few Rumanians who before 1941 tried to conciliate Russia, in his book *Prelude to the Russian Campaign*, quoted a passage from a manual of modern history compiled by a member of the Moscow Academy of Science: 'After the Crimean War a new State was created, the outcome of the enfeeblement of Russia and the diminution of its influence in the Near East: Rumania. To the creation of this State, the diminution of Russian influence and the increase of French influence in Eastern Europe have contributed in equal measure.'

Gafencu himself added: 'The comments of the Soviet historian are perfectly true: the Rumanian State was constituted after the Crimean War, when the thrust of the Russian Empire towards the south had been halted by a European coalition, and Russian influence was opposed by French influence: a political and military expression of European interest. The creation of the new State had thwarted the plans and ambitions of the policy of the Czars.'

Also after the Crimean War, the European coalition imposed on Russia the formation of the European Commission of the Danube, to prevent Russia from getting sole power over the mouths of the Danube. Gafencu wrote: 'The freedom of Rumania was therefore linked from the very beginning with the European conception that confirmed the freedom of the Danube.' At that time, Rumania also got the southern strip of the eastern province of Bessarabia, which bordered on the Danube delta. But just over twenty years later, at the Congress of Berlin in 1878, Southern Bessarabia was given back to Russia, who kept it until 1917. Then, after the Russian collapse and the Russian revolution, Rumania took the whole of Bessarabia, and Russia was again pushed back from the mouths of the Danube.

After the Russian revolution, the Rumanian educated classes in general decided that their country's mission was not only to be a bulwark against Russia but also to be a bulwark against Bolshevism. The new frontier, the river Dniester, was closely guarded, and there was very little traffic across it. Soviet Russia did not recognise the Rumanian annexation of Bessarabia. Rumania became part of the French—or Western—security system. When in the late 1930s, Nicolas Titulescu, Rumania's most intelligent inter-war Foreign Minister, tried to reconcile Rumania and Soviet Russia, the Rumanian right-wing parties reacted violently against his policy. The extreme right-wing anti-semitic Rumanian government of Octavian Goga, which took power in January, 1938, was clearly anti-Soviet. As, after that time, the various Nazi movements or groups gained strength in Rumania, the country tended more and more to become a satellite of Hitler Germany, and so ultimately a jumping-off place against Russia.

The Molotov-Ribbentrop Pact in 1939 finally discredited those Rumanian politicians who had sought conciliation with Russia. Rumanians believed that, as part of this pact, Germany gave her advance blessing to the Russian acquisition of Bessarabia and Northern Bukovina. This belief was justified when the Russians, after delivering their ultimatum, marched into the two provinces in June, 1940. From that moment anti-Russian feeling was at its highest pitch. It was inevitable that Rumania should—under the leadership of a reputedly pro-British General, Ion Antonescu—take part in the war against Russia at Germany's side.

Throughout that war, many Rumanians believed that, although they were fighting as the allies of the enemy of the Western Powers, Germany, nevertheless they had the tacit approval of the Western Powers in fighting against Soviet Russia, weakening her armed might, and driving her out of Europe. They almost expected Western gratitude. Up till the armistice in 1944, they received no encouragement from the Western Powers to cherish this belief. But it was not astonishing that the Russians, deeply suspicious of the traditional anti-Russian instincts of the Rumanian educated classes, became equally suspicious of supposed Western long-term plans to use Rumania as a pawn in an anti-Russian game.

The Russians' mistrust probably grew in proportion to the weakness of their own political influence in Rumania. During the war, their own friends in Rumania, chiefly the Communists, were very few and in very weak positions. The Russians had to rely almost entirely on British contacts with the Rumanian 'bourgeois', pro-Western, opposition which, if dilatory and procrastinating, had great popularity and had its men in powerful positions. This was a humiliating situation for Russia, in a country on her own border. Perhaps it explains partly why, after the armistice, the Russians were in such a hurry to get rid of the Rumanian 'bourgeois' leaders.

The leading pro-Western politician in Rumania, both before and during the war, was Iuliu Maniu, head of the National Peasant Party. There have been endless arguments about his character as a political leader. His friends said that he had always been genuinely democratic, in the Western sense of the word, had tried to introduce democratic methods into Rumania, had always sought to use constitutional means in the political struggle, and had genuinely tried to improve conditions for his country's peasants. His critics said that he had an essentially negative character, that his passion for constitutional forms had landed him in a purely unconstructive stalling policy, and that during the years between the two wars he generally preferred to be nobly irresponsible in opposition rather than take the responsibility of power in order to help the peasants. His friends said that he had always wanted good relations with Russia on condition that Rumania kept her full independence and integrity. They looked on him as the liberator of Rumanian Transylvania from the Hungarian yoke, in 1918. His critics said that at heart he could not help being instinctively anti-Russian, and that he supported the Antonescu government in the early stages of the war against Russia in 1941. They looked on him as a narrow nationalist and believed that under his leadership Rumania could never be reconciled with Hungary.

In spite of all criticism, very much of it justified, Maniu had for nearly thirty years been Rumania's most respected and influential figure among the masses of Rumanian peasants, particularly the Transylvanians.

When Britain, after the fiasco of her abortive 1939 guarantee of assistance to Rumania and the entry of German troops into the country, withdrew her diplomatic mission from Bucharest early in 1941, arrangements were made to maintain contact with Maniu. This contact was kept going, with certain very serious interruptions, up till King Michael's *coup d'état* in August, 1944.

For a very long time it seemed that this link was of very little practical use, except to get information about political developments inside Rumania. Maniu had no intention whatever of plunging Rumania into a desperate revolt against Germany which would end in bloodshed and reprisals. He had very little faith in sabotage and underground active resistance. He was working for the big-scale political coup, with full Allied backing in the form of co-ordinated air support and possibly also

I

British parachute brigades, when the time was ripe. It looked as though Maniu would not judge the time ripe until such a coup would be useless, or at least superfluous, from the point of view of shortening the war.

Throughout, Maniu worked closely with the Palace—young King Michael and his nearest advisers—and with Constantin Bratianu, elderly leader of the National Liberal Party, representing the pro-Western financial and business interests of Rumania. He had contacts with the two small left-wing parties, Communists and Social Democrats, but considered them unimportant. According to some sources, he first discussed collaboration with the Communists in 1943. According to Ion Constantinescu-Iaşi—later a member of the National Democratic Front government—who claimed to have acted as go-between for the Communists and Maniu, Maniu refused to enter an agreement with the Communists and Social Democrats 'until he was forced into it by the Russians after the Red Army crossed the Dniester in March, 1944'. Then a four-party 'Patriotic Bloc' was formed of the National Peasant, National Liberal, Social Democrat and Communist parties, which later became the political basis of the first government formed after King Michael's coup in August, 1944.

During the crucial period for Rumania—the summer months of 1944—there were two groups which were more important than the political parties. With both of these Maniu was in touch. One was a small nucleus of clever and bold men inside the Rumanian Foreign Office, mainly in its cypher department, who kept going one set of contacts between Maniu and the Palace, inside Rumania, and the outside world, and could also provide good information on what was going on in the outside world. One of these men was Niculescu-Buzeşti, son-in-law of Prince Stirbey, Rumania's first peace envoy to the Allies. (Buzeşti, less than three years later, was living in exile in Western Europe, and in the Maniu trial in November, 1947, was sentenced to fifteen years' imprisonment.) The other important group was formed by certain senior officers of the Rumanian Army. Very little is known about them, but General Mihail, of the General Staff, has been mentioned as the real organising power behind the coup of August, 1944.

The events which led up to the coup were confused. Eight or nine months before it, two British officers parachuted into Rumania. They had hoped to get into touch with Maniu, but were captured by the Rumanian police and shut up in a prison in Bucharest. Here various high officials of the Antonescu government visited them and, as the military situation got steadily worse, asked for advice on how to get out of the war. In the spring of 1944, the Red Army swept into Moldavia, north-east province of Rumania; the Germans fled before them, even riding on cows. There was panic throughout Rumania. Prince Stirbey went to Cairo to act as the representative of King Michael and Maniu in negotiating an armistice with the representatives of Britain, the United States and Russia. His journey had been organised with British help.

Early in April Stirbey sent a message to Bucharest transmitting the Allies' armistice conditions for Rumania. These conditions, which really represented Russia's minimum terms, were that Rumania should break off relations with Germany and fight beside the Red Army; that the 1940 frontiers should be restored between Rumania and Russia, who would get Bessarabia and Northern Bukovina; Russia would not insist on occupying Rumania during the armistice period provided she had freedom of movement for her troops in all directions through Rumanian territory; Russia regarded the Vienna Award, annexing Northern Transylvania to Hungary, as unjust and would help Rumania to get this region back.

A week later Maniu replied submitting counter-proposals which, he subsequently declared, were no more than a request for elucidation of certain obscure points in the Allied terms. On April 19th, Stirbey answered that the Allied representatives did not accept Maniu's telegram as a reply to their conditions. On April 20th Maniu sent a message saying he agreed to start negotiations on the basis of the Allied conditions and his own counter-suggestions, combined. He immediately sent a second envoy, Vişoianu, an extremely intelligent middle-aged man who had been associated with Titulescu, to help Stirbey in the negotiations. (Vişoianu, like Niculescu-Buzeşti, was sentenced *in absentia* to fifteen years imprisonment in November, 1947.)

Towards the end of May the Soviet representative in Cairo, Novikov, had an interview with Stirbey and Vişoianu, who as a result sent Maniu a message saying that the Soviet government would not discuss Maniu's counter-suggestions until he had said clearly whether or not he accepted the original Allied conditions, which might become more unfavourable if he did not accept them as quickly as possible.

On June 11th, Maniu sent a message to Cairo saying he agreed to conclude an armistice on the Allied conditions. He added that he was sending a plan of action for bringing Rumania on to the Allied side, which had been agreed by 'all responsible factors' in Rumania. On June 22nd details of the plan were sent to Cairo, saying—perhaps grandiloquently—that all that was needed to put it into action was a signal from the Allies. This meant, in fact, the Russians, since the Red Army alone was militarily concerned. But then came two months' silence from the Allied side.

Later, it seemed that this Allied, or rather Soviet, delay was due at least in part to separate armistice negotiations which Russia was conducting, through Madame Kollontay, the Soviet Minister in Stockholm, with the Antonescu government. In the early stages, at least, Britain and the United States did not know about these negotiations. Perhaps the Russians had become tired of the humiliation of depending on British contacts and British channels of communication, through Cairo, and wanted to pull off a coup of their own. Perhaps they had got weary of Maniu's desire to haggle and make conditions and delay action, and sceptical of his power to act. They may have thought an agreement with the government in power of greater military value than an agreement with an Opposition leader.

Meanwhile, in Bucharest, feelings got more and more tense as people waited for the Red Army, after long delay, to swoop down on the capital from Moldavia. The Communist Party became more active. So far, their resistance had not gone beyond publishing a clandestine newspaper, *Romania Libera*, and spreading underground propaganda—which, however, was as much or more than any other party was doing, apart from negotiating and planning. Now the Communists suggested to Maniu that they should start street demonstrations and factory strikes, to weaken the government. They asked, however, that the Army should guarantee not to shoot on strikers or demonstrators. Maniu said he could not provide the guarantee, so little happened.

By August 6th, even the Antonescu government had decided they must get out of the war. But then Marshal Antonescu, a vain and somewhat stupid man, was invited to visit Hitler, who appealed to his loyalty and convinced him that German secret weapons would suddenly change the whole course of the war. Antonescu came back determined to fight on with Germany.

The Opposition discussed immediate action without waiting for a reply from Cairo. This course was advised by certain senior officers. Critics of Maniu claimed that it was he who counselled further delay, and who as late as August 20th was still saying that 'one must not hurry'. Finally, in agreement with the King, the coup was fixed for August 26th. In the meantime, Maniu left Bucharest for the country for a few days. On August 23rd, the two Antonescus, Ion and Mihai, appeared at the Palace in Bucharest to see the King. The young King, seeing his chance, seized it, and had them both arrested in the Palace. On his own initiative and in the absence of Maniu, he put the plan for the coup into action three days ahead of schedule, and recorded an appeal to be broadcast to the nation and the world, declaring that Rumania had joined the Allies.

By his action he very probably caught the Germans off their guard; by August 26th they might well have known the details of the plan and forestalled it. The Rumanian Army and the people followed the King wholeheartedly, in spite of the vicious bombing of Bucharest by German Stukas, as a revenge. By the time the Red Army reached Bucharest, the Germans were out.

On the very day of the coup Buzeşti, who became King Michael's Foreign Minister, sent a message to Stirbey and Vişoianu in Cairo giving them full powers to sign an armistice on the basis of the Allied conditions of April, 1944. He added that Madame Kollontay had also offered Rumania certain concessions: that in fixing reparations Rumania's difficult economic situation should be borne in mind, and that the Rumanian government should be left a free zone where no Soviet troops should be allowed to enter. He asked that these concessions should also be taken into account in framing the final armistice terms.

The armistice negotiations were, however, shifted from Cairo to Moscow. From then on Russia played the decisive rôle. The final armistice terms were stiffer than the new Rumanian government, who considered they had done the Allies, especially the Russians, a great service, had expected. The Red Army occupied the whole of Rumania. There was no free zone for the Rumanian government. The Rumanians considered that the economic obligations laid upon them, in the form of reparations, restitution of property and maintenance of the Red Army troops stationed in the country, were far too heavy in view of their military services to the Allied cause.

This created a rankling sense of grievance, injustice and injury in the 'bourgeois' politicians, officials and officers who, with the King, had been mainly responsible for the coup and who formed the backbone of the first government after the coup. They had a grudge against the Russians; the Russians mistrusted them because they were pro-Western. So within a few months the split developed between the pro-Western politicians and the pro-Soviet politicians—the Communists and their comrades in the new left-wing bloc of the National Democratic Front. The Patriotic Front of the summer of 1944 ceased to exist. By the end of 1944 the Russians had already decided that it was only the National Democratic Front whom they could trust.

There were, however, six uncomfortable months of transition between King Michael's coup and the imposition of National Democratic Front rule. The parties of the Front could claim no more than a minor part in the coup (although eighteen months later Constantinescu-Iaşi solemnly told a foreigner that it had been the work of 'the King, the Communists and the Social Democrats'. These parties were also very weak in organisation and popular following. At the moment of the coup, it is likely that neither the Communist Party nor the Social Democrats nor Petru Grozea's Ploughman's Front had more than a very few thousand supporters each. In particular the Ploughman's Front, which had started some years before the war as a tiny local peasant group based on the Deva district of Transylvania, under Grozea's patronage, could not hope to win the mass of the peasants away from Maniu's 'historic' National Peasant Party without many months of intensive organisation and propaganda. The 'Union of Patriots', which was started on Communist initiative to attract the middle and professional classes to the Front, remained a minute and meaningless group.

The Front was therefore not ready for rule. Nor was King Michael ready to put them in power. Since, after the coup, the King's prestige and popularity were very great, his wishes mattered.

The King's first government after the coup was a broad coalition. Politically, the two most important men in it were the leaders of the two 'historic' parties, Maniu for the National Peasants and Constantin Bratianu for the National Liberals.

Lucreţiu Patraşcanu was chief representative of the Communist Party. He was a young Rumanian lawyer of middle-class family, highly educated, with a fine face and charm of manner. He was tolerated, even liked, by the 'bourgeois' politicians who looked on him as a 'Rumanian Communist', with some Rumanian patriotism, in contrast with the 'Moscow Communists', who had lived in Russia and were in several cases not of Rumanian blood.

Titel Petrescu represented the Social Democrats. He also was acceptable to the 'bourgeois' politicians: he was an idealistic dilettante rather than a revolutionary or a serious labour leader.

The Army was represented by General Sanatescu, who was close to the King as Marshal of the Court. He became non-party Prime Minister. The Foreign Office group, which had played an important part in preparing the coup, was represented chiefly by Niculescu-Buzeşti as Foreign Minister. Vişoianu, returned from Cairo, had later to take on the job of supervising the execution of the armistice from the Rumanian side.

Theoretically, it was a strong government, supported by practically the whole Rumanian people, and containing some capable men. The Rumanian Army, without dissent, swung around to fight with the Red Army against the Germans and Hungarians, and the campaign moved rapidly westwards out of Rumania into Hungary. The armistice was concluded in Moscow, in spite of the Rumanian sense of injustice and grievance against the Western Allies who failed utterly to support Rumanian claims for concessions.

It was probably a mistake that Maniu himself did not go to Moscow with the armistice delegation: he might have established relations of confidence with the Russian leaders. But Maniu, perhaps, was too anxious to preserve his personal dignity and to avoid personal identification with an armistice which was bound to be very unpopular in the country. His absence led to the belief among his critics that he and the other National Peasant leaders had never accepted in their hearts the cession of Bessarabia and Northern Bukovina to Russia, and were still fundamentally Rumanian nationalists.

There was probably, in fact, a good deal of foundation for this belief. Some months later Maniu told a foreigner that, although of course the armistice terms regarding their cession must be loyally carried out, the Atlantic Charter had not been applied to Bessarabia and Northern Bukovina, since the population had not been consulted. 'Naturally, as a Rumanian, one can only regret the loss of millions of Rumanians,' he said. The recovery of Northern Transylvania counterbalanced the loss of Bessarabia and Bukovina, he added; but Transylvania was now in the hands, not of Rumanians, but of Hungarians and Jews.

So Maniu's whole mental attitude, like that of his friends and of many Rumanians, was not one of appeasing and placating the Russian conqueror, but of standing out for what were considered to be Rumania's well-earned rights and of protesting whenever these were thought to be infringed.

The most serious grievance was the application of the economic clauses of the armistice. The Red Army applied wholesale, rough-and-ready methods, particularly in requisitioning for the Army and in removal of Rumanian industrial equipment and property under the title of restitution of property seized from Russia during the war. Constantin Vişoianu later complained that the reparations clause, Article 11 of the Armistice, was tolerable; but Articles 10 and 12, dealing with requisitioning and restitution, were far heavier burdens, particularly since they involved Rumania in unforeseeable and incalculable expenditure which made it impossible to budget for the future.

Given this serious cause of friction, the Russians quickly came to distrust the 'historic parties' and the Foreign Office group. At the same time, the Communist Party was gaining confidence, carrying on propaganda, organisation and agitation, and recruiting large numbers of members very rapidly. The floating population of opportunists, particularly townspeople and the economically insecure layers of the middle-class, including many minor government officials, were ready to inscribe themselves. Former members of the Iron Guard, the Rumanian anti-semitic Nazi organisation, were in a hurry to find refuge; in the past the Guard had had contacts both with the National Peasant Party and the Communists, and many found a home in one or the other, although the Communist Party was thought the safer of the two. As the Party grew, the Communists began to think that they and their political associates would soon be ready to take power, and that the essentially unreliable 'historic parties' could be eliminated. King Michael's broad coalition government began to crack up.

In November, 1944, General Sanatescu re-formed his government. This did not help. In December he gave up the task; with him, Maniu and Bratianu, and also Titel Petrescu who was worried at extremist tendencies on his left, quitted the government. The new Prime Minister seemed at first to be a man whom both the King and the Russians could like and trust. He was General Radescu, a soldier who had never been a politician and who spoke his mind sometimes with embarrassing frankness. He had been on friendly terms with some of the Communist leaders when they were together in the Targul Jiu concentration camp during the war, after Radescu had protested against the dictatorial methods of the German Minister in Bucharest, von Killinger. He was a stronger personality than Sanatescu, and it looked as though he might win the confidence of the Russians, work with the National Democratic Front, and at the same time keep its excesses in check.

Radescu started by giving the Front considerably more power in the new government. Grozea became Vice-Premier; other Front leaders held the Ministries of Justice, Labour and Communications. But Radescu kept the Ministry of the Interior for himself, in order to maintain order and quell agitation.

He did not succeed. The Front, although inside the government, acted against it. For long years past the Rumanian workers had not been allowed to form their own organisations or to fight for their rights. Now trade unions were given legal status, tasted power, and became very active. Here the Front could get an enthusiastic following, although there was a fair number of workers who stood aside. There were demonstrations and disturbances, mainly by National Democratic Front workers, in Bucharest and other towns. Radescu used the police to keep them down. A Communist, Teohari Georgescu, who was Vice-Minister of the Interior, resigned, accusing Radescu of keeping fascists in the police.

At the same time, there were disturbances and disorders in the countryside because of peasant agitation, exploited and stimulated by the National Democratic Front, for land reform.

Radescu found he had less and less power to keep order. He regarded his Cabinet colleagues of the Front as disloyal, men who were playing a double game. He was too stiff-necked, probably too conservative at heart, to go to meet the Front's demands, some of which—for whatever motive they were put forward—were really needed. In the end he lost his temper, and at a crowded public meeting in a Bucharest cinema, he bitterly denounced certain leading Communists as un-Rumanian and anti-Rumanian—particularly Ana Pauker, who was Jewish, and Vasile Luca, who was of Hungarian origin.

The Russians, in the early spring of 1945, were in serious military difficulties on the Hungarian front. Rumania lay directly on their lines of communications. They could claim that it was a military necessity for them that order should be restored in Rumania. They also apparently believed that they had serious grounds for mistrusting Radescu's personal attitude and aims in the event of a Russian military reverse in that area of Europe.

At the end of February, Vishinski descended on Bucharest from Moscow. There was some discussion; then Vishinski saw King Michael, and, it was said, executed one of his thumps on the table. The King gave way. Radescu went. A purely pro-Soviet National Democratic Front government, headed by Grozea, took power on March 6th, 1945. Maniu and Bratianu and the 'historic parties', together with the old foreign office group, in fact all the pro-Western leaders, went into full Opposition, with Titel Petrescu, the Social Democrat, hovering somewhere betwixt and between. The months of transition were over.

Although the National Democratic Front claimed to be a people's government, it was oddly remote from the people, except for the industrial workers. Somehow its leaders did not seem to be accepted as real politicians. It was felt that they were just playing the part. One reason for this feeling was that the Front had very few forceful personalities, and that these, for one reason or another, stayed very much in the background and left the showier rôles to less serious men.

Grozea, as Prime Minister, took most of the limelight. But he never seemed quite solid. His enemies called him a mountebank. To an outsider he seemed to mix a strain of genuine, if rather naïve and dilettante, idealism with a strain of disarmingly frivolous vanity. A man in late middle age, he was broad-shouldered, muscular and strongly-built. He had very blue merry eyes in a square face with strong cheekbones. He preened himself on his physique. One of the first things he told Sir Archibald Clark-Kerr (Lord Inverchapel) when the Three-Power Commission arrived in Bucharest at the end of 1945 was what physical exercises he did every morning. He liked to show off the muscles of his forearm. His enemies in Bucharest told many highly-coloured stories about his somewhat impetuous gallantry towards women.

Grozea was a man of comfortable means who in early middle age had awoken to the cause of social progress. He had identified himself with the small peasant group of the Ploughman's Front, and had been its only notable spokesman. But until the formation of the National Democratic Front, politics had been for him a hobby rather than a career. Although he was nominal chief of the Front, most Rumanians believed that certain Communists were the real power behind Grozea.

Most important of these was Emil Bodnaraş, who ran the Prime Minister's office. It was said that he could not hold the formal rank of Cabinet Minister, because King Michael would not accept the oath from a man who had once deserted his post as officer in the Rumanian Army.* Bodnaraş was one of the 'Moscow Communists' who had lived and presumably been trained in Russia. He was of Ukrainian blood, not purely Rumanian. Perhaps for this reason he had unusual energy, drive and organising ability. He was a good-looking man with a rather noble profile and grizzled sandy hair. He was a fluent and convincing speaker and talker, with some charm.

He was obviously a power in the Front. Enemies of the Front said that Bodnaraş ran not only the Prime Minister's office but also the

---

* In December, 1947, Bodnaraş at last attained Cabinet rank and became War Minister. King Michael abdicated a week later. Whether there was any connection between the two events is not known at the time of writing.

Prime Minister himself, and wrote his speeches for him. They particularly disliked him because they believed that he ran his own private political police, successor of the old 'Siguranţa'. He certainly collected numerous reports and dossiers containing snippets of political gossip, perhaps more, about all the Front's actual or possible opponents. He was also disliked because he was the man who finally decided whether or not any particular Rumanian should be given an exit permit from Rumania. Since a good many upper class Rumanians were anxious to leave National Democratic Front Rumania, for one reason or another, Bodnaraş had real power.

The two chief Communist Ministers in the National Democratic Front government—Gheorghiu Dej and Teohari Georgescu—were outwardly unimpressive. Dej's main concern was industry and the industrial workers, over whom he had considerable authority. He looked tough and was tough, and was the Communist Party's economic expert; but he did not seem a big personality. Teohari, to outsiders, was rather apologetic and defensive, but this was presumably not his real character. The Ministry of the Interior was effective enough.

The prophetess, some said the real leader, of the Communist Party was Ana Pauker. She did not hold Cabinet rank during the armistice period, and was content with relatively unimportant posts such as presidency of the Front's women's organisations. But she gave the impression of being the strongest and most powerful character in the Front.

She was a strongly-built, large-boned woman. She had short iron-grey hair swept back from her face, which, with its broad forehead and broad cheekbones, had a certain beauty. Although she was often flushed, there was a kind of brooding calm about her.

She was born of Jewish middle-class parents named Rabinsohn. After teaching in a Jewish school, she studied medicine for two years in Bucharest, but left the University to devote herself to the Socialist movement. When the Communists and Social Democrats split in 1921, she followed the Communist Party, which three years later was declared illegal. After that she had to work underground, often travelling abroad clandestinely to Switzerland and France. Once, when in Switzerland, she met an engineer, Marcel Pauker, who was a strong Communist, and married him. But she carried on her political work.

In 1936 she was arrested in Rumania, tried by court martial at Craiova for anti-State activity, and condemned to ten years' imprisonment. After nearly five years in prison at Mislea and Plataresti, she was exchanged, by agreement between Bucharest and Moscow, for a National Peasant Party deputy who had been arrested by the Russians when they entered Bessarabia in 1940. Ana Pauker went to Moscow, possibly for the first time, and was received by Stalin. Together with another Rumanian Communist, of Bulgarian origin, Boris Stefanov, she is said to have represented Rumania on the Executive Committee of the Third International until it was dissolved in 1943. (Stefanov later more or less vanished from the political scene.)

While in Moscow, Ana Pauker is said to have formed close friend-ships with Manuilsky, the Ukrainian Communist leader, and Maurice Thorez, exiled head of the French Communist Party. According to Bucharest gossip, her husband, Marcel Pauker, was eventually executed for Trotskyist activity. But when Ana Pauker reappeared in Bucharest after King Michael's coup, she brought her three children—the eldest a dark slim girl who often wore Rumanian peasant costume—back with her, and seemed very devoted to them.

During the war she was the chief broadcaster to Rumania on the Soviet radio, calling for active resistance to the Germans and pro-pagating the basic ideas of the National Democratic Front—which were closely akin to the basic ideas of the Bulgarian Fatherland Front. Later she is said to have played a big part in organising the Tudor Vladimirescu division from Rumanian prisoners of war captured by the Russians. Those who after indoctrination became good Communists were released and trained, and the Division, in which Ana Pauker is supposed to have held the rank of major, returned to Rumania with the Red Army.

In the first months after the coup, Ana Pauker was clearly very powerful, both in public political activity and behind the scenes. Later she seemed to recede into the background, and certainly appeared far less often at political meetings. But she remained powerful behind the scenes, waiting for her dramatic political reappearance as Rumania's first woman Foreign Minister in the autumn of 1947.

She was undoubtedly an idealist, a sincere and fanatical, if ruthless, Communist. Perhaps she preferred the early phase of dangerous under-ground struggle to seize power, to the later phase of the relatively safe if sordid manœuvring to maintain power.

Like Georgi Dimitrov in Bulgaria, Ana Pauker was well protected by tough-looking bodyguards when she appeared in public.

Ion Constantinescu-Iaşi, Minister of Information in the first National Democratic Front government, was a curious man in a curious position. There seemed little doubt that he had been a member of the Communist Party for some years past; he had been imprisoned for anti-State activities, which was the usual term used by pre-war Rumanian govern-ments for Communist activities. Yet in 1946 he denied indignantly that he was a Communist, although he claimed proudly that he had acted as liaison between the Communists and Maniu during the war.

The reason for this change of front was that in 1944, as a 'bourgeois' intellectual of the professional classes, he had been allotted the task of creating and leading the 'Union of Patriots', to draw these classes into the National Democratic Front. Although the employees of his own Ministry and a very small number of intellectuals joined the new 'middle-class party', in general no one took the Union of Patriots or

Constantinescu-Iaşi himself seriously. This attempt to rally the bourgeoisie was a fiasco.

The next hope of the organisers of the Front, in their effort to draw in the middle-classes, was George Tatarescu, who took one wing of the 'historic' National Liberal Party away from Constantin Bratianu. Tatarescu became the National Democratic Front's Foreign Minister, and was expected to bring a substantial section of the financial and business classes, always identified with the National Liberal Party, along with him. In this he had a certain limited success. As Foreign Minister, however, he started off on the wrong foot in that he was particularly unacceptable to the British, because he had not only been associated with King Carol of Rumania during the King's pro-German phase, but had also been concerned with Rumania's repudiation of Britain's guarantee. However, Tatarescu was a supple and skilful if devious politician, and had many reasons for loyalty to the Front. He could never have been a danger to it; it was presumably because the Communist Party thought his usefulness ended, rather than because they thought him a serious menace, that he was forced out of the government and compelled to make way for Ana Pauker in the autumn of 1947.

A third and last attempt to bring the middle-classes into the Front was made in January, 1946. The Union of Patriots was allowed to fade out, and Constantinescu-Iaşi launched a new 'National Popular Party', specifically declared to be the party of the middle-class, with a programme stressing the sanctity of private property, of family life and of the monarchy. Its titular leader was a sick man of untarnished political reputation, Mitiţa Constantinescu, but the moving force was Constantinescu-Iaşi himself. The Party gave a refuge for those men of the professional classes who felt that the time had come to think of their careers rather than their political prejudices, perhaps also a few sincere men. But on the whole it created very little stir in the country. The middle-classes remained an unreliable and doubtful quantity.

In the early days of the National Democratic Front, it had attached to it a tiny group called the 'Union of Democratic Priests', which aimed to rally the Orthodox Church to the Front. Practically its only known member was Father Constantin Burducea, who became Minister of Cults. On March 6th, 1946, Father Burducea quite suddenly handed in his resignation. Opposition circles said that the editors of one of the two Opposition newspapers had managed to get hold of a photograph showing the Father wearing Iron Guard uniform and playing a prominent rôle at an Iron Guard ceremony in 1940. The newspaper intended to start a propaganda campaign against him. So Father Burducea resigned quickly. After that the Union of Democratic Priests more or less lapsed. In any case, the Rumanian Orthodox Church showed no desire to make trouble. It was not in any way a danger to the Front.

The Social Democratic Party, the most important party in the Front after the Communists, was in a class by itself. Unlike most of the other little parties of the Front, it was a genuine party, with a certain history and tradition. But it had always been small and never very vigorous. After the split with the Communists in 1921, the more forceful of the left-wing youth went to the Communists rather than the Social Democrats.

Titel Petrescu, who undisputedly led the Social Democrats in 1944, was an intellectual theorist and talker rather than a man of action. He was not of the working-class, but was a fairly well-off lawyer. He was a man of French culture, and somehow the luxuriance of his grey locks, of his moustache, and of his bow-tie suggested the Quartier Latin fifty years ago. He had courage but was excitable rather than enduring.

In the early months after the coup, the Social Democrats and Communists worked together closely to get the industrial workers the rights which they had long been denied, and which the more conservative elements of the 'historic parties' were still hesitant to concede. But in the process of organising labour through factory committees and trade unions, the first friction arose. The Communists, being as usual more active and ruthless and better organisers, quickly seized the lead. The Social Democrats felt they were being left in the cold and were not being fairly represented on the committees. Squabbles arose over methods of electing the committees. The Communists, at least in the early stages, favoured election of candidates, usually Communist-nominated, by acclamation. The Social Democrats came more and more to see the advantages of secret voting.

Titel Petrescu himself left the government as early as December, 1944, partly because he was squeamish over the methods of trying war criminals before people's courts. But he remained leader of the Social Democratic Party, and the party remained in the National Democratic Front. When the Front's first government was formed in March, 1945, the chief Social Democratic representatives were Radaceanu and Voitec, two men of undistinguished and somewhat mixed political records, who had only come to the fore in the party through their close ties with the Communists. Petrescu was personally out of sympathy with them, and was soon at loggerheads with them.

After the National Democratic Front had taken power, Petrescu drifted closer towards the leaders of the 'historic parties', now in full opposition. He maintained his Social Democrat principles. but thought that Communist dictatorial leanings must be held in check. That was his common ground with the 'historic parties'. So, while the Social Democratic Party remained nominally united, and remained one of the leading parties of the National Democratic Front, Titel Petrescu's personal followers moved more and more openly into opposition.

This curious position brought the Social Democrats a flood of new recruits, many of them middle-class people who had little interest in the rights of the workers, but who thought that membership of the party combined the advantage of safety with the possibility of being mildly anti-Communist.

Inside the factory and union committees, and also in the local branches of the Social Democratic Party, a silent struggle developed between the two trends in the party. The one, represented by Radaceanu and Voitec, was towards full collaboration with the Communists inside the Front. The other, represented by Petrescu, was towards greater independence of the Communists.

A party conference held in Bucharest on December 1st, 1945, resulted in a partial temporary success for Titel Petrescu. The party remained united. It was provisionally agreed that the party should contest general elections, when held, with a separate and independent list, not on a joint list with the Communists. This decision was, however, liable to review at a later date. The Social Democrats were to continue their close collaboration with the Communists in what was loosely known as the 'United Workers' Front', but there was to be a redistribution of posts on the factory and union committees, so that the Social Democrats might be more fairly represented.

During the early spring of 1946 fresh elections were held for a number of these committees. Petrescu, however, considered that they were still not free and that the Communists were again imposing their candidates. The question whether the vote should be open or secret remained undecided and led to endless bickering. Petrescu claimed that, although two-thirds of the organised workers in Bucharest were Social Democrats, the Communists demanded fifty-fifty representation of the two parties; the Communists said: 'After all, we have more experience than you.' Stories trickled into Bucharest from the provinces about terrorist methods used by Communists against local organisers of the Social Democratic Party.

The climax came when the full party Congress was held in Bucharest on March 10th, 1946. The Congress was to take the final decision whether or not the party was to fight the general elections on an independent list. Everyone knew that the party was bound to split at last. The question was, who would get the majority of votes and so keep, or win, the party leadership.

On the eve of the Congress, Petrescu was confident that he had the mass of the party with him, although he complained of the 'pressure' that was being exerted against him by Radaceanu and Voitec, who, he declared, exploited their position as cabinet ministers to make promises and utter threats. There were signs, however, that Petrescu had lost ground and weakened his position inside the organising committee of the party. Even Şerban Voinea, a prominent Social Democrat and one of his most loyal friends, seemed to be wavering.

There was, both at the time and later, much dispute about the methods by which the delegates to the Congress had been elected by the local branches of the party. From Petrescu's side there were strong charges of irregularities. These, of course, could not be proved. It was certain, however, that there was a great deal of muddle. The mandate of nearly every delegate was contested by one side or the other on the eve of the Congress, and there was no time to check the facts.

The Congress opened, in private, in an atmosphere of great tension. The first speaker was Voitec. He spoke at length in favour of a common electoral bloc with the Communists. Voinea then asked him what representation the Social Democrats would get within the bloc, which would also contain the other parties of the National Democratic Front. Voitec produced his trump card: he said the Social Democrats had been promised the highest representation of any party. They would get 30 per cent. of the seats, while the Communists had undertaken to be content with a mere 20 per cent. This handsome promise naturally had a certain effect on the meeting.

The next bombshell was produced by Tudor Ionescu, who belonged to the Voitec-Radaceanu group. He brought out a photostat of a type-written document, which he declared to be a letter to Titel Petrescu from the secretaries of the two 'historic parties', the National Peasants and the National Liberals, promising Petrescu full political and financial support, together with transmission of instructions to this effect to the local branches of the two 'historic parties'. This document was, of course, meant to compromise Petrescu fatally by proving that he was in the pay of the two reactionary parties which had in the past prevented the workers from obtaining their rights. The opinion quickly spread, however, that the document was a forgery, and its authenticity was never proved.

Petrescu himself, a delegate later said, was 'too much in the clouds' to play any decisive rôle at the meeting. The vote was finally held by a curious mixture of open and secret voting; 232 votes were recorded in favour of the joint electoral bloc with the Communists; 29 delegates voted against, and 60 abstained. Şerban Voinea rose and made a speech strongly calling for party unity in spite of everything. But Petrescu got up and walked out with a 'handful' of his friends.

Next day Petrescu declared the procedure of the Congress invalid, split the party and took his wing of it out of the National Democratic Front and into full opposition. He was later allowed to start his own newspaper, and to contest the general elections with his own private party list. But, according to the official results, he was only allotted 55,528 votes in the whole country, and was not granted a single seat in the Rumanian Parliament. He had been completely eliminated.

The Radaceanu-Voitec Wing, on the other hand, contested the general elections along with the Communists in the National Democratic Front electoral bloc, and were rewarded. They did not get the 30 per cent. that had been promised at the Congress, but they got over

20 per cent. of the bloc's 348 seats. They had 81 seats, compared with 72 for Tatarescu's National Liberals, 70 for the Ploughman's Front and 67 for the Communist Party. But these figures did not represent the relative power of each party inside the government that resulted from the elections.

It remained a mystery whether the majority of members of the Social Democratic Party were with Titel Petrescu or with the Radaceanu Voitec group and the National Democratic Front. This question however, soon became academic and politically unimportant. The cadres and organisation of the party, on the whole, went with the Front. A year later, in November, 1947, the pro-Government Social Democrats decided, willingly or unwillingly, to fuse with the Communists in a new 'United Workers Party'. So they lost even the show of independence. A few days later it was announced that Titel Petrescu was to appear before a military tribunal; so his wing of the Social Democrats was also at an end.

The Party had split over the question, whether to fight the Communists openly or whether to temporise and appease them in order to survive. To appear to yield in order to remain alive is more in accord with Rumanian tradition and character than the romance of a hopeless fight to the finish. In the case of the Social Democrats both strategies failed.

A fight to the finish, which they could not believe hopeless, seemed the decision of the Opposition, the 'historic parties'. In part, it was forced upon them. Neither the Russians nor the National Democratic Front were inclined to offer them a serious compromise. The Russians mistrusted them because of their long-standing ties with the West originally France, later Britain and America. The leaders of the Front weak in Rumanian following but strong in Russian backing, saw no need for an unsatisfactory sharing of power.

But in part, the uncompromising fight to the finish was the natural choice of the Opposition. Temperamentally Maniu, the Transylvanian was better suited to it than to practical compromise. It was commonly said that he had learned his political strategy and tactics as an Opposition deputy in the old Hungarian parliament, before the break-up of the Austro-Hungarian Empire, had never forgotten them, and persisted in using them in very changed circumstances. During many of the years between the two wars, the National Peasant Party was the most powerful in Rumania; yet it was for months, not years, that Maniu was prepared to accept the direct responsibility of government. He was most at home in opposition, upholding the righteousness of his own position and putting those in power into the wrong. He probably found his greatest moral satisfaction when indicting his lengthy, statesmanlike, sometime biting protests and memoranda to Marshal Antonescu during the war

After the coming of the Red Army, the rôle of upholder and champion of the independence of the Rumanian nation against the threat from

without and within was one that fitted him well. Having survived to
many years of opposition to different régimes, he perhaps did not
realise quite how dangerous a rôle it was. It brought him, in accordance
with the political logic of the times, a sentence of life imprisonment,
delivered on November 11th, 1947.

The National Liberal leader, Constantin Bratianu, although his
record showed him to have a more practical and less formalistic
temperament than Maniu, was an old and venerable man. His party
tradition had become one of conservatism. He could hardly adapt
himself to a rapidly changing Rumania in which the financial and
business interests which his party represented were bound to suffer.
And as the National Liberal Party was very much of a family affair,
the patriarchal Bratianu set the tone.

The differences between the Opposition and the Front were not
fundamentally differences of political programme. The stock criticism
of the National Peasant Party was that it had no constructive programme. In fact, though few of its members seemed aware of it, the
party had a sound and progressive programme, issued on October 15th,
1944, and adapted from its pre-war programme. It proposed the redistribution of land to the peasants, on the two principles: 'the land
belongs to him who tills it', and 'property is a social function'. It
advocated the progressive nationalisation of heavy industry and of the
Bank of Rumania. It said that the unionisation of workers and of
private employees should be free, that collective labour contracts
should be obligatory. In social insurance, it proposed an adaptation
of the Beveridge Plan. Except perhaps for the last point, there was
nothing to divide the National Peasants from the National Democratic
Front.

The real thing dividing the two was difference in attitude towards
Russia. Both, in their programmes, accepted the principle of close
collaboration with Russia as Rumania's closest and most powerful
neighbour. But the Opposition, in their hearts, felt any appeasement of
Russia to be a form of betrayal, and looked forward, with blind
unthinking optimism, to the time when Rumania would again be
miraculously free of Russian control or even influence. The leaders of
the Front, although their enemies may have exaggerated their sub-
servience, were certainly not inclined to oppose Russia's wishes in any
serious way. They hoped at best to wheedle concessions from Russia,
as, in the economic field, they sometimes did.

At the risk of ingratitude for hospitality, it must be said that the
Opposition was seen at its worst in the drawing-rooms, and dining-
rooms, of Bucharest. The lawyers and business men and a few relics of
the aristocracy sat gloomily yet eagerly swopping political gossip, either
on Rumania's grievances against Russia, or on any fresh worsening in
relations between Russia and the Western Powers. There was a strong
undercurrent of resentment against the Western Powers for their failure

K

to 'stand up' to Russia. There seemed a sad lack of realism or real thought, let alone discretion. At one tea-party at which foreigners were present, photographs of Rumanian peasants in national costume were handed round. On the back of one was stuck the caption: 'Rumanian peasant types from North Bukovina, occupied in 1940 by Soviet Russia, after Stalin's agreement with Hitler. Bukovina, this "holy land" of all Rumanians, has never before been under Russian domination.'

There were, of course, a few exceptions, genuine idealists of the Western liberal type, but they were very rare.

The better side of the Opposition could be seen in the countryside, in the villages, among the peasants. Here also the better-off farmers and small local officials, many of whom had done well and prospered while Rumania was in the hands of the Germans, were narrowly and selfishly conservative and looked back nostalgically to the good old days. To judge by them, there was something in what the extreme Left said, that the National Peasant Party was a party of 'kulaks'. But the Party also still had a big following among the real peasants, who had not gone over to the Ploughman's Front because the rumour had got round that it was only a stooge party for the Communists.

In one village in Transylvania, the villagers pointed out seven or eight men, sitting isolated in the corner of the café, as the only 'Communists' of the place. Asked whether they were really members of the Communist Party, the villagers answered: 'No, perhaps they are members of the Ploughman's Front, but it is all the same thing.'

The more constructive and genuine element of the National Peasant Party was shown at a meeting held in January, 1946, in Campulung, a small town in the hills north-west of Bucharest. It was practically the first Opposition meeting held after the visit of the Vishinski-Harriman-Clark Kerr Mission had given full legal status to the Opposition parties and allowed them to resume activity. The speaker was Ion Michalache, probably second in importance to Maniu himself in the party. He was a younger, more energetic and positive man than Maniu. Unlike nearly all Rumanian politicians of all parties, he was not a lawyer and a townsman, but was of peasant stock and had started as a schoolmaster in the countryside. Most of his life he had lived and worked among peasants, and had turned his own village, near Campulung, into a model village. His great disadvantage was that he was considered hopelessly compromised in the eyes of the Russians, because he had served in the Army as a reserve officer during the campaign to recover Bessarabia from the Russians in 1941. It was said that he had volunteered for this service; and the fact that he had somehow avoided service in the later stages of the war against Russia did not wipe out this blot. When his name came before the Vishinski-Harriman-Clark Kerr Commission as possible representative of the National Peasant Party in the government, it was turned down out of hand by Vishinski. A man so suspect to the Russians could hardly last long as a free Opposition politician; eighteen months later, in July, 1947, he was arrested for attempting to escape from Rumania, and later sentenced to life imprisonment.

The meeting was held on a bleak frosty Sunday, with deep snow everywhere. The peasants came into Campulung on sledges, wrapped in their long shapeless winter coats and with sheepskin hats pulled down over their ears. Mihalache, adding a picturesque touch, said that they had arrived with icicles on their moustaches. They looked simple, honest straightforward men. They gathered in a small dingy cinema, with little interference from the police, who had been reinforced for the occasion. They stood and cheered Mihalache enthusiastically when, himself dressed like the peasants, he came on to the platform. Everyone sang the royal Rumanian anthem with extraordinary emotion. Mihalache, who was a clever speaker, simple, direct, forceful, was heard with devoted attention, though probably not with full understanding. It was an intelligent speech.

'The social and economic life of the world has hitherto followed the course of so-called political and economic Liberalism, with all its advantages and disadvantages. It was good because it saved mankind from serfdom through the liberties it gave, and the right to be one's own master. It was bad because it left the weak paralysed at the mercy of the strong, who had inherited their wealth, when the race of free competition began. To use the popular expression, it was the time of "everyone for himself, and devil take the hindmost". . . .

'To-day, willy-nilly, world economy has left the old channel and is seeking a new one.

'Communism points out its road: a State-directed economy entirely excluding private economy, and a political system in keeping with a single party and a single will. . . .

'But many people—democratic people in the Western sense—recognising that the road of economic Liberalism has been abandoned, nevertheless do not wish to enter the road of totalitarian Communism. They seek for a middle road, where private initiative and economy can collaborate with State initiative and economy, each having its own framework and together pursuing the widest possible satisfaction of the needs of the working-classes. . . .

'The National Peasant Party has set out again on the struggle, having as its ideal the creation of the Peasant State. . . . We are not in favour of unlimited rights for the individual nor of the unlimited rights of the State; we favour the joint economy of collaboration between private initiative and the State. . . .

'Of a peasantry until recently enslaved, physically weakened and spiritually abandoned, we wish to make the determining factor of power. . . . We shall be guided by the need—greater here than anywhere else in Europe—to find a new use for labour, by creating new industries, beginning with agricultural industries, and beginning with great public works, road-building, canalisation of rivers, irrigation, draining of marshes, and so on. We shall strive for a just balance between the prices paid for the peasants' labour and produce, and for the production of the factories and towns. . . .

'Communism is a clear creed, pursued with sacrifices, with heroism and with well-known methods and programmes, and does not differ from one country to another. . . . We ask ourselves, however, why, here in Rumania, do the Communists not speak to us openly and sincerely in the name of this programme, their only real one? Why do they speak to us on behalf of other interests, even on behalf of big finance and private industry? Why do they hide behind improvised groups using the same methods, even the same men, as have already been discredited under the dictatorships of King Carol and Marshal Antonescu? Every day new parties and new groups spring up. We are not impressed by this mushroom growth from the moral rottenness of society and the dregs of serious political parties. It is not difficult to perceive the manœuvre: all are led by Communists who have filtered into key posts. . . .

'This is what a peasant in Oltenia said: "I stood seven years on my right foot; it went to sleep and I could not stand on it. And now for a year and a half we have been asked to stand on the left foot. This too, we feel, has gone to sleep. But we know that the world cannot stand on one foot. The time must come when we shall again stand on both feet, for that is the will of God." '

This speech, although probably rash and politically unrealistic in the circumstances, had something honest and straightforward and positive about it. Unfortunately, neither Mihalache's words nor the peasants to whom he was talking represented anything like the whole of the National Peasant Party or the Opposition. There were many in the Opposition who had little interest in the peasants or in constructive programmes. The one question which obsessed them, and which they often put openly to foreigners, was: 'When do you think the war against Russia will start?'

It seems likely that no Rumanian, except for the sincere Communists, wanted Russian influence over Rumania to last permanently. Some of the more intelligent and progressive might feel that temporary Russian influence would be a spur for the speedy carrying out of reforms which otherwise would have been delayed for years. Others, the opportunists, might feel that they could exploit Russian influence in order to make quick careers. But in either case, it was not the same as wanting Russian influence to last for ever.

Leaving the sincere Communists on one side, the main difference of opinion between Rumanians was over the question: how long Russian influence was likely to endure? There were varying answers.

Most of the Opposition believed, in their heart of hearts, that war between Russia and the West would come quickly, in the first few years after the war. They usually denied that they wanted war, saying that Rumania would suffer the most heavily of all European countries. But, perhaps unconsciously, they let expectation of war become the assumption on which most of their thinking was based. So they tended just to wait passively, with a strange mixture of hopelessness and hopefulness, for the outbreak of the war.

One or two of the small fractions which broke away from the National Peasant Party in 1945 and 1946 did so because they based their calculations on a different assumption. They believed that relations between Russia and the West would remain 'normal' for the next fifteen years. Russia would therefore keep her influence over Rumania for that time. It was necessary to placate Russia and try to meet her wishes for the time being, in order to preserve some kind of Rumanian national independence during the period of waiting.

This view seems to have been shared also by members of certain of the parties of the National Democratic Front. Sometimes Social Democrats of the government wing would stress that, although they wanted to collaborate loyally with the Communists, their chief aim was to keep Rumania in existence as a more or less independent State and nation. Among such people, however, war between Russia and the West did not seem necessarily inevitable even in fifteen years time; they believed that some peaceful stabilisation of the balance between East and West might lighten pressure from the East on Rumania.

Only if undeniable proof could be given of lasting settlement between Russia and the West, or if Russia softened her methods so as to make Russian influence generally desirable, could the average Rumanian be induced to stop speculating on big Power politics and look to the needs of his own country.

9

Portrait of Rumania

RUMANIA, or at least Old Rumania, is a land of maizefields. In the autumn the full maize stands tall and yellow. Here and there in the fields are little shelters, made of woven maize stalks, under which the peasants can go to sleep shaded from the midday sun, or chew a lump of cold mamaliga, their yellow maize porridge. Sometimes a peasant sleeps in the tiny patch of shade cast by a fruit-tree growing beside the road, which is deep in soft yellow dust. Peasants in Rumania seem to do a lot of sleeping.

In winter, the flat white plains of old Rumania stretch away into a distance where the snow melts into the misty grey of the heavy sky. A few peasants, in long shapeless shaggy coats which hang around them like tents, trudge through the deep snow under which, here and there, winter wheat is already springing. Many of the roads are blocked; only sledges can get through.

Most Rumanian villages are practically nothing but a long main street, often the highroad itself, lined with narrow one-storey houses, usually set sideways on to the road. Deep ditches on each side of the main street pass for a drainage system. There is a rabble of dark-haired children with big black shiny eyes, hens, ducks, and mongrel dogs. There is a small stucco Orthodox church, usually modern, a village pub with a bare wooden floor where the men of the village drink the local plum spirit or rather sour wine. One half of the pub may be a dingy village shop, where among pots and pans and brushes they sell crudely-coloured, childish prints showing bible scenes or picture-diagrams of the Tree of Life, starting with Adam and Eve and the serpent and rising to the Kingdom of Heaven.

A great deal of gossip, grumbling and argument goes on in the pub. It is probably the centre of any political discussion that there is in the village. It can create the atmosphere needed for passive resistance by the peasants to government orders. Peasants who are blacklegs may sit at tables by themselves, cold-shouldered by the rest.

There is often resentment not only against the government, whatever it may be, but also against the towns, in particular the nearest market town. The townsman is looked on as a profiteer and exploiter of the peasant. This is because, traditionally, the price of the manufactured goods which the peasant goes into the market town to buy—cloth, shoes and boots, pots and pans, tools for field work—is very high in proportion to the price at which the peasant can sell his crops, his eggs, butter, chickens and fruit in the market. So the ordinary peasant has a deep-seated unreasoning grudge against the towns, which in normal times have him in their power.

When crops are bad or when for any other reason there is a food shortage, the peasant takes his revenge. For once he has power over the towns. He sells as little as possible of his crops at the fixed official price, as much as possible at enormous black-market prices. He cares so little for the towns that he would often rather hide his produce or let it rot than sell it at the fixed price. Even though villagers may be kindly and tolerant among themselves, they feel little kindness and tolerance towards townsmen.

Few peasants' children get more than the most elementary education. They remain simple, superstitious people, biddable enough except when they believe that their land or their crops are threatened. If a politician comes and makes a political speech in a big village, the peasants will not heckle or ask questions. They will stand, hat in hand, sweating gently in the sun, listening with apparent rapt devotion, some even smiling blissfully. They are not violent, ambitious, aggressive. The younger ones would often like to find jobs in the towns, but without skill it is difficult to find work, and the difference between the way of life and way of thought in town and village is so great that it may be hard for the ordinary peasant boy to adapt himself. So most stay in the village, often idle because there is not enough land and so not enough work. And more and more children are born, to tumble about in the dust or mud of the village street among the ducks and chickens.

The towns, of course, are not really as rich and thriving as the peasant thinks. Round the outskirts, even of the big towns, are bits of wasteland pocked with primitive-looking wooden shacks, where the unskilled and unsuccessful town workers live—among them the peasants who have come in from the village and failed to make good. Here again there is a rabble of scrawny hens and mongrel dogs and children, and the atmosphere is not so very different from the village, except that there may be even greater poverty.

But the main part of the town has an air of rather bogus modernity, of would-be American progress. Bucharest, architecturally a maddening jumble of pseudo-oriental, pseudo-baroque and pseudo-American styles has, lining its French-type boulevards, giant garages with spiral runways, smart petrol stations, newish concrete-built cinemas with neon signs, big blocks of flats. These jostle with nineteenth-century private houses standing back from the road, which in spite of their pomposity have a certain dignity. There are plenty of shops, particularly dress-shops, shoe-shops, chemists, hairdressers and shops selling cosmetics, and plenty of slickly-dressed women and men staring at the windows. Even if there may be a crisis and inflation at the moment, the city, though rather shabbier than usual, still shows that for some years past money has been thrown about and the middle and upper classes have had their luxuries and amusements and their sophistication. It is a world very far from the world of the village.

A lot has been written about the Athénée Palace, the chief hotel of Bucharest. It sums up the wealthy, smart life of the city. A pleasant, even dignified building, it looks across the enormous formless open space cleared by King Carol, King Michael's father, in front of the royal palace, which is like most other European royal palaces of the last 150 years. Standing on a balcony of the Athénée Palace, your eye strays nervously across this vast space and finds rest only in a royal equestrian statue facing the palace and a huge advertisement painted on the windowless wall of a big block of flats on the far side of the space.

Inside the hotel there are thick rich carpets, soft lights and doe-eyed lift boys. The heart of the hotel is the big lounge hall, lined with gilt-bordered mirrors and sprinkled with lushly-upholstered sofas and arm-chairs. Nothing is very modern; the Athénée Palace seems to belong to the period of the 'Grand Babylon Hotel'. The hall is crowded, at almost any time of day, with smartly-dressed women and men. It is said to be the breeding-ground of many high-level intrigues, private, political or black-market. Leading members of the National Democratic Front are practically never seen there, only the Front's lesser officials, engaged on affairs of some kind or other.

But in 1946 big business and finance, a few relics of the aristocracy, foreign ministry officials, aspiring would-be politicians, a small sprinkling of foreign business-men, and an obscure layer of what can only be called 'contact men', all stared, chatted discreetly, strolled or drank coffee or spirits among the mirrors and palms. Most of them knew most of the others, at least by sight and reputation. They were the nucleus of that section of pre-National Democratic Front Bucharest which had so far survived and still hoped to survive, by hook or by crook, for many years yet.

They were people of great sophistication, quick-brained, sometimes witty. They spoke excellent French—a good many had been partly educated in France—and quite often good English and German. They prided themselves on their cosmopolitan outlook and polish, though all would have claimed to be good Rumanian patriots. They had a frank, even exhibitionist, cynicism which either disarmed or repelled foreigners according to their temperament.

All had grown up in an atmosphere of easy-going but inescapable corruption. The young men who had started as sincere idealists, wishing to live up to the best standards of Western Liberalism, found themselves faced by a bitter dilemma at the very beginning of their careers: either they must reconcile themselves to being eccentric, slightly despised failures all their lives, or they must adopt the habit of corruption which pervaded the Rumanian civil service, business, even professional life. Few chose the first course: most felt they would do little good by clinging uselessly to their ideals. They comforted themselves by reflecting that corruption does not necessarily mean ruthlessness and gives opportunities for easy kindheartedness and geniality.

Few of them knew or cared about the peasants—three-quarters of the Rumanian people—except former landowners or those who had somehow managed to keep remnants of their estates. These looked on the peasants in quite a kindly, if possessive way, but regarded them as a totally different type of being from themselves. The rest felt a vague sentimental benevolence towards the peasants, but this feeling was most unlikely ever to take practical form. They were fundamentally, if amiably, selfish.

The National Democratic Front could obviously not hope to make any lasting impression either on the Bucharest bourgeoisie or on the mass of the peasants, who between them summed up the Rumanian people, during its first years of rule. The Rumanian people is rather like a sponge growing on the floor of the sea. New influences and forces may flow through it; the sponge may swell and sway in the tide, but does not change its structure or way of growth.

The ordinary Rumanian, in town or country, grumbled and fretted at the new government's laws, decrees, regulations and efforts to impose economic or political controls. But then as far as possible he ignored them or got round them or at best paid them lip service. The Front had practically no success in awakening or creating a sense of social responsibility or social solidarity or loyalty to the State.

In general, the Front irritated and frightened Rumanians into a certain loose solidarity of opposition. Although the government and its organs were for the most part weak and ineffective in imposing their will, their sporadic use of violence against 'the public' provoked bitter resentment and a kind of moral indignation, which at moments took the form of unaccustomed courage and obstinacy. Because the National Democratic Front government had been put in power by the Russians, the government and all its works were felt to be 'un-Rumanian', and any gesture of opposition became a sign of Rumanian patriotism.

One particular weakness of the government was that they could not trust their own administrative organs. Before the Front took power— from August, 1944, to March, 1945—comparatively few changes were made in the police force and gendarmerie by the Sanatescu and Radescu governments. Then the Front, through the Communist Minister of the Interior, Teohari Georgescu, started a purge of the police and the local administration, to remove 'fascist elements'. A year later Teohari Georgescu said that between 30 and 40 per cent. of the personnel of the police had been changed. Similar changes had taken place in the local administration, from prefects and mayors downwards. But these changes did not seem to have been sweeping enough to produce effectiveness, honesty and loyalty. They introduced a certain number of Communists into the police and local administration: in the spring of 1946 Teohari Georgescu said that the proportion was roughly one-sixth in both. Ten out of sixty prefects were Communists, and ten out of seventy mayors of big towns. But in Rumania this leavening of Communists—probably most of them very newly-fledged Communists—did not succeed in altering the whole organisation, or make it politically reliable.

So the Front government had to fall back on other weapons to keep the political demonstrations or activities of its opponents in check. One useful weapon was organised groups of factory workers, either in Bucharest or the provinces, who could be despatched in lorries to points where the opposition were concentrating. There, by violence or a show of violence, these shock-groups of workers could scatter or terrorise or paralyse Opposition supporters.

Another weapon was the Tudor Vladimirescu Division, formed in Russia during the war from Rumanian prisoners who had undergone political conversion and training. Units of this division, which was said to be of more than normal size, were dispersed through the country among other formations of the Rumanian Army. They were thoroughly reliable and could be called out in case of emergency by the Ministry of the Interior, to quell demonstrations. The other division formed of Rumanian war prisoners—the Horia, Cloşca şi Crişan Division—was supposed to be much less reliable, since a number of its members had volunteered and feigned political conversion merely in order to escape from prison camp life. Officers and men of normal units of the Rumanian Army were, at least in the early phase, quite unreliable for the purposes of the Front, and, in a popular demonstration, were more like to intervene on the Opposition side than to quell it.

In the very big, relatively spontaneous, Opposition demonstration outside the royal palace in Bucharest on November 8th, 1945, which left bitter memories on both sides, it was lorry-loads of Bucharest workers who provoked the first real violence. The lorries drove at what seemed high speed into the massed crowd, weaving about in figures of eight to scatter the people. But the crowd—mostly middle-class people, students, some army officers—did not scatter; a lorry was stopped and overturned; shots were fired. Detachments of the Tudor Vladimirescu Division were called out; some young men in the crowd were arrested and taken into the Ministry of the Interior. The rumour got around that they were being tortured during interrogation; the crowd surged towards the doors of the Ministry of the Interior; fresh firing started. Most observers said that machine guns were used on the crowd from the roof of the Ministry. There were a number of injuries, some fatal.

After that there were seldom disorders on so big a scale. Both sides, perhaps, were shocked by what had happened. Outsiders were astonished at the courage and obstinacy shown by the crowd, which had held its ground for several hours.

But smaller demonstrations, often only of a few hundred young men and girls led by the National Peasant and National Liberal youth organisations, would still gather before the royal palace, sing the royal anthem over and over again, and chant 'Regele şi Maniu'—'The King and Maniu'—or just 'Regele, Regele, Regele', in endless chorus. After November 8th, provided the crowd did not grow too big, they were normally left in peace.

Even the crowd of several thousands which gathered on the evening of February 7th, 1946—the day when Bucharest radio rather prematurely announced that Britain and the United States had recognised the Rumanian government—demonstrated and marched undisturbed. In the afternoon there had been a long and not very cheerful National Democratic Front procession, mainly of workers and government employees called out for the occasion, to celebrate the government's international triumph. Then, as dusk fell, hundreds of young people gathered around the equestrian statue in the royal square, wishing by one means or another to demonstrate against the newly recognised government. The crowd swelled. When darkness had fallen, they formed a procession and marched towards Bucharest's main boulevard.

As they passed along the streets, nearly every window opened and beams of light streamed out. The people in the crowd sang the royal anthem and chanted 'King and country'; the people inside the houses took up the singing and chanting, and many came out into the street to join the procession.

Then part of the crowd turned off down the narrow street leading to the British Legation and stopped outside its tall iron gates, which had been quickly closed, to shout 'Long live England and America', 'Long live Bevin', and 'We want free elections'. A young man was heaved up on the shoulders of the crowd and made a speech declaring: 'We protest against the infringement and restriction of our liberties'. Then the crowd moved on to the American Legation. Throughout the evening small crowds of Opposition supporters gathered in the middle part of the city, and tried to cheer, seize and carry on their shoulders any British officer passing by.

It was a curious way to protest against Anglo-American recognition of the National Democratic Front government. Earlier that day the manservant in a big Bucharest household had threatened to bar the door to any British or American visitors who might come: that was his form of protest. But the conflict and mixture of feeling, if illogical, was typically Rumanian.

One tactic of the Communists was to insist on admission to Opposition indoor meetings on grounds of democratic freedom. A group of Opposition industrial workers, belonging, curiously, to the National Peasant Party, arranged a Sunday morning meeting on the outskirts of Bucharest, in a quarter near the main railway yards, known to be a Communist stronghold. When they came they found their meeting-place —an inn—half-filled with Communist workers. Fearing trouble, the Opposition workers trooped off to another small building 300 yards away. The Communist workers trooped after them and demanded entrance to the building. But the organisers of the meeting only allowed in those who could show a National Peasant Party membership card. The Communist workers protested plaintively and indignantly: 'This is contrary to the four freedoms laid down by the four Foreign Ministers at Moscow. Do you call this liberty, democracy? We demand, in the name of democracy, to be allowed in to the meeting.' It was an ironical reversal of rôles.

Out in the provinces, actual violence was more frequent. According to what seemed an authentic story, a deliberate attempt was made on the old Opposition leader, Constantin Bratianu, when he was on his way to make a big speech at Campulung at the end of February, 1946. Bratianu was travelling in one car with other members of the National Liberal Party; lesser lights of the party were driving in a second car. Not far from Campulung they were met by a lorry belonging to the Braşov aircraft company, filled with workers, who shouted insulting remarks as they passed. Then, it seems, the lorry turned and pursued the two cars. It grazed the second car and then drove into the first car, in which Bratianu was riding, forcing it into the side of the road and almost into a deep ditch. The car was damaged, but Bratianu himself was, surprisingly, unhurt. The government promised an enquiry into the happening, but nothing ever came of it.

At intervals the two Opposition parties, through their representatives in the government, would make long protests against alleged acts of terrorism. The instances they gave could not be verified and may have been much exaggerated but were seldom refuted. At the beginning of March, 1946, Emil Haţieganu put in a detailed protest on behalf of the National Peasant Party:

'At the beginning of February, Mr. Romul Pop, former commissioner for Transylvanian refugees, Mr. Zeno Bianu and Dr. Fielt were wounded in Sibiu by blows struck from behind by seven Communists armed with crowbars. . . .

'On February 5th, about 1,000 to 1,500 Communist workers, most of them under age, demonstrated in the streets of Timişoara. Groups of demonstrators struck and wounded passers-by whom they knew to be National Peasants. . . . There were eleven wounded. . . . The demonstrators were armed with crowbars and shouted "Down with Maniu and Bratianu". Instead of restoring order and arresting the aggressors, the police detained all the wounded at the police station. . . .

'On February 16th at 12.30 hours our party headquarters in the Borough of Arad were devastated by Communists armed with crowbars. Those of our party organisers who were in the building were seriously wounded. Dr. Botioc had the base of his skull split. Professor Teodorescu and Dr. Ungureanu are in a serious condition. Dr. Drincu, Dr. Emandi, M. Mladin and M. Mircea Emandi were wounded. . . . Our headquarters are situated opposite the police station. . . . The authorities refused to do their duty. This proves their complicity. . . .'

Such sporadic outbreaks of violence were not new in Rumanian life. They were in line with the practices of the Nazi Iron Guard, even of more reputable parties. If the positions of the Opposition and the Communists had been reversed, the Communists could have hoped for little tolerance, There is a thin streak of sadism in the Rumanian make-up, shown in anti-semitic outbreaks, or in occasional political assassinations, which contrasts oddly with the usual Rumanian easy-going amiable laziness. The Communist Party, by recruiting the young and poor townsmen and some of the Iron Guards, had admitted hot-headed and irresponsible and stupid people into its ranks. The more solid and respectable peasants and middle-class people in the Opposition felt outraged.

The oilfield district of Rumania, north-west of Bucharest, around Ploeşti and Campina, led a life of its own. Ploeşti after the war was a dingy battered town, badly shattered by American bombing, its unrepaired streets deep in mud or snow for half the year. A few British and other foreign oil engineers had come back to live there in what remained of their pre-war villas on the outskirts of the town. They could still get a delicious meal—perhaps with trout from nearby mountain streams—in the town's best restaurant, but the restaurant was now unpainted and dilapidated.

Outside the town were some of the big refineries, where the smell of oil hung heavy and smooth. Grotesque tower-like structures dominated the jumble of sheds, laboratories, furnace-houses, machine-repair shops. The foremen and supervisors were intelligent, smiling and polite to outsiders. The workers looked sullen and aloof. On the walls were scrawled in chalk National Democratic Front slogans, usually: 'Death to the executioners, Maniu and Bratianu'. The foremen and administrative employees glanced at the scrawls nervously, disgustedly as they passed, but dared not rub them away.

Some miles away the black, skeleton-like, rather monstrous derricks, rearing out of long low ridges of hills, marked the oil wells. The slopes of the ridges were pock-marked with the scars of exhausted or abandoned wells. Below each derrick, round the mouth of the well, lay piles

of long metal pipes of different diameters, to be screwed together and
forced many hundreds of metres down into the earth. Here the smell of
the oil, even fumes of it, seemed to surge up out of the ground, even
richer, heavier, somehow appetising. Oil oozed along the muddy
ditches and gullies.

Older engineers told how, many years ago when the oilfields were
newly exploited, sometimes great bursts of gas would break out as a new
well was being sunk, and sometimes a great fire would flare up, burning
for several days and visible many miles away. But now, they said, these
fields were getting tired, and the time had come to prospect in new
fields, away up in the north, perhaps around Bacau—if only there was
the equipment, the transport and the necessary permission from the
Rumanian government.

Transylvania, high-lying rolling land almost circled by a horseshoe
of mountains, seems to shut out old Rumania and follow a life of its
own, more orderly, self-respecting and earnest. There was little of the
steaminess and indolence of the plains; in Transylvania there was a
certain freshness and briskness in the air; outlines were clear-cut.

Perhaps centuries of semi-independence in spite of Turkish pressure,
together with the natural rivalry between the three races of Transylvania, had made the people proud. In Transylvania there lived, very
roughly, three million Rumanians, one and a half million Hungarians,
and over half a million Germans. The land had never been purely
Rumanian—though there have been many inconclusive learned disputes
on this question. From the Middle Ages onwards, the Saxon settlers,
living mainly in their walled towns, good craftsmen and merchants,
trading widely, had been the most prosperous, most civilised of the
Transylvanians. The Rumanians and Hungarians were the countryfolk.
But by the nineteenth century the Hungarians were the great landowners, the feudal lords; the Rumanians—and many of the Hungarians
—were the labourers on the land, the shepherds in the hills. The Saxons
remained the prosperous townsfolk or the rich farmers living in villages
where the houses were as strongly built as tiny fortresses.

Transylvania, as part of the Austro-Hungarian Empire, came under
the thumb of the Hungarian government in Budapest and in the later
part of the nineteenth century Budapest started a campaign to 'Mag-
yarise' at least the Rumanians of Transylvania. The Rumanians, afflicted
with inferiority complex, were bitterly resentful.

In 1918 the Austro-Hungarian Empire broke up; Rumania, with the
blessing of Britain and France and the help of the Rumanian Transylvanian leader, Maniu, won all Transylvania. The Hungarian lords
were driven from their big estates by the Rumanian land reform. The
Rumanians became the governing class, although the upper-class Hungarians—those who did not leave Transylvania for Hungary—still

regarded themselves as the socially elect, and the Saxons remained the most solid, prosperous element. The Rumanians got a good deal of their own back on the Hungarians, although their natural lazy tolerance saved them from consistent vindictiveness, and left the Saxons to themselves.

In 1940 fortunes changed again. Hitler thought that, while intimidation and threats would be enough to make Rumania toe the line, bribery and promises were needed to secure Hungary for his war plans. The Vienna Award, dictated by Ribbentrop, and, as a sop to Italy, by Ciano also, split Transylvania between Hungary and Rumania. Hungary got the more important part, Northern Transylvania. But the division, although it took some rough account of ethnographical factors, made both sides bitter and discontented. The Rumanians saw no reason why they should give up anything; the Hungarians wanted much more. For the next four years they bickered constantly. Both sides hoped and planned to gain their wishes, somehow or other, during the course of the world war, perhaps by changing sides at the crucial moment, perhaps by a little private war between Rumania and Hungary.

In Southern Transylvania, the Rumanians indulged in petty persecution of the Hungarian peasants. In Northern Transylvania the Hungarians came back as the governing class, and ruled with an iron hand; and some of the Hungarian landlords came back to their estates. The Rumanians, both in Transylvania itself and in old Rumania, grew very bitter.

Just as Hungary had profited in 1940 because she lay nearest to Germany on Hitler's march east, so in 1944 Rumania profited because she lay nearest to Russia on the Red Army's march west. As early as the spring of 1944 the Soviet government was ready to give all Transylvania back to Rumania. When King Michael brought his country over to the Allies in August, it was on the understanding that Rumania would get back the whole of Transylvania or 'the major part thereof', subject to confirmation at the Peace Conference. This understanding was confirmed in the armistice terms.

In Transylvania itself, this decision came as something of a surprise. Soviet thought had seemed, in its general principles, to favour autonomy for much-disputed, racially mixed areas, as for example in the case of Macedonia. Soviet propaganda during the war had seemed to back the idea of an autonomous or even independent Transylvania. The Hungarian and Rumanian Communists of Transylvania had worked and consulted together with this end in view. Now Russia, together with the Western Powers, was giving back Transylvania unconditionally to Rumania.

But very soon it seemed that Russia had changed her mind once again. As, in the autumn of 1944, the Rumanian Army and the Red Army pushed the Germans and Hungarians out of Northern Transylvania, Rumanian refugees and officials from old Rumania streamed in behind them. The new Bucharest government of Sanatescu was in a hurry to send in prefects and local administrators from old Rumania. Bands of armed Rumanians, calling themselves the 'Maniu guard' but officially disowned by Maniu, started to terrorise Hungarian villagers. There was friction, disorder, administrative confusion.

The Soviet military authorities, presumably on Moscow's orders, decided that this chaos on their lines of communication endangered the military prospects of the campaign. They cut off most of Transylvania administratively from the rest of Rumania; it was placed under Soviet military authority and ruled in practice by a joint Hungarian-Rumanian 'Liberation Committee', with its seat in Cluj (Kolozsvar). There again seemed chances that Transylvania might become permanently an autonomous unit.

The committee was made up of Communists or men of Left-wing sympathies. They believed sincerely that an autonomous Transylvania, in which both Hungarians and Rumanians were fairly treated, was the best solution for all. Questions of schooling, universities, prefects, mayors and local officials—which had so long been running sores—could be settled, if dealt with honestly and fairly, on the basis of the numbers of Rumanians and Hungarians living in each district, town or village. Each people could have its rightful share in local administration, its own culture and its freedom. If Transylvania were too small a unit to stand alone, it could either be an autonomous unit attached to Rumania or an autonomous unit in a confederation of Rumania and Hungary.

Most members of the 'Liberation Committee' were young. One Hungarian was a young trade union organiser. One Rumanian was a university lecturer in mathematics. A few were older, but were intellectuals, not politicians, and so had something youthful in their approach to politics. All were Transylvanians, coming neither from Hungary nor from old Rumania.

They tried to run Transylvania on their own principles, so as to bury old hatreds. They planned carefully that Hungarians and Rumanians should receive just representation in local administration. Hungarian members of the committee later boasted that they had even made a Rumanian mayor of Cluj, the chief town, although 70 per cent. of the townspeople were Hungarian, as a token of good faith towards the Rumanians. The Committee claimed to have balanced Transylvania's budget out of taxation, to have paid the salaries of officials and schoolteachers and university professors, both Rumanian and Hungarian. They felt they were laying a good basis.

But they met many difficulties over what they called the 'reaction' or the 'chauvinism' of both Rumanians and Hungarians, particularly farmers and peasants. Racial hatred might be damped down, but still smouldered. The committee suffered under the doubtful advantage of Red Army backing. It was mistrusted by the Rumanians, partly because they thought it Communist, partly because they thought it was favouring the Hungarians and was even plotting to give Transylvania back to Hungary. The Hungarian peasants mistrusted it because they also thought it Communist and imagined it was favouring the Rumanians. In old Rumania, people of all parties bitterly resented having Transylvania cut off from the rest of the country, just when they thought they had won it back.

Nevertheless, the Cluj Liberation Committee made a start on building up an autonomous Transylvania. But within six months things changed again. At the beginning of March, 1945, Vishinski installed the Grozea government. The Russians must have known clearly that this government would have very little prestige in Rumania. Somehow its position must be strengthened. On March 9th, 1945, Moscow announced that Transylvania would be returned to the administration of the Rumanian government. It would come under Bucharest once again.

This meant the end of the Liberation Committee and of Transylvanian autonomy. Its members went back to their old jobs a little sad and disillusioned. Prefects and representatives of the various Rumanian Ministries were again appointed by Bucharest. Mayors were still elected locally, but under the auspices of the National Democratic Front.

Petru Grozea was himself a Transylvanian. One of his most cherished hopes was to play the dramatic role of conciliator between the Rumanians and Hungarians of Transylvania, between Rumania and Hungary. He spoke good Hungarian. Although it would have been too dangerous, politically, to agree to autonomy, he tried to carry on some of the Committee's ideas on equality between the two peoples.

His government kept Hungarian prefects in the three predominantly Hungarian counties of Eastern Transylvania—the 'Szekler' counties. There were still a number of Hungarian mayors. In Cluj, four Hungarian daily newspapers were published, in addition to the Rumanian dailies. In the bookshops there were more Hungarian than Rumanian books. People could talk Hungarian freely. Cluj university, which had been originally Hungarian, then Rumanian from 1918 till 1940, then again Hungarian until 1944, then for six months a joint undertaking, now became a Rumanian university once again. But the Hungarians were also to be allowed to have their own university in Cluj, with a medical faculty in another town. The Rumanian authorities allocated them certain buildings. Theoretically they were also to receive financial support from the Rumanian government; but early in 1946, money was still not forthcoming, and the Hungarians were still suffering from crippling difficulties through lack of equipment, books and funds to pay the teaching staff. The Hungarian university was more theoretical than real. Still, it had been allowed in principle, and that was important.

In spite of Grozea's enlightened principles, the first year of his government's rule in Transylvania pleased very few. It left both Ru-

L

manians and Hungarians disgruntled, and suspicions and resentment between the two seemed if anything to be growing. The Hungarians of Transylvania were nervous and scared because they feared that, in spite of Grozea's good intentions, small local Rumanian chauvinists would get back into the saddle and oppress the Hungarians. The more conservative Hungarians—and outside the towns most of them were conservative-minded peasants and farmers—were mistrustful of the Grozea government because it was a 'Communist government'. The few surviving members of the Hungarian aristocracy still in Transylvania naturally shared this mistrust and were still ardently revisionist: they hoped Transylvania would yet go back to Hungary and cherished reprints of a map, alleged to have been published in a leading London newspaper in January, 1946, showing Hungary in possession of all Transylvania.

Still, most Hungarians in Transylvania realised that they were in many ways better off under Grozea than they could hope to be under Maniu and his Transylvanian followers. So, whatever their political views, they rallied to the one permitted Hungarian political organisation, the 'Hungarian Popular Union', which was closely linked with the National Democratic Front. The Union polled over 500,000 votes in the general election of November, 1946, and was allotted 29 seats in the Rumanian parliament. But this relatively strong position depended entirely on the Union's keeping in step with the National Democratic Front.

As for the Rumanians of Transylvania, even the Left-wingers had certain reserves about the Grozea government. They said that it meant too much centralisation, that too many officials had been sent in from Bucharest, a good many with dubious pasts. But the bulk of the Rumanians were followers of Maniu, the 'liberator of Transylvania' in 1918, and they naturally were all against the Grozea government. They said, unfairly, that Grozea had sold out Transylvania to the Hungarians—and of course the Communists and the Jews—who were running everything.

There were two wings of Maniu's National Peasant Party in Transylvania, the one intensely nationalist, the other rather more broadminded. On the one hand there was Emil Haţieganu, a bullet-headed, stubborn-jawed but intelligent Transylvanian who had stayed in Cluj throughout the Hungarian occupation to defend Rumanian rights, and suffered in the process. Publicly, he accused Grozea of failing to bring to trial Hungarians who had persecuted and killed Rumanians under the Hungarian occupation from 1940 to 1944, or to restore their homes to Rumanian refugees who had fled from Transylvania as a result of Hungarian oppression. Privately, he believed that the only final solution of the Transylvanian problem was the deportation of all Hungarians to Hungary. This, after all, was the decision reached by Czechoslovakia over the Hungarians of Slovakia.

Deportation of Hungarians was, however, never the official policy of the National Peasant Party, nor of its more broadminded wing. For example, Ionel Pop, a youngish vigorous and pleasant man who was Maniu's chief representative in Transylvania, thought the Hungarians a necessary element in Transylvania and believed that Rumanians and Hungarians must find a way of living together peacefully. He also had a certain local patriotism, considering that there should be a large degree of decentralisation from Bucharest.

But in general, members of the National Peasant Party, even if they were on quite friendly terms with the Hungarians of their own towns and villages, were suspicious of what they believed to be the Hungarian desire to domineer, Hungarian excess of energy, and Hungarian wiles and manœuvres. They thought Hungarians should be kept very firmly in their place.

So great was Maniu's prestige in Transylvania that Grozea's Ploughman's Front, which, partly through Grozea's popularity in his own small district of Deva, had made considerable headway among Transylvanians in the early months after King Michael's coup, soon seemed to lose its impetus. Transylvania, apart from the Hungarian minority, became an Opposition stronghold.

So Transylvania remained a restless, divided and dissatisfied land. People were even divided over the question of the Saxons—the hardest hit by all the political changes.

During, even before, the war, the Saxons, normally solid conservative people, had been subjected to intensive blasts of Nazi propaganda and organisational fervour. Although the older people were nervous and hesitating, feeling that they were getting along very nicely as they were, most responded willingly enough to the call of the fatherland. They joined the powerful Volksbund and the subsidiary Nazi youth, women's and economic organisations, and during the war came to be a highly privileged group within Rumania. The younger ones enrolled in German S.S. formations, while keeping their Rumanian nationality.

Then came the German retreat from Transylvania in the later part of 1944. The most notable and compromised of the Saxon Nazis went with the German armies. The great bulk stayed at home: locally, in the towns and villages, there had not been so very much friction between Saxons and Rumanians, so they were not particularly afraid.

In the winter of 1944-45 the blow fell. The Russians suddenly decided that they would deport all Germans of working age—up to forty-five—from Rumania for forced labour in Russia. In actual fact, arrangements for deportation were so rough-and-ready, the whole thing was carried out in such an impromptu way, that probably not more than 30,000 were actually deported, mostly in January, 1946. A year later those who were sick or unfit for work—and a few perfectly healthy men—started dribbling back home again. No one really knew whether the Russians intended in the end to send back the whole lot, although Grozea was supposed to have asked for their return on one of his visits to Moscow.

While in Russia, the Saxons led hard lives but were not ill-treated by Eastern European standards. This was one man's story:

Although he was over age he was carried off to his local railway station at a few minute's notice, and taken to the Rumanian frontier in a truck holding forty people. At the frontier he and the others were put into Russian trucks. There were, he said, 100 people in each truck. It was bitterly cold; there was a stove in his truck but no wood to burn in it. No food was provided during the many-day journey to Stalino, but some of the deportees had had time to collect food before they left, and they shared it out.

When they got to the end of the journey at Stalino they were deloused and taken to barracks. Here the Russians in charge said that they had not expected the deportees for another two months, so nothing was ready. The Germans spent several days cleaning out the barracks. Then they were sent down a coal-mine, where they were set to work with White Russian and Soviet Russian internees. The mine was flooded; it had been out of use for some time, owing to devastation carried out both by the Russians themselves and by the Germans. At first they had to work thigh-deep in water.

Normally they worked eight hours down the mine. Sometimes they had to put in overtime loading trucks at the pithead. Their food was monotonous and scanty, mainly salt gherkins and cabbage soup, but they got plenty of bread. They were paid wages, which varied greatly according to skill. On an average the wages left very little over, after paying for keep, to buy extra food.

The Russians never beat up the workers. Punishment for bad behaviour was two days' imprisonment.

Some of the workers complained because the women were given heavier work than the men. Men would be employed to shape oak pit-props; women had to carry them about. The Russians said that this was the way the work was arranged and there was no changing it.

Later this particular German was moved to a kolkhoz. Here he thought the work very hard; he had to work from dawn to dusk, although Russians employed on the same kolkhoz only worked eight hours. A typhus epidemic broke out in the kolkhoz: the man got frightened and just walked out. He started walking westwards, from one kolkhoz or labour camp to another, staying a few days in each. No one seemed to take much notice of him: there were no camp records. Only rough total numbers were known. When he got to the Rumanian frontier he was caught by frontier guards when trying to cross the river Pruth, sent before a Soviet military court and condemned to twenty-one days' imprisonment. While he was serving this sentence an order came through 'for the release of all Rumanian citizens', and he was sent back to Rumania on a goods train. When he got home he discovered that his middle-aged wife had also been deported to Russia, and had been working not far from him. He started trying to get her home.

Another Saxon, a powerful-looking, perfectly healthy man, came home about a month later. He declared that it was only sick Saxons who were being sent home. Asked how he himself had managed to get away, he said he had held 'a very important post' in a Russian concern, and had been on good terms with 'important Russians'. So, it appeared, he had been able to fix things.

Those Saxons who had been farmers or peasants usually found, when they got home, that their land had been confiscated and given to others. Under the law for the confiscation of Saxon property, only those who had been members of Nazi organisations or formations, or were 'collaborationists', were to lose their land. But this definition covered most of the Saxons; and in any case land reform was carried out by rough-and-ready methods. As a result, some of the Saxon villages looked deserted and poverty-stricken, in spite of their fine solid houses. The Saxon townspeople, however, suffered little. The shopkeepers kept their shops and the merchants their businesses. Sibiu—Hermannstadt— one of the loveliest old Saxon towns, stayed predominantly Saxon, and looked rather more prosperous than many Rumanian towns.

The National Democratic Front and the Opposition were divided over the Saxons as over every other question. Although the National Democratic Front government, unlike the new governments of Yugoslavia and Hungary and Czechoslovakia, never suggested that the German minority should be deported to Germany, they believed that the Saxons should be treated sternly and were in no hurry to restore their political rights or to allow them to get back their old privileged economic position. Members of the National Peasant Party were much more lenient towards the Saxons; perhaps they thought that they could be a useful anti-Hungarian and anti-Communist force. What they said was that the Saxons had always been a valuable economic element in Transylvania and that oppression of the Saxons would have a bad effect on Transylvania's prosperity. They particularly criticised the confiscation of land from the Saxons. They declared that the land had been given by 'the Communists' to gypsies, in order to purchase gypsy votes, and that the gypsies were lazy and feckless and left the land untilled. This, they said, was damaging to Transylvania.

So old and new quarrels and grievances poisoned the Transylvanian air in spite of Grozea's well-meaning plans. There were the old quarrels and grievances between Rumanians and Hungarians, and the new ones between the National Democratic Front government and the Opposition, between the 'Communists' and the National Peasant Party. There were the new grievances of the Saxons. And there was the disillusionment of those who had hoped for Transylvanian autonomy to bring

peace at last to the three peoples who had lived together in Transylvania
for hundreds of years.

In spite of everything, life in the smaller towns and villages of
Transylvania was going on, early in 1946, in very much its old comfortable way. Probably the mayor had been changed, and was now a member
of the Ploughman's Front or a Social Democrat; but the new man
probably interfered very little in local happenings.

Some farmers would complain bitterly that Transylvania had been
much more prosperous in the wartime days of the Germans: then the
German Army had been staggered to find a land of milk and honey and
butter, but had paid good prices and had not eaten up too much. Now,
they said, the Russians had come and had eaten up everything and
Transylvania was poor. To the outsider, however, there still seemed to
be a fine supply of hams and eggs and butter and venison, although
they were very expensive for the few Transylvanian townsmen who had
not got relatives among the peasants.

Still, the rolling uplands looked well tilled and tended, and the beech
woods and pine forests were full of wild animals that could be hunted,
birds of all kinds, deer, wild boar, hares, even bears.

For a boar shoot, hunters came by car, or by sledge if the snow was
deep, from little towns like Sighisoara or Rupea, where tall solid houses
clustered under a mediæval castle or church perched up on a hill, to
the meeting-place in a village near the woods. The hunters were local
officials, merchants, schoolmasters, even priests, together with farmers
from the neighbourhood, most wearing tight-fitting breeches, leather
leggings, and peaked caps. To warm themselves before the shoot, they
gathered first in the inn or the schoolhouse and passed round bottles of
particularly fiery plum spirit and chewed lumps of raw bacon. As they
warmed up they grumbled more and more fiercely at the government,
the Communists and the Russians, and sighed more and more sadly for
the good old days. Outside the beaters—if it was a relatively big shoot—
stamped in the snow. Mostly they were shaggy, sly-looking, merry
gypsies.

Then the shoot began, a long uphill trudge through the snow, into
the woods. The snow was very shiny and crisp and smooth, except for
the footprints of hares and deer and birds, under the bare black trees.
Then along a ridge or hill-slope the hunters would string out in a long
line and wait, grumbling bitterly at the incompetence and inferiority of
all gypsies, while the beaters far below them tried to beat up a boar
with wailing cries and harsh shouts.

Some time after noon, when everyone was wet and rather weary, they
would meet in a sheltered spot in a little white valley, where a great
wood fire had been lit on a circle of earth that had been cleared of snow.
They sat around and ate cold meat and cheese and toasted big lumps of

bacon fat and thick slices of bread on long sticks over the flames, letting the hot grease from the bacon drip on to the smoky bread. There was plenty more plum brandy. The hunters cracked jokes at the gypsies, and the gypsies cracked jokes back. Politics were forgotten for the moment, perhaps until the end of the day when, in the whitish misty dusk, everyone trudged heavily back through the snow, down the hill-slopes and then through pastures and bare orchards to the village. In the village inn, of course, once boots were beginning to dry and clothes to steam and coarse red wine to go the rounds, politics started up once again.

Sometimes the hunters, all Rumanians, met in a Hungarian village. In the village inn the Hungarian innkeeper, very tall, dignified, with upward-curving black moustache and a grand manner, was welcoming, even gracious. His black-eyed daughters pressed food and drink, and brown paper to line boots, on the strangers. The baby was shown off to the visitors. The villagers admired the hounds belonging to one of the hunters—a priest; they were heavily built, with powerful shoulders and big heads. Some had cruel-looking scars, from earlier struggles with a boar.

At last the hunters went off in rickety sledges, the horses driven with much whip-cracking by Hungarian drivers. The sky was a soft bright blue. The snow was very white and shiny. Delicate, intricate black skeletons of flowers and grasses rising out of the snow all had little glittering ice-caps or crowns, or tiny glassy icicles hanging from them. The great black skeletons of the beech-trees stood out sharply against the white of the earth or the blue of the sky.

The Hungarian drivers spent the day building the big wood fire in the snow, drinking spirit out of the bottle, cracking jokes and waiting for the Rumanian hunters to come down from the hills. When at last they straggled in, there was more drinking, eating, stories of old hunts and fierce boars. Then there was the drive home down the valley, as the sun was setting behind the line of beech trees at the top of the hill, turning the western sky golden and lighting up the snow. The Hungarian drivers, now a little drunk, let out wild cries and peals of laughter as they whipped up their horses recklessly. The sledges creaked and swayed and nearly broke to pieces as the horses plunged down steep gullies at a canter, crossed frozen streams and struggled up the other slope. The Hungarian children scattered as the sledges squeaked and clattered into the village and up to the inn door, where the Hungarian innkeeper was waiting, with dignified courtesy, to welcome back the Rumanian hunters.

On such days, racial and political quarrels slumbered for a little.

Greece and the West

On the smooth golden evening of May 15th, 1946, the new Greek Army, British-trained and British-equipped, held its first great public initiation ceremony. It was in the vast deep oval of the Athens Stadium. Over ten thousand Athenians sat on the steeply-rising tiers of white steps that curved around the sandy arena, sucking sweets, chewing figs or smoking. Hawkers with trays full of yellow and pink lollipops did good trade. The low sunlight spilt into the great bowl through the pine trees that fringed its upper rim. Greek police, British-trained and quietly uniformed in grey, patrolled the arena.

In the middle of one side of the Stadium sat the Regent, Archbishop Damaskinos, a massive muscular man, with a clever determined face; he would have been impressive even without his great curling grey beard and his flowing black robes. He was acting head of the Greek State, holding the throne for King George, who was then still in England. Around him sat General Sir Bernard Paget, British Commander-in-Chief Middle East, dwarfed by the towering Regent; high-ranking British officers of British Land Forces, Greece, and the British Military Mission; members of the new Royalist Cabinet of Constantin Tsaldaris, formed after the first post-war Greek elections on March 31st, and high Greek Army officers.

A day or two earlier General Rawlins, head of the British Military Mission, which, through liaison units attached to every Greek unit of any size, was training up the new Greek Army, had said that he was proud of the Army he had helped to build. With its seven divisions stationed throughout Greece, but in greatest strength near her northern frontiers, he said that it would give a wholesome shock to anyone who tried to break in over the border. Modern-type British equipment had been arriving faster than it could be absorbed. The Greeks themselves wanted their Army to be modelled entirely on the British Army. Drill and methods of training were practically identical. British Army handbooks were being translated into Greek as quickly as possible. British N.C.Os, old-timers, said that the quality of the Greek recruits now being trained was as fine as that of British recruits. The officers and men of the Greek Army might, of course, have their political views. But that was a matter of temperament and was inevitable. It was nothing to do with the British Military Mission. The Mission's one task, General Rawlins said, was to help train up an efficient non-political Army; and results seemed good.

In fact, everything was hopeful. It was only Left-wing cynics who said that the new Greek officers' corps was almost exclusively Royalist and anti-Communist, or complained that the new Greek Army was being integrated in the British Army and trained to hold a Greece that was no more than a Mediterranean outpost of the British Empire.

Now the Army was having its official birthday, or rather christening. The evening opened with a religious service, chanted by a body of black-bearded Orthodox priests, standing in the yellow sand of the arena. A network of loudspeakers, wired to the portable microphone set up near the priests, relayed the chants throughout the great crowd. Just before the end of the service, the loudspeakers suddenly went dead, with a click. To most of the crowd the chanting became a faint far-away hum.

The ceremony continued. There were to be solemn speeches. A sleek announcer took the microphone, put it in front of the seats of honour, and through a momentarily restored relay system introduced the Greek Minister of War, Mavromichalis, a short nervous rather angry-looking little man. The Minister peered up at the microphone and started his rolling phrases. The microphone clicked and the loudspeakers again went dead. The Minister flushed, made irritable gestures, went on mouthing his opening sentences in vain, and stopped. There was a pause, men rushed to and fro, there was a crackle, the microphone came to life, the Minister started again. A few more echoing periods and then for a third time the relay system died. The Minister shrugged, gesticulated, remonstrated, turned and sat down. Then should have come the big speech of the evening, from General Paget. The General sat firmly in his seat and did not budge. The military display started in a hurry.

After physical exercises of classic type by Greek men and girls, the show developed on sound British lines. The battle-dress, the smartness of the drill, the brisk marching of the new Army's picked men, the barking of the N.C.Os, all conformed to type except for the bright black eyes and swarthy skins of the men and a certain loose smoothness of their muscular movements which British training could not quite disguise.

Later the display warmed up and the crowd got excited as at a football match. The Greeks rode and jumped British motor-bikes over British-designed obstacles, plunged them through sheets of flame. As a climax came a fine mock-battle, with smoke-bombs, crackers, machine-gun fire, desperate charges against the enemy, realistic rescues of the wounded. The arena was filled with glowing smoke and noise. Sections of the crowd, carried away, shouted 'Sofia, Sofia'—anti-Bulgarian war-cry of the anti-Communist Greeks.

The sun had set and the thick dusk had fallen, smelling of mimosa-trees and pepper-trees, as the crowd streamed cheerfully away, pleased with the evening's fun. The lemonade-vendors at their little stalls, the

popcorn-sellers rattling their sieves over the charcoal, did a lively trade.
The police relaxed their would-be British dignity and strolled off,
lounging like ordinary Greeks.

Most people forgot the fiasco of the thrice-dead microphone and the
paralysed battery of loudspeakers. A few spread the story, apparently
a true one, that E.A.M. had three times cut the connecting wires, in
spite of the police patrols, as an ironic protest against the new Army's
British-blessed christening.

A few days earlier, on May 1st, E.A.M., the Communist-inspired
Left-wing coalition that had fought the Germans during the main war
and the British during the civil war, had held its own big celebration.
It was a grey dreary morning, with heavy showers of rain. From the
early hours, processions of E.A.M. supporters had marched from the
workers' districts around Athens, through the wealthy and official
centre of the city, to a big football ground in a poor district. The processions, striding manfully, carried dripping banners and sang E.A.M.
and partisan songs. They had throaty throbbing voices. In the open football field itself and on the crowded stands, several thousands gathered,
some in formations representing factories or unions or clubs or youth
organisations or women's organisations, some just jumbled individuals.

The leaders of the Greek Communist Party and the small Left-wing
groups linked with it in E.A.M.—Agrarian, Socialist and so on—stood
bareheaded, in everyday shabby clothes, unguarded among the throng
on one of the stands. The crowd cheered them warmly and enthusiastically, especially Nico Zahariades, the youngish Communist leader who,
after arrest under the Metaxas régime, had spent most of the war years
in a German concentration camp. With his broad forehead, his large
deep-set eyes, his hollow cheeks under strong broad cheekbones, he
had a fine face and a pleasant, rueful smile.

The crowd on the field, standing in the pelting rain, many holding up
umbrellas, sang with growing fervour the International and the Red
Flag. Finally they sang their own hymn for dead heroes—the E.A.M.
partisans and prisoners—to a simple beautiful tune. As the hymn
started all the thousands on the field knelt on one knee in the wet grass and
mud. The hundreds of black shining umbrellas sank towards the earth.
The banners dipped. Real feeling seemed to bind the big crowd together.

E.A.M. was still in the phase of an oppressed revolutionary movement. In spite of Communist intimidation and tyrannical methods and
the bitter disillusionments of the civil war, in the winter of 1944-45, it
was still, in part, a movement of the persecuted, the underdogs, the
men who made sacrifices and took risks. Although the experts said it
had lost much of its moral sway during the sixteen months since the
civil war, on that May 1st, E.A.M. still had a fervour and spontaneity
which the Fatherland Front, its political counterpart in Bulgaria, after
twenty months of success and undisputed power, had already lost by the
wayside.

It was hard to tell whether the crowd felt their chief enemies to be the British or the Greek 'monarcho-fascists'. On the whole, the British seemed to come first. One big crudely-painted poster held high in the crowd showed British soldiers flogging a Greek worker with chains. Another showed a Greek worker being dragged along the ground behind a jeep driven by jeering British soldiers. The banners bore slogans calling on the British to quit Greece.

Two British Labour Party Members of Parliament, who were present as guests, were in an awkward position. Although they were against the Labour Government's policy towards Greece, they felt that party unity and discipline must be upheld in public, before a foreign crowd. They made emotional but perfectly non-committal, even evasive, speeches. They neither condemned nor endorsed Mr. Bevin's policy. The crowd did not like this caution. When one of the M.P.'s spoke of 'British democracy', the crowd shouted in protest and had to be hushed by Greek communist spokesmen. The crowd then cheered politely for a little. But when an M.P. mentioned Bevin, they burst out again: 'Bevin and Churchill—it is all the same.'

For the rank and file of E.A.M. there could have been no more sweeping condemnation of Bevin. For them Churchill was, first, the man who insisted on putting King George II back on the throne of Greece; second, the man who personally directed the 'civil war'—really a war between the E.A.M. and the British troops in Athens—at the end of 1944. They forgot the measure of help, if strictly limited and given under reserves, which the British, under Churchill's leadership, had sent to the E.A.M. forces—the E.L.A.S.—during the main war.

Perhaps E.A.M. should really have been grateful to Churchill. It was British wartime insistence that the Greek throne should be held open for 'George Glucksberg' that pushed many Greek republicans, most of them far from Communist, or even anti-Communist, into joining with the Communists in E.A.M. and E.L.A.S., as a Left-wing anti-monarchist alliance. It was the monarchy question which kept some republicans unhappily loyal to E.A.M., even when, towards the end of the German occupation, they had begun to shrink away from the dictatorial ruth- lessness of the Communists in many parts of Greece, and to quail at the more and more open signs of conflict between E.A.M. and the British.

Most Greeks traditionally and sincerely liked the British. It was only on the extreme Right that certain royalist groups had been traditionally pro-German. On the extreme Left, the Communists naturally were pro- Russian and mistrustful of capitalist Britain. But up till the war the Greek Communist Party had only been a very small group, although it was made up of energetic and single-minded men who were driven into prison or hiding by the Metaxas dictatorship.

When in October, 1940, the Greeks, led by King George II and

General Metaxas, defied the Italian invasion, they acted probably less
from love of Britain than fury and scorn at Italian insolence and a wild
burst of national pride. But when, just over six months later, the British
arrived, too few and too late, to help Greece resist the far more powerful
German invasion, and when the British were forced into helpless retreat
and evacuation of Greece, the Greeks showed a kindliness and understanding which were warm and generous. There was little reproach,
little suggestion that the British were deserting Greece. Greek peasants
along the line of retreat were open-hearted and fearless in helping
British troops. When the British were huddled under the olive trees
near the shore at Navplion, waiting for ships to come from Alexandria
and take them off before they were strafed to bits, and when incoming
ships were sunk by German bombing just off shore, the Greeks did not
look on this as humiliating for the British. They seemed to keep their
old affection for their allies.

As Greek armed resistance grew up during the three and a half years
of German-Italian occupation, the British, when they first established
liaison in October, 1942, supported all resistance groups—E.A.M. on the
left, Napoleon Zervas's forces which were originally centre republican
and later Right-wing royalist, and the tiny Left-centre group of Psarros.

There was no friction between the British and Zervas, nor between
the British and Psarros during the months before his force was eliminated
by E.L.A.S. Zervas, who was a broad, jovial, easy-going, professional
military man, with a great spade beard grown to solemnify his position
as guerilla leader, was particularly biddable and loyal. His force was
based in the wild mountain country of north-west Greece. The British
on their side helped him with gold sovereigns to pay his men and with
arms to carry out sabotage and small-scale attacks on the Germans, in
accordance with British plans. Zervas's forces were built up by, and
almost completely dependent upon the British. There were few com-
plications between the two sides.

Relations between the British and E.A.M./E.L.A.S. were very
different. E.A.M./E.L.A.S. were not dependent on the British and were
far from biddable. They wished to run resistance their own way, and
for their own ends; and they thought they had the right to absorb or
swallow up other resistance groups, such as those of Zervas and Psarros,
which they looked on as artificial creations of the British designed to
curb the power of E.A.M.

Colonel Christopher Woodhouse, who for the later part of the
occupation was the senior British liaison officer in Greece, wrote a letter
published in *The Times* on January 14th, 1947, to answer 'the accusation
against the Allied policy of support of the Left-wing resistance movement during the occupation of Greece'.

Colonel Woodhouse's argument was that already before the first
contact between the first British Military Mission and the E.A.M.
Central Committee in Athens, on January 31st, 1943, 'E.A.M. and

E.L.A.S. were firmly established, capably organised, increasingly well armed, and, in effect, entirely controlled by the Communist Party of Greece.' While the British supplied all Greek resistance movements with gold, arms and ammunition, 'it can be deduced from the prodigious quantities of all three which E.A.M./E.L.A.S. have been found to possess since the end of the occupation that our supplies were a drop in the ocean compared to their other resources'. Among their other resources were arms captured in battle with the enemy, arms surrendered by the Italian Pinerolo Division after Italy's capitulation in 1943, and arms left behind by the Germans when they withdrew from Greece.

Colonel Woodhouse did not in his letter specify any other sources of supplies, but let it be understood they might have existed.

It is, however, still a mystery what these sources could have been. During the war years, no serious suggestion was ever made that E.A.M./E.L.A.S. were getting arms or material support from Russia, Yugoslavia or Bulgaria. Towards the end of the occupation a tiny Russian mission dropped into Northern Greece, without consulting the British. Its members said their aim was to look after Russians captured while serving in the German forces in Greece. More probably they wanted to get first-hand information about the strength of E.A.M./E.L.A.S. There was no evidence that they organised the supply of arms to E.L.A.S. As for the northern neighbours of Greece, although in the later stages E.A.M./E.L.A.S. had frail political contacts with Tito in Yugoslavia and the partisan leader Enver Hoxha in Albania, perhaps also locally with the Fatherland Front in Bulgaria, in practical terms their only working link with the outer world was through the British.

Friction between E.A.M./E.L.A.S. and the British started early on. The E.A.M. leaders were always mistrustful. British liaison officers, before arriving in Greece, were so briefed as to look on E.A.M. with almost equal mistrust.

However, as Colonel Woodhouse stated in his letter quoted above, 'it was resolved at the beginning of 1943 that our relationship with E.A.M./E.L.A.S. should be hopefully friendly rather than fruitlessly hostile.' He added: 'With periodical deviations that relationship was accepted by E.A.M./E.L.A.S.; by their Communist leaders half-heartedly, because they regarded us as only temporarily less dangerous enemies than the Germans; by their non-Communist rank and file as wholeheartedly as their Communist leaders would allow.'

In practice, relations between individual E.L.A.S. bands and individual British liaison units varied greatly from one district of Greece to another. It seemed that in those areas where E.L.A.S. had strong support from the local population, and where E.L.A.S. put the fight against the Germans before local politics, relations were fair, sometimes excellent. This happened particularly in certain districts of Eastern Greece, south of Salonika. Where E.L.A.S. lacked local support and were more concerned with preparing an internal political coup than with fighting the Germans, relations were bad and got steadily worse. This happened especially in the Peloponnese, a Right-wing, royalist, stronghold. In North-west and North-central Greece, where E.L.A.S., in spite of a series of abortive 'frontier' agreements, clashed with Zervas's force, relations were rancorous, although appearances were generally observed.

The overall picture was of mutual suspicion and damped-down hostility. The underlying cause was conflict of post-war political aims. Although the average British liaison officer and many of the E.L.A.S. men genuinely wanted to get on with the war job and to fight or harass the Germans, on both sides the big men behind the scenes had other considerations in mind. On the British side it was calculated that it would be a mistake to let E.A.M./E.L.A.S. get too strong or to send them too many arms, because E.A.M. wanted to swallow up all its possible Greek opponents and aimed at a post-war Left-wing dictatorship which would probably be anti-British. On the E.A.M. side, some leaders wanted to conserve arms and manpower so as to be as materially powerful as possible at the moment of liberation and to become the decisive political force in Greece.

In this E.A.M. followed a different political strategy from Marshal Tito's National Liberation Movement. Tito believed that it was only by fighting to the utmost against the Germans, not by conserving strength, that he could secure the post-war political position of his movement in Yugoslavia. Some leading Yugoslav partisans privately criticised E.A.M. for mistaken strategy on this point. Yet whether, if E.A.M./E.L.A.S. had followed Tito's course, long-term relations with the British would have been better, it is difficult to guess.

By 1944, the British realised that they would have to yield Bulgaria and Rumania to Russian influence, and at best share Yugoslavia with Russia on a fifty-fifty basis. Greece was the only country in the Balkans where they could hope to keep supreme influence. So they must take a strong line in Greece. Further, the Churchill Government laboured under a peculiar sense of obligation and gratitude to King George, who, they felt, must be given a fair chance to take back his throne: if E.A.M. seized power, he would have no hope. But if King George went back to Greece, a debt of gratitude for Greek resistance to Italy and Germany in 1940 and 1941 would have been repaid; also, a régime would be established which would guarantee Britain's influence in a corner of the Balkans which was strategically important to British interests in the Eastern Mediterranean and the Middle East.

Sentiment mixed curiously with strategic calculation in the minds of British politicians, officials and officers. Strategy apart, they genuinely believed in 1944 that an E.A.M. government could only be a government of a tiny minority, resting on brute force and opposed by most Greeks. They reflected rosily on the ancient glories of Greece, the birthplace of democracy, and on the historic ties of friendship and culture between Greece and Britain. Dangerously, they believed that these traditions were so powerful that the great mass of Greeks would follow whatever lead Britain might give, and would do whatever Britain wanted. In this gay confidence, they thought that by 1944 the tide had already set against E.A.M./E.L.A.S.: they would soon melt away, if only they could be prevented from grasping power at the moment when the Germans withdrew.

British efforts to forestall an E.A.M./E.L.A.S. armed coup led to complicated political negotiations in 1944. Since 1941 there had been a series of crises and changes in the Greek government in exile, even mutiny in the Greek forces in the Middle East. The government had been narrowly based, moderately royalist in tendency, although moderate non-Communist republicans were co-opted in the later stages. Twice E.A.M. representatives—together with other politicians—had been smuggled out of Greece, for British-sponsored conferences with the government, once in Cairo, once in the Lebanon, the first abortive, the second conciliatory. The British Ambassador to the Greek exiled government, Mr. Leeper (later Sir Reginald), had played the role sometimes of a discouraged but conscientious hen with a brood of particularly anti-social ducklings, sometimes of a sheepdog with a flock of particularly goat-like sheep.

Finally, in the summer of 1944, when German withdrawal from Greece and the threat of an E.A.M. coup were drawing close, British mediation brought E.A.M. representatives into the exiled government headed by the moderate republican, George Papandreou, who belonged to a small centre political group. Among the E.A.M. representatives, the man who in public played the biggest part was Professor Alexander Svolos, a non-communist intellectual who seemed a genuine idealist. In practice the Communist Party representatives among them said less and did more, and had the final word on E.A.M. policy and tactics within the Cabinet.

After further British-sponsored negotiations a military compromise was made to complete the political compromise. General Sarafis, commander of the E.L.A.S. forces, together with General Zervas, his rival, were induced in September, 1944, to accept the overall command of the Supreme Allied Commander, Mediterranean—a British general—who was to be represented in Greece after the liberation by General Ronald Scobie, commander, British Land Forces, Greece.

By such painstaking negotiation and diplomacy, the British hoped to tame and subdue E.A.M. politically, to forestall the use of armed violence by E.L.A.S., and to prepare the way for disarming E.L.A.S. under General Scobie's supervision. Then they hoped to sponsor and consolidate a moderate coalition government based on the centre groups, which would be conciliatory but firm with the extreme Left and would be amenable to British guidance. The question of King George's return would be kept decently in the background for the time being, until passions had cooled off. Later, when the centre government was well settled in Greece and when British prestige and material aid had done their work, a plebiscite could be held which could be expected to be favourable to the King. Greece could then become a moderate constitutional monarchy which would naturally want to keep the closest ties with Britain.

The British poured out far more forethought, tact, planning, diplomacy, and expert study on Greece than the Russians ever devoted to any of the Balkan countries in their sphere. During the German occupation, the British had far more liaison units in Greece than the Russians had in the other Balkan countries. But British planning somehow miscarried.

The higher British authorities consistently underestimated the organising capacity, armed strength and hold over the population of E.A.M./E.L.A.S., and over-estimated the power of British prestige and popularity. On their side the E.A.M. leaders were badly handicapped by the affection which most Greeks felt for the British, and against which E.A.M. propaganda could make little headway. But they could profit from the indecisions and fluctuations of British policy and the disunity and amateurishness of the Greek centre politicians on whom the British relied. The British authorities were hampered by British public opinion at home; the E.A.M. leaders made the mistake of exaggerating the power of British public opinion.

As the political and armed struggle developed after the German withdrawal, it grew clear that the opposing forces were fairly evenly balanced. Neither side could win lasting victory. So the struggle dragged on and on, in one form or another, and became more and more bitter.

Hope of compromise or conciliation with E.A.M. vanished within a few weeks of the liberation of Greece.

The Germans began to withdraw from Greece in the early autumn of 1944, under the strategic pressure of the Red Army's drive westwards through Rumania and Bulgaria into Hungary and Yugoslavia. Greece became for the Germans a strategic outpost which had to be abandoned lest it should be completely cut off. They only suffered small loss in their gradual and orderly withdrawal. This fact was later exploited by the enemies of E.A.M., who said the E.L.A.S. had reserved its arms and men to use against fellow-Greeks and the British. There was some truth in this accusation, but a parallel charge could also be brought against the British Command. Only a very few British troops could, it appeared, be spared from the Italian front or the Middle East for Greece—not enough for any large-scale action against the retreating Germans; the Americans would not help because they did not at that time want to get entangled in the Balkans; and the British Command had too little faith in E.A.M.'s political aims to arm E.L.A.S. heavily for independent E.L.A.S. attacks on the Germans during the withdrawal.

When the Supreme Allied Commander, Mediterranean, judged the military situation ripe, a few thousand British troops, perhaps the equivalent of half a division, landed in Greece. But by this time the German withdrawal had gone far enough for E.L.A.S. to take power in most of the towns and villages. Athens and the neighbourhood were just saved for the Papandreou government and the British Command. So were one or two other easily accessible towns such as Patras, in the Gulf of Corinth. Elsewhere the British forces, when they came, had to undertake delicate and often unpleasant negotiations with the local E.L.A.S. commanders whom they found already in practical control. In some places the E.L.A.S. commanders were, on the surface, polite to the British. In others there was very nearly open bloodshed. But there were E.A.M. representatives in the Papandreou government, and the watchword was still conciliation and co-operation; so direct clashes were usually avoided, often by a hairsbreadth.

For the first weeks the Papandreou government sat in Athens desperately trying to start organising the country. Outside the Athens area they had no real power and no administrative machine. The countryside was mostly in the hands of E.L.A.S., except in so far as the scattered British units limited their authority. The loyalty of E.L.A.S. to the Papandreou government was doubtful, just as the attitude of the E.A.M. Ministers inside the government was ambiguous. The British Command and the non-E.A.M. members of the Papanderou Cabibet decided that one of their first tasks must be to persuade E.L.A.S. to hand in their arms and to disband or enrol in the regular Greek Army. This Army, after repeated purges in the Middle East, was mainly royalist. It was obedient to the British Government and so to the Papandreou government.

The real aims and plans of the E.A.M. leaders at this stage are still not clearly known. It would have been strange if, before liberation, they had not toyed with the idea of seizing power through the country, including Athens itself, and holding it in defiance of the British and of all agreements with the Supreme Allied Commander, Mediterranean. This would, however, have meant a head-on collision with the British, and E.A.M. probably did not know in advance exactly how small the British landing forces would be.

So, after the British landings, E.A.M./E.L.A.S. found themselves still theoretically subject to the Papandreou government and the British Command. But there were compensations. So long as they still controlled the Greek countryside, they were still in a very strong bargaining position, and through the E.A.M. Ministers in the government could hope to dictate their own terms. Then, in November, 1944, E.A.M./E.L.A.S. were asked to disarm and disband voluntarily, to lay down their power, to become helpless.

To many, to obey seemed pointless suicide. The simple-minded rank

M

and file believed that the British would at once exploit the disarming of
E.L.A.S. to strengthen the Right wing in Greece, to maintain the
German-sponsored anti-Communist Security Battalions in existence,
and to force 'George Glucksberg' on an unwilling people with the help
of the strongly royalist Sacred Battalion—the crack unit of the Greek
regular army formed in exile. Those E.L.A.S. bands which had been
particularly ruthless towards the Greek villagers under the occupation
feared vengeance once they gave up their arms. The few key-men in
E.A.M./E.L.A.S. probably thought, quite cold-bloodedly, partly in
terms of the personal struggle for power, partly in terms of the question:
was Greece to be yielded up lock, stock and barrel to the British, or was
it to be held open for Russian influence, so that in the end it could be
joined to the Soviet sphere?

The open clash came on December 3rd in Athens. A big E.A.M.
crowd came up against the police in the centre of the city. Shots were
fired, according to most accounts, by the police. The E.A.M. Ministers
walked out of the Papandreou government, the non-Communists
perhaps with some reluctance. E.A.M. called out their organised groups
and their unorganised sympathisers. Street fighting broke out through
most of Athens. Originally it was between Greeks and Greeks, but
within a matter of hours the British troops in Athens were called in
against E.A.M./E.L.A.S. The rump Papandreou government's position
was too dangerous for the British to stand aside.

Very soon the British Command, the British Ambassador and civilian
officials, the Papandreou government and its officials, were hemmed
into a tiny area in the middle of the city, around the royal palace, a big
department store building used as British Headquarters, and the Hotel
Grande Bretagne. This was called 'Little England'. Outside it there was
sporadic sniping and machine-gunning. The British and Greek government forces made little headway in their efforts to clear other parts of
the city. The chief 'rebel' stronghold was round about Omonoia Square,
only ten minutes' walk from 'Little England'. It even seemed possible
that 'Little England' might be overrun.

The situation was saved for the British and the Papandreou government by the arrival of British reinforcements from Italy—the men who
could not be spared for the original British landings during the German
withdrawal. Now they forced their way up the broad exposed five-mile
road from the Piraeus to Athens. The tide turned. Omonoia Square was
recovered, after many of the neighbouring houses had been blasted,
burned or holed by mortar fire. The Acropolis which, apart from a small
British dump, had remained a no man's land, escaped with a few shallow
marks of glancing bullets on the pillars of the Parthenon.

Athens was gradually cleaned up, district by district, by the British
troops, by the Greek police and regular forces, and by hastily enrolled
Athenian volunteers, mostly fanatical monarchists. The more highly
organised military formations of the 'rebels' started their long slow

retreat northwards, taking with them captured British troops and air-men and upper- and middle-class Athenians, men and women of all ages, as hostages. The hostages, as British planes searched the country-side, had to make long and weary forced marches on foot—the 'rebels' had practically no transport—and got very little food or sleep. Some had jewels or money taken from them. After negotiation, the British were recovered, exhausted, but mostly unharmed. But not all the Greek hostages got home. Some presumably died of the hardships they had to undergo. Others were presumably killed for fear of later reprisals if their captors were identified. The fate of the hostages left a corroding poison in the minds of most non-Communist Greeks.

Altogether, the ruthlessness and above all the efficiency with which E.A.M./E.L.A.S. had waged war in Athens so horrified and frightened the middle-class and upper-class Athenians, and others who liked a quiet orderly life, that an unbridgeable gulf was cleft between the hard core of E.A.M./E.L.A.S. and other Greeks, between the Communists and the anti-Communists. E.A.M./E.L.A.S. lost many of its sympathisers and members drawn from among the moderates, the intellectuals, the more progressive element of the upper classes and middle-classes. It almost even lost some of its non-Communist leaders such as Alexander Svolos.

Greece was split sharply into the extreme Left and the extreme Right. On the one side was pro-Soviet, Communist-guided E.A.M./E.L.A.S. On the other were the relatively pro-British royalists, to whom the anti-Communist republicans and moderates of the Centre drew closer and closer. The real middle-of-the-way men, who still wanted concilia-tion and compromise, became fewer and fewer and had less and less public support. They were pathetic survivals.

The civil war also greatly stiffened the attitude and sharpened the feelings of the British in Greece against E.A.M./E.L.A.S. It confirmed and strengthened the worst fears and most lurid suspicions of the British diplomats and officials. In the Army, by the end of the fighting there were few British officers and fewer men who still had a good word to say for E.A.M. Among those who had been stationed away from Athens, there was a small number, mainly officers, who continued to see some justification for E.A.M. or who at least believed in concilia-tion. But they were regarded by the rest as at least mildly eccentric.

In Britain itself, on the other hand, feeling had been violently divided over the Greek civil war. A first-class political crisis, coming at a time when the overall war situation was still dangerous, was probably only just averted by Bevin's uncompromising declaration of loyalty to Churchill over the Greek question. E.A.M. had been counting on the hope that the Labour Party might quit the National Government; Bevin dashed this hope, and E.A.M. never forgave him.

Still, during December and most of January important London newspapers, particularly *The Times* and the *News Chronicle*, strongly criticised government policy over Greece, and there were tense moments in the House of Commons.

Churchill, who had always taken a particular personal interest in Greece, was shaken enough to make a sudden dramatic dash to Athens during the December fighting, and drove in armoured convoy up the dangerous five miles from the Piraeus to the British-held heart of Athens. He achieved little immediate result; but his visit probably convinced E.A.M. that he would never yield. He was determined to push on relentlessly and uncompromisingly until E.A.M./E.L.A.S. had been militarily defeated.

The defeat was achieved and the military threat from E.A.M. was removed for nearly two years. But E.A.M. remained a political danger, not only inside Greece itself. Many people in Britain had been seriously disturbed and distressed. The British government felt that, politically, they must follow a policy of moderation and apparent conciliation. They delayed the coming to power of the Greek Right Wing for another fourteen months.

In February, 1946, the Varkiza Agreement was concluded between the Greek government, now led by a veteran strong man of Greek politics, General Plastiras, and the 'rebel' leaders. Endless British tact combined with strong British pressure had been needed to get it signed. In form it was essentially moderate. At the end of the fighting there had been an outcry in Greece, not only from the extreme Right, for vengeance and reprisals and the wholesale suppression of E.A.M./E.L.A.S. The Agreement provided for the surrender of arms by E.L.A.S.; it also provided for the replacement of martial law by ordinary civil law procedure. A plebiscite was to be held on the monarchy. The Agreement left E.A.M. and the Greek Communist Party as legal and recognised bodies, with their own newspapers, in spite of the demand for their outlawry. In practice both sides infringed its spirit and its letter. E.L.A.S. kept many of their arms. Right-wing extremists took private vengeance on those who had taken part in the 'rebellion'. Both sides kept in being armed bands in the remoter parts of Greece. Yet Varkiza was a fair attempt at compromise, which would never have been made without British intervention.

The British spent the next year and a quarter trying to create a broad centre party or bloc to stabilise Greek political life. They failed. There was a succession of would-be moderate coalition governments or governments of experts, headed in turn by General Plastiras, Admiral Vulgaris, the Regent Damaskinos himself, Panayotis Canellopoulos and finally the eighty-six-year-old Liberal leader, Sofoulis. All tried in one way or another to pacify Greece and bring order into economic and financial chaos. But they had a hopeless struggle against Greek extremism and Greek individualism. They had very little support or authority in the country. They depended almost entirely on British moral backing and British material aid. Neither the extreme Right nor the extreme Left, neither the royalists nor E.A.M., were represented in these governments. Since Greece was roughly divided into these two extremes, the moderate governments were quite unrepresentative. And since the British would not back them with consistent force, they were also powerless.

The British did, however, try, rather despairingly and inconsequently, to make them strong and make them popular. The British Liaison Mission, under General Rawlins, armed and trained the new Greek Army. A British Police Mission, under Sir Charles Wickham, who had had long police experience in Northern Ireland, helped to train and equip a new Greek police force, theoretically following the British model. A large British economic mission tried to advise and help the Athens governments in the economic reconstruction of their country. British financial advisers, including high Treasury officials, tried to stop inflation and stabilise the currency. British labour advisers tried to help in the creation of trade unions on the British model and to heal the breach between Communist-led and anti-Communist workers. Britain sent goods and gave loans. Two British divisions remained in Greece, stationed at key points all over the country: the theory was that they should give confidence and stability and strengthen the authority of the Athens government.

Results were poor in comparison with the British effort. By the time the first post-war general election was held in Greece on March 31st, 1946, the successive Athens governments had made practically no serious start on economic reconstruction. The currency had been temporarily stabilised, but its basis was still most precarious. Greece had been saved from famine, but mainly through the temporary blessing of UNRRA supplies. Industry was still almost at a standstill. In spite of the new British-trained army and police, there was still terrorism by extreme Right and extreme Left bands in different parts of the countryside—by the Right mainly in the Peloponnese and by the Left mainly in North-eastern Greece. The new army and police could not be relied upon to enforce order upon the extreme Right. The prefects and local officials sent to the provinces by the Athens governments had only dubious authority. British occupation meant that there was plenty of freedom, of a kind, in Greece. But it was a doubtful and precarious freedom, permitting the existence of little local tyrannies and carrying in itself the danger of a great tyranny.

Sofoulis, the Liberal Prime Minister, under whose nominal rule the first general election was held, himself said that the country was not peaceful and orderly enough for a fair and free election. The Prefect or Nomarch of the province of Serres, north of Salonika—Yanni Theophanopoulos, who had been appointed by Sofoulis—said much the same.

'It is too early. I have not yet had time to bring order to the province,' he said four days before election day. 'First I was sent to the Drama area. There I made a mistake. I tried to deal with the extreme Right with a strong hand, sternly. What good did it do? They only denounced me as a "Communist" and a "Bulgarian". I, who am a Liberal from Athens. Since I came to Serres I have followed different tactics: I have tried first to convince the extreme Right that I am a reliable and under- standing person. Then when I have won their confidence, I shall be able to bring them into line, to establish authority over them. But I haven't got to that stage yet—it takes time. So, as things are now, if elections are held on Sunday, they will be held in this province under threat of terrorism both by right and left. What can I do?'

But the British Government had decided that the election could not be put off any longer. They apparently hoped that a Greek government based on an elected parliament would have more authority in the country and make a more vigorous start on reconstruction. With the Sofoulis government—the last of the governments created in a political vacuum—the British had made positively their last effort along this line. According to Athens gossip, the list of the Sofoulis Cabinet had been drawn up by the British Ambassador himself and his advisers at the Embassy. On paper it was more broadly based and had a better chance of popular support than its predecessors. Sofoulis was a highly intelli- gent, far-sighted, even wily old man. But even he and his colleagues had failed to do more than keep up appearances. Some laid the blame for this failure on the inadequacy and inconsistency of British backing. But by now the British were beginning to tire. They felt that they could no longer go on pouring money and experts into Greece to prop up ineffective governments. Something new had to be tried.

To meet charges that the elections would not be free and orderly, an 'Allied Mission for Observing the Greek Elections' was called in. British, Americans and French all served upon it; the Russians refused, saying that the appointment of such a Mission would be interference in Greek internal affairs. A.M.F.O.G.E. set up an elaborate system of teams to tour the country and observe conditions before election day, making a kind of preliminary Gallup poll of political feeling, and also to observe conditions of voting on election day itself. The Mission created around itself an atmosphere of Western efficiency and activity.

Nevertheless, E.A.M. decided to boycott the election. Partly, perhaps, they genuinely feared that there would be so much Right-wing terrorism that it would completely distort the results. Partly, perhaps, their leaders realised that the strong tide of popular feeling against the Left, resulting from the civil war, had not yet turned, and that even in relatively fair elections they could not hope for victory. In either case, boycott seemed the safest course.

The E.A.M. leaders organised a big campaign for abstention, in Greek 'Apohé'. The word 'Apohé' was bill-posted on the Athens trams, on the walls of houses and public buildings, scrawled in chalk all over the poorer quarters of Athens. Little boys peddling black-market Lucky Strikes and Gold Flakes in the heart of Athens raised a clenched fist and proudly announced that they were all for 'Apohé'. On the eve of the election a crowd of over 5,000 E.A.M. supporters, mostly boys and girls, gathered outside A.M.F.O.G.E. headquarters and the Grande Bretagne hotel to listen to long speeches, to sing, and to chant over and over again: 'Démokrátes ápohé'—'Democrats, abstain'. They denounced the Greek 'monarcho-fascists' and called on the British to quit Greece.

Marching away, at last, towards Omonoia Square, the crowd clashed with the police. Five civilians and five policemen were reported injured.

During the election campaign, E.A.M. made far more show in Athens than did the royalists. The royalists did their share of scrawling on walls, 'Long live the King' or the big 'X' sign with a rough crown drawn over it; the 'X' was the symbol of a small fanatical extreme Right organisation which carried out acts of terror particularly in the workers' suburbs lying between Athens and the Piraeus. In one E.A.M. stronghold, Kokkinia, a sprawling collection of tenements and rough hut-like dwellings, where some tenements had been gutted by the Germans as a reprisal for wartime resistance, workers complained bitterly that 'X-ites' had swooped on the local café, dragged off an E.A.M. boy and shot him.

Otherwise the chief outlet of the royalists was to drive at speed around Athens in cars and lorries chanting and tooting rhythmically on their horns the royalist slogan, 'Ér-, Ér-, Érhetái'—'he is coming, he is coming'. 'He,' of course, was King George II, still in London waiting for his cue to enter the scene.

Election day in Athens and Attica passed off apparently in complete calm and order, even in such 'red' workers' quarters as Kokkinia and Nea Smyrna. An outsider had as little chance of guessing what intimidation and terrorism had gone on behind the scenes as in the Bulgarian election four months earlier. Perhaps there were rather more Greek armed police and lorryloads of armed Greek troops to be seen in the Athens area than there had been Bulgarian militiamen and troops in Sofia. On the other hand, in the 'red' districts around Athens, there were sometimes pickets of two or three men lounging outside the polling stations—apparently E.A.M. men noting down who was going against the 'Apohé' and casting a vote. This would have been a daring action for the Opposition in Bulgaria. In Megara, a little market-town north-west of Athens which was a royalist stronghold, there was dancing and singing in the main street, very much as there had been in the Bulgarian towns.

The usual picture in the Athens district was of long tidy queues of men—women had not been granted the vote, as they had been in all

Soviet-occupied Balkan countries—standing patiently in their Sunday suits in the early summer sun, waiting to cast their votes. The polling station was often the local Orthodox church, where electoral officials sat or lounged, smoking, drinking and munching snacks with cheerful disregard of ecclesiastical proprieties. Jeep-loads of A.M.F.O.G.E. observers roared up at relatively rare intervals on their final rounds of inspection.

In what might be called the lower middle-class districts of Athens there seemed some prospect, during election day, that the centre groups might do better than most people expected. A fair number of men volunteered the information that they had voted for the centre politicians, for Canellopoulos or Sophocles Venezelos or Papandreou. But it was easy to exaggerate this impression. A more typical Athenian was a better-class artisan who said: 'I work part-time for two different employers. One is royalist, the other is E.A.M. The first has said he will sack me if I don't vote, the other has said he will sack me if I do. I am not going to tell you which I have done.'

It would, however, be a fair guess that, although there was undoubtedly sporadic localised terror in Greece, on an overall picture there was considerably less systematic intimidation in Greece than during elections in the Russian-occupied Balkan countries.

For one thing, the British might inspire dislike and resentment, even in some cases hatred; but they did not inspire fear in the way that the Red Army somehow did. This was clear from the whole attitude of the E.A.M. leaders and journalists when talking to Englishmen. Even those who had earlier been in prison or under arrest were normally jaunty, cocksure, on the attack. They could slang the British as violently as they liked in their speeches and their newspapers: a public word of criticism of the Russians, in the Russian-occupied countries, carried the risk of a treason charge.

For another thing, the Greek anti-Communist forces, although they were brutal and savage on occasion, were also anarchic and poorly organised. They were too inefficient to carry out a highly systematised terror. Further, their leaders wished to keep up some show of being in the vanguard of Western civilisation, too cultured to stoop to merely 'Balkan' methods.

Trickery was probably more widely used than violence. Everyone admitted that the lists of voters used for the election were highly inaccurate. According to A.M.F.O.G.E. the lists could be regarded as 71 per cent. valid, 13 per cent. invalid, 16 per cent. of doubtful validity.

Using this estimate, A.M.F.O.G.E. reached the conclusion that, of the 'valid electors', 60 per cent. had cast votes, either for the royalists or the Centre. Of the 40 per cent. of 'valid electors' who did not vote, A.M.F.O.G.E. rather surprisingly estimated that only 10 to 20 per cent. could be counted as 'party abstentions'. This suggested that only between one-tenth and one-fifth of Greece was behind E.A.M.

On their side E.A.M. claimed that the election showed that they had over half the population behind them. They estimated that 55 per cent. had abstained.

Most outsiders watching the election results as they came out from one district after another thought that the truth lay somewhere between the two estimates. At one point, almost complete results showed just about 50 per cent. of the possible voters abstaining, though the final figures, possibly after some high-level jiggery-pokery, reduced this percentage to about 34. At a rough guess, it seemed probable that the royalist bloc and E.A.M. each had a little over one-third of the Greek people behind them. Of the rest—rather less than one-third—perhaps half had voted for the Centre groups and the other half were genuine non-political 'abstainers' of the kind that never voted in any election.

Whatever the real state of feeling, Greece's first post-war election in practice gave a big parliamentary majority to the combined royalist groups. They were allotted 216 seats out of a total of 354 seats in parliament, and they felt that they had won an undisputed victory and had a clear right to rule the country.

British officials in Athens had mixed feelings about this result. They had hoped to the last that there might be strong representation of the moderate centre in the new parliament. The royalists were not altogether convenient collaborators: many were disgruntled extremists, resentful of British interference aimed at reducing anti-Communist excesses. The old royalist tradition, up till the 1939 war, had been pro-German and anti-British.

British pressure was brought to bear, so that the new government resulting from the election should be a coalition of Right and Centre, not purely a government of the Right. As a result the three closely allied Centre politicians—George Papandreou, Panayotis Canellopoulos and Sophocles Venezelos—hesitatingly aligned themselves with the royalists, and in the following months of 1946 drifted in and out of the royalist government. In the process they drew closer and closer to the royalists; abandoning their republican views, they accepted the monarchy, and they became more and more strongly anti-Communist. They could no longer be said to represent a real moderate centre in Greek politics.

Only the old Sofoulis, the Liberal, was left as a middle-of-the-way man, seeking to work out compromises between Right and Left, between the royalists and the Communists. Otherwise the political split, cleaved deep by the civil war, was gaping and unbridged. British attempts to secure moderation became more and more defeatist and half-hearted. From the formation of the first royalist government of Constantin Tsaldaris in April, 1946, the British drew more and more into the background.

The threat of outlawry again hung over E.A.M., or at least over the Communist Party. As the Tsaldaris government felt its strength, there were more and more arrests and internments of E.A.M. men and Communists. The Communist newspaper *Rizospastis* survived for the time being, although the government, if it had not been for Western opinion, would certainly have liked to ban it.

On September 1st, 1946, the Tsaldaris government held the referendum for which Greece had waited so long—not, however, on the constitutional question of the monarchy, but purely on the practical question of the return of King George II to Greece. The Greeks were not given the chance to vote straight out for a republic. This time the task of the Allied observers was only to supervise the revision of the lists of electors. There was no full-blown A.M.F.O.G.E. The results gave a big majority for the King. Out of 1,801,140 electors registered on the revised lists, 1,691,592 cast votes.; 1,166,512 voted for the King and 521,267 against; there were 3,815 invalid votes.

This majority seemed a surprisingly big one, even though many Greeks were obsessed by fear of Communism and by panic about Slav invasion from the North, and looked to the King to protect Greece from both. Yet less than three years earlier the King had still been bitterly disliked for his association with the pre-war Metaxas dictatorship. Things had changed since then, and most outsiders would have expected him to get a majority of votes. But few thought that in a perfectly fair plebiscite it could have been so large.

By this time Greek internal strife had openly become a bone of contention between the great Powers, between East and West. The Ukrainian Foreign Minister, Manuilsky, had brought the case of Greece before the United Nations. The Security Council debated whether or not British troops should stay in Greece. Already there were rumblings of the coming guerilla rising in the mountains of Northern Greece, led by the Moscow-trained Communist and former tobacco worker, General Markos Vefiades.

During the winter of 1946-47 and the following year, the guerilla forces developed their strength and widened their field of operations. They found at very least moral and political support, and shelter when hard pressed, over the northern border in Yugoslavia, Albania and Bulgaria, countries lying within the Soviet sphere. On Christmas Eve, 1947, Markos felt strong enough to proclaim an independent government led by himself, in rivalry to the Athens government. The Athens government retaliated by declaring the Communist Party illegal and banning the last Communist newspaper. At the start of 1948 the Greek government, in consultation with British and American military advisers was planning a fuller mobilisation and the placing of the Greek Army on a complete wartime footing, so as to fight its second 'spring offensive' against General Markos.

In these circumstances neither the British Government nor the United

States Government was likely to cavil at the shortcomings of the Athens governments. These had to be backed and reinforced by the Western Powers, or else Greece would have to be abandoned to the East, to Russia and her smaller Balkan associates.

The Americans, it was true, had, after taking over chief responsibility for Greece from the British in the summer of 1947, felt embarrassed at sponsoring a royalist-dominated government. After delays and involved negotiations, the Liberal Sofoulis, old as he was, had been induced to head a fresh coalition government, stretching further towards the Left than its royalist predecessors. But by that time the guerilla movement was so formidable that the new Sofoulis government merely maintained the policy of the royalists: its main aim seemed to be to get increased United States support, if only financial, for fresh attempts to liquidate Markos.

The Americans, even if they were not prepared to increase their total expenditure on Greece straightaway, agreed to transfer to military purposes funds originally allocated to civilian aid. On this basis, it was announced in January, 1948, that America had sanctioned the increase of the Greek government's armed forces to a quarter of a million men. At the same time there were still, at the opening of 1948, British troops stationed in Greece, in the face of reiterated Soviet demands to the United Nations that they should be withdrawn.

So Greece, over three years after her liberation from the Germans, was one of the most tense points of stress in the trial of strength between East and West. Ernest Bevin, speaking in the House of Commons on January 22nd, 1948, delivered a sharp warning to Russia and the Balkan neighbours against intervention in Greece. 'It is dangerous in international affairs to play with fire,' he said.

In these circumstances the Greeks themselves were by then divided simply into the anti-Communists and the Communists, and it did not matter much whether a man was a Left-wing Liberal or a man of the Centre or an out-and-out royalist. But the lack of strong characters among the anti-Communists was an embarrassment for the Western Powers.

The royalist, Constantin Tsaldaris, soon after his electoral victory in 1946, gave the impression of a short-tempered, harassed, irritable, probably dyspeptic man of middle age. He was stoutly built. Deep lines slanted downwards from the corners of his mouth. There were dark pouches under his eyes. Although he came of a wealthy family of politicians he seemed to feel that he had got himself into a job that was too big for him. He was therefore straining himself to play the strong man, the man of rapid and irrevocable decisions. Yet in his comfortable, richly-furnished villa in the fashionable quarter of Athens, he seemed overshadowed by his big, blonde, nordic wife, widow of a German scholar. In the crowded parliament, when he made his first speech as

Prime Minister before a smartly-dressed audience of fashionable Athenian men and women, he spoke monotonously, lifelessly, hurriedly, like a man doubtful whether he could dominate the house.

Nevertheless, among the royalist politicians, most of them men of narrow minds, interests and experience, Tsaldaris was probably the strongest man. His policy was essentially nationalist and conservative. It appealed to the narrowest patriotic instincts and fears of the Greeks, and was hampered by the moderating admonitions of the British. Its main basis was anti-Communism and resistance to any incursion from Greece's northern neighbours. A further popular plank was its demand for fresh territory in the north, from Albania and Bulgaria.

'Greece, who contributed so significantly to the victory of the democratic camp and made so many sacrifices, does not put forward thousand-year-old historic claims, as she would be justified in doing,' he said in April, 1946. 'She asks for no more than justice. . . . She asks to be given a few territories which have always been Greek, and which either are still inhabited by a predominantly Greek population, or which have been de-hellenised by fire and the sword during recent years. She also demands that her frontier with Bulgaria be rectified in such a way that her northern provinces, on which her economic life depends, should be secured from fresh invasion.'

Britain's failure to fight for the territorial claims of Greece when they came before the Peace Conference in 1946 was bitterly resented in Greece, especially by the Right-wing. The royalist government decreed a day of mourning and protest against the treaties, reserving the right to press the claims of Greece in the future.

At home, Tsaldaris at first phrased his policy in moderate but warning words. E.A.M. and the Communist Party were to be allowed a legal existence—so long as their activities were 'within legal limits'. Since his constant contention—which had a good deal of factual foundation—was that E.A.M. was fundamentally disloyal to the State and exceeded the limits of legality, he could hold the permanent threat of outlawry and proscription over the heads of E.A.M. When in February, 1947, General Zervas, the old guerilla opponent of E.L.A.S. became the Royalist Minister of Public Order, many prominent members of E.A.M. discovered themselves outlawed in practice, if not formally. Thousands were arrested and sent to the islands in the spring and summer of 1947.

By this time Tsaldaris was no longer Prime Minister. Some months earlier he had handed over this post to a little-known royalist, Demetrios Maximos. Tsaldaris remained, however, the chief among the royalist politicians, and was also the chief negotiator for royalist Greece with the Western Powers.

If the Greeks had not been obsessed by fear of Communism and Slav invasion, Tsaldaris was not the man to hold the loyalties of a majority of the people. But things were abnormal. The Greeks saw in Tsaldaris, above all, the man who had brought back King George II and served the monarchy. The monarchy since the civil war had become to all anti-Communist Greeks the symbol of Greek nationalist resistance to the Communist threat within and the invasion threat from the north. It was only the monarchy, they believed, that could keep Greece outside the Soviet sphere and bind her to the Western Powers.

The Greek Communist leader, Zahariades, had just the opposite aim: to break down what he considered a purely artificial barrier between Greece and the rest of the Balkans, to prevent Greece from becoming permanently a mere 'colony' of the Western Powers, and to link Greece with the Soviet sphere.

Somewhat illogically E.A.M., of which the Communist Party was the driving force, backed the Tsaldaris government's claims to territory from Albania and Bulgaria. This was, however, a purely tactical move by the Communists. They did not expect the pro-Soviet governments of Albania and Bulgaria to take E.A.M. declarations seriously on this point.

Zahariades explained in May, 1946, that originally it had not been the wish of the Communist Party to back these claims. The party had wanted to have the northern frontier questions settled 'on the principle of the self-determination of the populations concerned.' The average Greek peasant or worker, he said, had small interest in territorial demands. It was mainly the *petit bourgeois* and upper classes who backed them. However, the non-Communist groups allied with the Communists in E.A.M. had wanted to support them; so the Communist Party had agreed, in order to preserve the unity of E.A.M.

As for the supposed claims by Marshal Tito's Yugoslavia on Greek Macedonia and Salonika, Zahariades said firmly: 'Territorial questions between Greece and Yugoslavia do not arise.' His public policy, at least, was that the population of Greek Macedonia was 90 per cent. Greek and only 10 per cent. Slav, and that E.A.M. stood for the territorial integrity of Greece.

What the private policy of the Greek Communist Party over Macedonia may have been, it was hard for outsiders to fathom. But it seemed unlikely that the Greek Communists would ever willingly agree to cede any part of Greek Macedonia, since such a step would have been the last fatal blow to the Party's prestige in the rest of Greece. On the Yugoslav side, also, it seemed probable that, whatever rash demands the local hotheads in Yugoslav Macedonia might proclaim, the real leaders of Marshal Tito's régime were much more interested in procuring a pro-Soviet government in Greece than in acquiring a slice of Greek Macedonia.

Nevertheless there was a general feeling in Greece that the Communist Party's attitude over the northern frontiers was at best weak and watery, if not downright treasonable. To distract attention from this weakness, the Communists, through E.A.M., ran their own campaign of territorial claims, reaching in other directions—into the sphere of the Western Powers and their associates. They strongly claimed the British colony, Cyprus, thereby seriously embarrassing the royalist government, who dared not press this particular claim. The royalists knew that their British patrons had no idea whatever of relinquishing a strategically important island in the Eastern Mediterranean at a moment when the British were being pushed out of Egypt and threatened in Palestine.

To alarm and annoy anti-Soviet, pro-Western Turkey, the Communist Party and E.A.M. also demanded the Turkish province of Eastern Thrace. They declared that thousands of Greeks, former inhabitants of Turkish Thrace, were waiting to go back there and cultivate the lands left empty by an exchange of populations after the first world war.

These Communist claims were first and foremost a matter of internal political tactics. The positive foreign policy of the Communist Party was to develop close long-term relations between Greece and the rest of the Balkans.

In the spring of 1946, Zahariades visited Prague and Belgrade and was very much impressed by the economic activity he saw there, particularly in Czechoslovakia's industry. The future of Greece, he concluded, lay in the closest possible economic ties with the countries lying to the north, inside the Soviet sphere. To them Greece could sell her tobacco, currants, olive oil and other agricultural produce. In return they could sell Greece most of what she wanted. Czechoslovakia could send agricultural and industrial machinery, tractors, motor cars. Rumania and Hungary could send wheat. Yugoslavia and Bulgaria could send meat.

There was something almost childlike in the enthusiasm of Zahariades as he expounded these ideas, toying with a hard-boiled Easter egg painted crimson and inscribed with his name by a political admirer. He would not admit that he might be over-optimistic in his estimate of economic recovery in the countries of the Soviet sphere, or that Greece, as a seafaring Mediterranean country, needed close economic links with the Western Powers. He was convinced that Greece, by trading with the Balkans and Central Europe, could find economic stability and also independence. She could free herself from 'colonial' enslavement to the West.

He claimed, rather naïvely, that the British were, for example, deliberately delaying reconstruction of the Greek railways 'so as to make profits for British cars and petrol'. To get the British out of Greece would solve everything. That was what E.A.M. were working for, 'by all political methods'.

Every British soldier in Greece, Zahariades said, would be made to feel that he was unwanted; his life would be made 'impossible',

'Greece to-day is nothing but a British colony,' Zahariades added, smiling a charming but melancholy smile. 'If the British leave we shall be able to settle our own affairs in our own way—even in the economic field.'

Britain certainly could not claim that her economic aid had brought Greece stability or recovery in the first thirty months after liberation.

When, in the spring of 1947, the United States decided to take over the economic burden of Greece from Britain, who could no longer bear the strain, official figures of British aid were given in London. The British Government had wiped out obligations incurred by the Greek government during the war period, amounting to over £40,000,000. Early in 1946 Britain had made a loan of £10,000,000 to assist in stabilising the Greek currency. Between January 1st, 1946, and March 31st, 1947, Britain had provided £18,000,000 for the maintenance of the Greek Army, and had placed a further sum of £11,000,000 at the disposal of the Greek government for the purchase of equipment for the Army. These sums made up a heavy total for impoverished and weakened Britain.

British aid was not the only aid that flowed into Greece from the West. According to one expert estimate, up till the moment when the United States took over responsibility, the Western Powers—including UNRRA under that heading—had spent altogether £250,000,000 on Greece, a small country of 7,500,000 people.

The report of the United States Economic Mission which the American expert, Paul Porter, led to Greece in the spring of 1947, gave a lower total of 700,000,000 dollars, or £175,000,000 of 'foreign assistance'. During the year 1946 alone, it estimated the total of UNRRA aid and British military subsidies at 300,000,000 dollars, or £75,000,000.

Delivering its gloomy verdict, the American report said:

'There is the inescapable conclusion that, in spite of 700,000,000 dollars in foreign assistance, Greece during the past two years has merely managed to survive. There are exceptions, of course, but, in general, economic conditions have improved but little over those prevailing at the time when the Nazi forces were expelled from the country. . . .

'Since the war there have been seven changes in the Greek government. No government has been able to develop an effective economic policy and to inaugurate necessary controls. Those controls which have been attempted have failed as a result of various causes, among which is the lack of effective government machinery for impartial administration. Partly because of these factors, private capital instead of devoting itself to reconstruction and development has been preoccupied with schemes to hedge its risks, outside the Greek economy.'

The American report gave the civil war of 1944 and the later guerilla rising in the north as important causes of the 'desperate economic crisis' facing Greece. But it also said:

'There has been a sense of helplessness, and in some quarters a feeling that, because Greece suffered so much during the war, it is now entitled to the care of its richer Allies. . . . The lack of confidence among government officials and the people in the ability of Greece to save itself financially and the belief that it must depend on aid from abroad have contributed to an appalling inertia. . . .

'There exists a wide disparity in the living standards and income throughout Greece. Profiteers, that is traders, speculators and black-marketeers, thrive in wealth and luxury, a problem with which no government has effectively dealt. At the same time the masses of the people live on bare subsistence. . . .

'It appears that in the absence of substantial foreign assistance and the adoption by the Greek government of strong control measures, another round of extreme inflation with all of its disastrous economic and political consequences is a certainty.'

Even if this report was drafted partly in order to impress the American home public and to get support for President Truman's foreign policy, few outsiders could quarrel with its gloomy conclusions.

It was the Greek sense of helplessness, of apathy—except among the black-marketeers—that seemed most dangerous to outsiders. Both officials and individuals were always finding excuses for doing nothing, or as little as possible.

A Greek official publication, issued in London in May, 1947—two and a half years after liberation—quoted the Minister of Finance, Demetrios Helmis, as explaining the difficulties of collecting taxes:

'Under present circumstances, many of the ordinary sources of revenue cannot render an appreciable yield. This applies especially to income from houses and land, owing to the existing Rent Restrictions Act, which fixes very low rents both for houses and shops; to income from company dividends or interest on bonds, as companies for the moment are unable to pay dividends, while inflation has wiped out all the pre-war government bonds issued in drachmæ; to income from salaries and wages owing to the fact that neither of these categories has kept pace with the rise in the cost of living; to income on agricultural enterprises owing to the heavy losses sustained by peasants and stock-raisers during the war.'

The Minister did go on to explain that the Greek government were trying to get taxes from the only remaining source, commercial and industrial profits. But his whole argument revealed the underlying sense of hopelessness.

One of the most depressing things about Greece, for any foreigner, was the appalling state of the roads, even the main Athens-Salonika highroad, the main link between Northern and Southern Greece. Twenty miles an hour was a good speed for any jeep; in some places it was impossible to drive at more than fifteen; even at these speeds, jeeps often collapsed under the strain. The roads in western Greece were even worse. Practically no repair work had been done since the war started, as far as anyone could see, except on a very few tantalising half-mile stretches. These, according to an old Greek custom, were the result of a brief pre-election outburst of energy by the local Prefect, designed to win votes for his party. No other Balkan country, two years after the end of the war, had roads anything like those of Greece.

A booklet issued by the Greek Embassy in London in March, 1947, *Reconstruction in Greece since the Liberation*, gave this answer to criticisms of Greek roads:

'Local supplies of stone and cement are available and so is the labour. But any large-scale road repair programme would have entailed an immediate heavy outlay in drachmæ for the payment of wages and local material. Under present conditions this would inevitably have led to fresh inflation, as the amount of consumer goods is still far from sufficient to satisfy the wants of the population. It is this haunting fear of inflation (there have already been two inflations since the liberation) which has so far deterred the government from embarking at once on a big programme of road restoration. The labour is there, and people are only too anxious to work, but until the financial programme has been solved, it would be risky to increase the amount of purchasing power in the people's hands by the issue of paper currency.'

Arguments like this, based on liberal economic theories run to seed, made more understandable, if no more palatable, the totalitarian economic methods, the systems of forced or half-forced labour, imposed by the pro-Soviet Balkan governments.

Greek villagers who had suffered heavily from the war seemed paralysed by the same apathy as the officials. In the small village of Lidoraki, north of the Gulf of Corinth, the Germans had gutted all the houses except two. Only the sturdy stone outer walls were standing; there were no inner walls, no floors or ceilings, no windows, no roofs. In May, 1946, the villagers had been living in those conditions for two years—for two winters. Practically nothing had been done, even in a makeshift way, to patch up the houses, except where thin woven straw coverings had been slung across between the gaunt stone outer walls. If you asked the villagers why they had not done more, they answered: 'The B.B.C. told us during the war that the Allies would rebuild every house in Greece destroyed by the Germans as a reprisal. Well, let them come and rebuild Lidoraki. We are waiting.'

The only people who seemed really active and really successful economically were the speculators and black-marketeers, mainly in Athens and Salonika. For one thing there was a brisk illicit trade in UNRRA goods. People commonly said that in Salonika, before ever an UNRRA ship reached port, its cargo had been sold to the black-market dealers. There were many other profitable forms of speculation in currency, gold and goods.

That was presumably why the excellent and expensive dancing-places

N

and restaurants of Athens were crowded with Greeks as well as British
officers; why in the summer of 1946 there were a good many excellently-
groomed Athenian women who could buy light sandals costing the
equivalent of £7 or £8, and frocks at proportionate prices; why the
elegant quarter of Athens, Kolinaki, still breathed an air of quite
un-Balkan and un-post-war luxury.

Trading and speculation of this type did not bring much benefit to
Greece as a whole, since profits were very seldom put into schemes of
reconstruction or development. It was often said that those Greeks who
possessed or acquired wealth were mainly interested in transferring it
to safety abroad, if possible to hard currency countries. It was not used
to rebuild Greece. Much of the money which the Western Powers put
into Greece found its way first into private pockets and then out of
Greece again.

The only Soviet-controlled Balkan country which reached a state of
economic and financial disorder and decay at all like that of Greece
was Rumania. Partly, perhaps, this was because Rumanians and Greeks,
not being Slavs, had rather the same kind of temperament, the same
individualism, scepticism and lack of community conscience. But there
was one very big difference between the two countries. In the one case,
Rumania was badly handicapped because she had to pay out heavily
in goods, materials and money to the occupying Power, Russia. In the
other case, Greece was heavily subsidised by the occupying Power,
Britain, and from 1947 by the United States.

It was very doubtful whether the Western Powers would ever be able
to make Greece a self-supporting economic concern. It seemed most
likely that Greece, under her pro-Western régime, would become more
and more apathetic, more and more torn by guerilla warfare, and more
and more reliant on outside aid. The price of keeping Greece outside
the Eastern sphere would continue to be very high.

II

Portrait of Greece

THE Greeks ought by rights to be a nation of calm clear-sighted people with candid simple minds. Then they would match the lucidity of air and sky and colour, the bare sharp lines of the mountains and hills, the clarity of the sea.

Perhaps some of the shepherds and goatherds and peasants are men of that kind. But most of the townspeople and a good many of the villagers, however poor, look somehow ironically knowledgeable, sceptical, oddly sophisticated, often disillusioned, unyouthful. They seem argumentative, indirect in their thinking, changeable, spasmodically violent. Yet many have charm and rapid intelligence. The Greeks are more quick-witted and versatile and subtle than other people in the Balkans. Even though many till the land, as a whole the Greeks lack the solid peasant virtues; instead they have the sharpness and flexibility of seafarers and traders. Their curse is their lack of stability and common plodding endurance. If they were more weighed down by plain stupidity they might have more ballast.

These people live, apparently unnoticing, in a country so lovely that nearly every foreigner feels a weary sense of flatness when he first leaves it. Almost all of Greece is beautiful. But it has many differences within itself.

The Peloponnese, Attica, Euboea, the gulf of Corinth, all the coast and the islands, are of the Eastern Mediterranean. But the mountains and plains of Central and Northern Greece, especially inland from the sea, have more of the roughness and wildness of the Balkans. They merge into the mountains of Albania, Yugoslav Macedonia and Bulgaria. There is a continuity as well as a contrast between Greece and the rest of the Balkans.

Athens, the political, social, intellectual and financial heart of Greece, is at once more Western and more Oriental than the other Balkan capitals. In its administrative, upper-class residential and wealthier commercial quarters, it is more spacious, more sophisticated, more Western. Here Athens has something of a south German town, even of Southern France. In its poorer residential and trading quarters, in its great sprawling haphazard workers' suburbs, it is more nearly oriental, and has touches of old Istanbul. A lot of the charm of Athens lies in its sharp contrasts.

Athens is poised on the long gentle slopes between the mountains of Attica and the sea. It is guarded by three bare ridges, two of them rising in long smooth curves. On the one side is Pentelicon, scarred with old quarries from which much of Athens was built. On the other side is the naked mass of Hymettus, once wooded; now there are one or two villages lying in small clusters of trees in the folds of the slopes. Behind Athens, more remote and lofty, Parnes rises, sharp and angular.

Hymettus, where there are still sweet herbs for the bees that make the honey, changes during the day. In the morning it is a bright rusty brown in the deep yellow of the early sunshine. In the evening, as the sun sets, it changes from soft camel-colour to shadowy violet and purple.

Set against the hills, Athens looks out to the sea, shining five miles away beyond the Piraeus and Phaleron, with small steeply-curved islands, sharp as shark's fins or dolphins, breaking out of the blue or grey or silver of the water.

Through the 'western' part of the city runs the Boulevard of Queen Sophia, with its row of flower-shops, its grey feathery pepper trees, its legation and embassy buildings and government offices set in walled gardens like pretentious villas. Then there is Constitution Square with its mimosa trees and flowering shrubs and little red-painted café tables, its smart 'dancings' and sweet-shops and hotels; there is the Hotel Grande Bretagne, once elegant and comfortable, made dreary after the liberation by British military administration; the royal palace, of agreeable but undistinguished south German classical style; the Zappeion Gardens, with their palm trees and green dank pools and climbing roses and honeysuckle and dusty paths and broken seats and unkempt grass and perambulators and children; the dull pseudo-classical university buildings; the heavy modern department stores and the expensive shops and cafés of Churchill Street.

Even this part of Athens is not altogether Western. There are—or were under the British occupation—the swarms of black-eyed impudent little boys peddling British and American cigarettes and chewing-gum and toothpaste, as well as shoelaces and ribbons and pocket-mirrors and combs. There are the melancholy, moaning, professional beggars, loquacious old men, boys, girls with filthy babies, children, one silent, angry, small boy with two short stumps for arms; many wear scraps of old British battledress. There are the sellers of popcorn, sweets and sickly-coloured drinks, the small dark shops where they sell sour milk and Turkish-type cakes soused in honey. There is the turbulent traffic of screaming and clanging trams, dashing cars and lorries with shrieking brakes violently jammed on. The centre of Athens is noisy, restless, nervous, except for the well-dressed, middle-aged men with carnations in their buttonholes, the smart women in 'Kolinaki' hats, who sit unconcerned and complacent, idle, staring and chatting, at the small outdoor café tables.

Kolinaki is the wealthy residential quarter lying behind the Boulevard of Queen Sophia, where there are quiet shaded streets, comfortable villas set in small discreet gardens of semi-tropical trees and shrubs, a few blocks of smart modern flats. The richer Athenians, merchants and bankers and politicians and unusually successful professional men— mostly royalists, almost all violently anti-Communist—live in Kolinaki. During the civil war they lived in peril, almost in a state of siege, and they have not forgotten it.

The 'oriental' parts of Athens are in curious and sudden contrast. Hermes Street starts from Constitution Square as a respectable shopping street and ends in the atmosphere of a bazaar, with rugs and carpet-slippers and copper pans hung out to catch the passer-by. It leads into Plaka, the quarter lying under the steep northern slope of the Acropolis. Plaka is all small twisting streets and alleyways, some so steep that there are flights of steps; tiny squares where there are beds of gay flowers or perhaps a tiny old brown Orthodox church. There are small flat-roofed houses of the old-fashioned Turkish style, a few with minute gardens shut in by high stone walls. Looking down on the flat roofs from the Acropolis, you can see family parties sitting sunning themselves on hard wooden chairs, babies sleeping, lines of washing hung out to dry, cats stalking other cats, cats asleep, perhaps a young man playing a guitar and singing.

The poorer commercial districts of Athens, and the grey shapeless streets of the Piraeus, are more modern but have the squalid dreariness of an Eastern Mediterranean port. Then there are the workers' suburbs, lying on the lower slopes between Athens and the sea, strange ram-shackle rambling places. There are practically no built-up roads, only rough, sandy, grassy tracks. Goats, sheep and hens stray around. Houses are often no more than rough, tiny, wooden shacks, run up to shelter the refugees that flooded in from Asia Minor after 1923. There are a very few gaunt tenement buildings, stranded in the jumble of shacks. In the slightly better quarters there are modest flat-roofed villas set in small arid gardens, dumped down haphazardly and without plan; during the occupation, Jews, resistance men, a few British officers, took refuge here and lived 'underground'—although living underground might mean lying and sun-bathing on the roof, screened only by the low parapet. There are a number of new large ugly Orthodox churches, considerably more small bars and cafés, very few shops, practically no cinemas.

These poorer workers' districts are still mainly Communist strong-holds, just as they were anti-German strongholds during the occupation and 'rebel' strongholds during the civil war. Young thugs of the Right-wing semi-fascist organisations sometimes make raids in order to chalk up their royalist, anti-Communist anti-Slav slogans, or even to beat up a few Communists if they are particularly daring. But usually the people living in these districts lead their own lives apart, pleasantly enough though in poverty. Families sit and sun themselves outside the door of the house; the men meet at the little shack-like bars and sit and talk in the sun; sturdy-legged sunburnt children, raggedly dressed, play and brawl in the dust and sand and on the wasteland.

There is great vitality in them all, if also great bitterness towards the rich, the police, the Greek troops garrisoned in the neighbourhood, and the British.

For the outsider, the typical Greek is the man of the city or the town. Even the small remote country towns, with their cobbled streets and sleepy tumble-down look, have plenty of cafés and eating-places which often stay open until midnight; they have a talkative, argumentative liveliness which seems more characteristically Greek than the life of the countryside.

Out in the country life can be strangely isolated and primitive, once you are away from the highways. There are villages of little rough stone houses. Often there is the big village plane-tree, with its smooth chequered bark, throwing its cool chequered shade over a pond or stream. Usually there is the village *taverna*, the inn, with wooden benches set outside the door and more benches inside on the bare wood floor; in the more prosperous districts there are big copper pans of rich-smelling stew and vegetables on the stove, and on the counter bowls of eggs and big dishes of sour milk stood out to set.

There are great differences in the countryside of Greece. Peloponnese, although its countrypeople are supposed to be among the most backward and narrow of the Greeks, has a gentle delicate look. Ruins of mediæval castles or forts are perched on oddly-shaped rocky hills jutting suddenly out of the plain. In early summer there are judas-trees in purple flower, masses of poppies, big white daisies and scabious; the early wheat and the young vine-shoots are very green. Near the Gulf of Corinth there are grey-green olive groves and flowering fruit trees.

North of the Gulf of Corinth the country changes. The mountains rise higher and steeper and wilder. There is snow on the long distant ridges of Parnassus, often hidden in cloud. The valleys are deep, often wooded; there are sudden rocky gorges. The country seems more savage, less gay and gentle.

North again, the big flat plain of Thessaly, ringed around with mountains, is bare, shadeless, and seems endless when the midday sun makes a heat haze.

Further north again, Macedonia is mostly bare, rocky, lonely and dry, apart from the few stony rivers and the curious deep green lakes; but there are clouds and rain and mist, and the air is no longer clear and light as in the rest of Greece. There are strange birds with blue-green or powdery-blue wings. In the north-west, Epirus has beech-woods and oaks and pinewoods; the meadows in early summer are a soft living mosaic of small flowers, blue, yellow, red, purple and pink.

Macedonia and Epirus are the link between Mediterranean Greece and the rest of the Balkans. They have, or have had, their un-Greek minorities. Epirus has had its Albanians—their total is hopelessly disputed, but there were perhaps around 15,000—living to the south of the Albanian border, just as there has been a Greek minority living over the border in the southern tip of Albania.

In the summer of 1946, however, it seemed that the Albanian minority had somehow mysteriously vanished from Greek Epirus. The new Albanian government of Enver Hoxha said that they had been brutally persecuted and driven out by the 'monarcho-fascist' Greeks and the Zervas bands. If you asked the Greeks of Jannina, the main town of Epirus, what had happened to the Albanians, they at first looked innocently blank. 'Albanians, what Albanians?' they said. 'Oh well, the Albanians—they collaborated first with the Italians and then with the Germans. They persecuted the Greeks of Epirus and when the Germans were retreating they got frightened. They had a bad conscience. So they fled with the Germans—all of them. There are none left now. We are all Greeks here.'

So they all seemed to be, and intensely nationalist Greeks too. Their nationalism was sharpened and embittered by the Greek refugees who were steadily trickling in from Albania.

Unbiassed observers in Albania always reported that the Hoxha régime did not in any way persecute the Greek minority as such, but gave it full minority rights—schools and local representation—provided that its members followed the régime's political line loyally. Some of the Greeks were therefore well enough off in the new Albania. But a good many had always been anti-Albanian and now were also anti-Communist and showed their views. They suffered accordingly. The Greeks of Jannina said that 8,000 had fled from Albania to Greece during 1945 and the first half of 1946, most of them 'illegally'.

There was one particular group that had been hard hit. These were the Greeks, living for many years in the small towns of South Albania, who had for one reason or another always kept Greek citizenship. Early in 1946, according to the Greek account, the Albanian government had suddenly decided to expel them. They were turned out at very short notice and, they said, were allowed to take with them only the barest personal possessions. A watchmaker complained that he had not been allowed to take the tools of his craft. All these Greeks gathered in Janinna and the neighbourhood, and they made the feeling of the Greeks of Epirus even more violent against the Albanians.

A body called the 'Association of Northern Epirus' had its head-quarters in Janinna. It was run by local business and professional men, all fervent nationalists. Their most urgent job was to look after the refugees, which they did fairly well with the help of UNRRA and the Greek Red Cross. But they were much more interested in the political task of getting 'Northern Epirus'—that is, Southern Albania, possibly up to the River Skumbi—for Greece, and avenging the real or fancied wrongs of the Greek minority, which, they fantastically claimed, numbered 240,000—a figure probably five times too large.

The Association ran an extremely polemical anti-Albanian newspaper called *Boreios Epiros*, which told tales of killing, imprisonment and persecution of Greeks in Southern Albania, particularly the main town, Argyrokastro.

Its members whispered that they had good underground lines of contact over the border into Albania, and got plenty of information from the other side. More openly they boasted that—if only the Athens government would let them—they could 'easily' march over the frontier and seize all 'Northern Epirus' by force for Greece. If the Albanians had their informers in Janinna, who reported this kind of boasting, it was no wonder that there was so warlike an atmosphere on the Greek-Albanian frontier.

Janinna itself, a little town full of faded oriental charm, with crumbling minarets and the ruins of a Turkish mosque and fort and baths and bazaar, set on a headland running out into a deep hill-ringed lake, had the atmosphere of a frontier town. There was a relatively big Greek Army garrison. The barracks were well guarded. For a stranger to go up to the border, he had to get a special military permit from the garrison commander, who after many formalities gave it with warnings of Albanian ferocity and stray shots over the frontier.

The frontier post on the highroad leading, in peaceful times, from Janinna to Argyrokastro lay on a low mountain pass among flowery mountain meadows. The Greek frontier guards, all armed—except for those who were kneading bread in a wooden trough—pointed out the peasants tilling the fields on the slopes and in the valley below, some on the Greek side, some on the Albanian side. It was a risky life for them, according to the guards: it was dangerous to stray a foot over the line marked out by white frontier stones. The guards told the story of a Greek shepherd who had crossed a little way to bring back a strayed sheep: he was shot dead by the Albanians, and when his brother went to look for him, he was killed too.

Over the frontier, a few miles away, the black jagged mountains of Albania reared up into the sky. On the hillside just facing the Greek post, white stones, neatly ranged, spelt out Albanian slogans: 'Long Live Enver Hoxha', 'Long Live the People's Republic of Albania'. Big five-pointed red stars were scarred in the earth. The Albanian frontier guards wore high boots and greenish-khaki stiff-looking uniforms of the new Yugoslav type, with red stars on their caps. They did not like being stared at. At the sight of a camera they retired coyly behind their guardhouse or behind bushes up the mountainside.

The Greeks said that they and the Albanian guards never talked nor passed the time of day with one another, hardly even when travellers crossed the frontier. Travellers were very rare, practically all foreign officials. Apart from the warlike feelings between Greeks and Albanians, it was almost impossible to get an Albanian entry permit.

The lonely mountain frontier post divided not only two small Balkan countries but also two worlds—the East and the West.

Further east, in Macedonia, south of the Yugoslav frontier, the district around Florina and Kastoria also had, as early as the summer of 1946, a tense and threatened frontier atmosphere. The people of Kastoria, a lovely old town standing, rather like Janinna, on a headland running out into a dark green, hill-ringed lake, were frightened: first of the Communists, then of the 'Slavophones', or Slav-speaking Macedonian minority, and then of the supposed threat from over the Yugoslav frontier. There were a good many 'Slav villages' around Kastoria; Greek schoolmasters, mayors or police officials sent to these villages were, they said in Kastoria, in great danger. Already some had been killed or had vanished. The Slavs and Communists were forming armed bands which were threatening decent Greeks.

The 'Slavophone' menace was both new and old. It recalled to the Greeks of Kastoria the old violent three-sided feuds between Greeks, Serbs and Bulgars that had torn Macedonia before the Balkan War in 1912, and even later. But after the 1914-18 war there had been an exchange of populations between Greece and her Slav neighbours. The 'Slavophones' who stayed in Greece were people who themselves chose to stay. According to reasonable neutral estimates, they numbered somewhere between 80,000 and 120,000. They were nearly all simple and uneducated peasants, speaking their own Macedonian Slav dialects, who did not want to leave their land. Up till the second world war, they seemed relatively contented, although the Greek authorities were anxious to absorb them as full Greeks and to prevent them from developing any sort of Slav culture. But the war, the German-Bulgarian occupation of Northern Greece, and the growth of armed bands and partisan movements, unsettled them and revived old pro-Slav, anti-Greek feelings among them.

In the later part of the war there was formed among them, on Communist initiative, a Left-wing resistance organisation called S.N.O.F.—meaning the Slav People's Liberation Front—which was linked, over the Yugoslav frontier, with the Macedonian branch of Tito's National Liberation Movement, and on the Greek side with E.A.M./E.L.A.S.

The revival of Slav feeling among the minority, which was now inspired to claim cultural and national rights and was suspected of wishing to join Greek Macedonia to Yugoslav Macedonia, shocked and frightened the non-Communist Greeks of the region. After Greece was liberated, E.A.M. officially disowned any connection with S.N.O.F., because it lost too much prestige by backing Slavs.

Marshal Tito and his Yugoslav Macedonian representatives were for a time left as the only open and outspoken patrons and protectors of the Slav minority of Greek Macedonia. They did the job with a great deal of noise. From 1945 onwards the Belgrade and Skoplje newspapers—echoed by the press of Fatherland Front Bulgaria—broke out periodically into bursts of horror stories about Greek 'monarchofascist' persecution of the Slav minority and about the influx of Slav refugees driven from Greece over the borders into Yugoslavia and Bulgaria. (According to a standard Soviet official figure, 30,000 fled from Greece.) It was certain that after the civil war of winter 1944-45 several thousand people fled from Greece over the frontiers; but probably many of these were not really Slavophones, but were ordinary Greek Communists afraid of reprisals.

Behind the scenes, the Greek Communist Party in Macedonia throughout kept up discreet contacts with the Slav minority leaders, just as they kept up their links with the Yugoslav Communists. This combination of circumstances made Macedonia the particular stronghold of the Greek Communists. It was mainly in Macedonia that late in 1946 'General' Markos Vefiades developed his new guerilla forces, linked with the Greek Communist Party headquarters and discreetly helped by the Yugoslav Macedonians over the border.

This did not mean that Markos's guerilla movement was primarily Slav. It was not limited to Macedonia but was also strong in Thessaly. It was essentially Greek and was in part a natural reaction to the first months of unintelligent and autocratic and sometimes brutal rule of the Greek royalists. But it was helped by the special conditions in Greek Macedonia—a newly aroused Slav minority and a Yugoslav frontier friendly to the guerillas.

For the average non-Communist Greek these special circumstances, even before the Markos 'rebellion', combined to swell out the old bogey of the 'red Slav menace' to gigantic and terrifying size.

The Greeks as a whole detested and despised the Albanians, feared and mistrusted the Yugoslavs, but hated the Bulgarians more than all. Their hate was a blind deep-rooted feeling, grown from old historic rivalries and jealousies, natural temperamental antagonism, and three recent experiences of Bulgarian military occupation within thirty years.

Very soon after the second world war, the average Greek felt quite kindly towards the Italians, in spite of the humiliations of the Italian occupation, and quickly forgot the Germans in spite of the burnings, executions and reprisals of the German occupation. But they could forget nothing of the Bulgarian occupation of Eastern Macedonia and Thrace, and allowed the memory to become a sore that spread and festered.

Because after September, 1944, there was a new pro-Communist régime in Bulgaria, it was easy for the Greeks to identify the Bulgarians and the Communists as hateful objects. During the civil war days, in the heart of Athens, it was enough for a man to have the word 'Bulgarian' hurled after him in the street for bystanders to set on him and beat him up, perhaps kill him. Even after the civil war, to call a Greek 'Bulgarian' was a violent form of abuse.

For a foreigner to admit that he saw any good in the Bulgarians was folly. To argue, however mildly, against Greece's territorial claims on Bulgaria was an almost unforgiveable social blunder. To mention Bulgaria's claim to an outlet on the Greek Aegean, except to denounce it as treacherous impudence, was to damn yourself utterly.

This feeling against Bulgaria was roughly the same all over Greece, and was not limited to the border area or the north. It was perhaps even more virulent in Athens—where there must have been plenty of people who had never seen a Bulgarian—than elsewhere.

The Greek-Bulgarian frontier, like the Greek-Albanian frontier, was an almost impassable barrier between two worlds, East and West. Serres, the ugly little garrison town guarding the main road from Salonika to the border and to Sofia, was full of troops. In 1946 there were a good many British troops as well as the Greek garrison. During the war the Germans and Bulgarians had started extending a normal-gauge railway across the border from Bulgaria towards Serres and Salonika; but after the liberation the Greeks stopped all work and grass and flowers grew up on the newly built track. There was also an older narrow-gauge line running over the frontier. On the Greek side, by 1946, the rails had grown rusty and poppies were growing between them.

The frontier post at Kula was a little wooden bridge over a shallow stream swirling down from the mountains to flow, about a mile away, into the Struma, or Strymon, the turbulent rusty-brown river from Bulgaria, overhung with willows and aspens and thick bushes.

On the Greek side, there were water-meadows with deep lush grass. In the evenings of early summer hundreds of frogs croaked harshly and throatily. The Greek frontier post was made up of one small building housing a handful of troops and a couple of stone cottages, one of which was the customs and passport office. There were also a couple of ruined houses, devastated by the Germans or Bulgarians during the war. A tribe of cats and kittens roamed around; the guards treated them affectionately. A dark-haired young peasant woman in black did the cooking and hung out the washing.

The Greeks nominally wore British battledress; most of them lounged around with shirts wide open, some were unshaved. They led an isolated carefree life, little troubled by instructions or inspection by higher Greek authorities in the interior. The passport official was a gentle charming young man with rimless spectacles from the Peloponnese who might have been a country schoolmaster. He spent most of his time drinking Turkish coffee and studying an illustrated English grammar. He particularly enjoyed one conversation in the grammar which ran something like this: 'Do they drink coffee in England?' 'Yes, but English coffee is very bad. In Turkey and in France the coffee is very good, but in England it is undrinkable.' This seemed to him a great joke.

Behind his gentleness he was a fervent monarchist, like the rest of his comrades. He mildly blamed the English for having 'kept the King away from Greece' for so long. As for his Bulgarian opposite numbers on the other side of the frontier stream, he said he never spoke to them if he could help it, and would be happier if he could not even see them. Laughing merrily, he said: 'Once, about twenty years ago, one of our generals with a small private Greek force made an expedition over this bridge and about twenty miles into Bulgarian territory. The Bulgarians couldn't stop them. But the Greek government had to disown them and pay a big cash indemnity to the Bulgarian government.'

He added mildly and jokingly, but with some underlying seriousness: 'Soon perhaps we will do the same thing again, only this time we will go further, and we will stay.'

But in the spring and summer of 1946, everything outwardly seemed placid and peaceful at the little bridge. Very rarely there was a warlike touch. If British units in the Serres area were holding exercises, a small convoy of British armoured cars with signals equipment might roar up to the Greek side of the bridge, stare across to the forbidden territory on the other side of the 'iron curtain' fifteen feet away. The Bulgarian guards on the far side would run out agitatedly in a body and stare back. Then the British would roar off again. No Russians ever came to the Bulgarian side of the bridge, to peer across into the Western sphere.

The Bulgarian guards were more smartly uniformed, striding about in their high leather boots, and looked more brisk, soldierly and business-like than the casual easy Greeks. Their frontier officials were brusque, exasperatingly thorough and meticulous and slow, sometimes deliberately obstructive, and were apt to treat anyone crossing the frontier as a highly suspicious character. It was up to the traveller to prove his innocence of espionage, currency smuggling and contraband in food-stuffs. Any doubtful point—and there were usually many of them—had to be referred over a highly erratic telephone system to Sofia, to the Bulgarian War Office or Ministry of the Interior, or to the Allied (Soviet) Control Commission.

But once a traveller had cleared himself, the Bulgarians could be kindly and helpful and even mildly, though unrelentingly, apologetic for their strictness. They would turn out and carry the traveller's luggage over half a mile to the nearest railway station and lend money for train fares, while the more educated officials talked largely and enthusiastically about international friendship and the brotherhood of all humanity.

Delivering a traveller from one side of the frontier to the other was a solemn little ceremony. The senior Bulgarian official—if the traveller came from his side—would send a soldier to the middle of the bridge to ask a Greek soldier to bring up the senior Greek official. The two officials met in the middle of the rickety little bridge, by the frontier pole, saluted, and shook hands formally and unsmilingly. The traveller's papers and luggage were handed over. At last after more ceremonial hand-shaking the traveller himself was allowed to cross. The handshake seemed clearly to be no more than a momentary truce, to prevent two opponents from stabbing or shooting one another.

Yet, very rarely, the Greeks and Bulgarians unbent. Once a cormorant, which had somehow made its way inland, suddenly squatted on a small sand-spit in the middle of the frontier stream, and started to sick up the fish he had just caught. There was a rush of Bulgarians and Greeks from both sides. The guards quickly unslung their rifles. After hurried shouts across the water, a Bulgarian was told to fire first. He missed the cormorant which flapped casually a few feet further upstream and settled down again. From both banks soldiers waded into the stream up to their thighs, then their waists, apparently hoping to to grab the fish-glutted bird with their hands. Bulgarian and Greek guards gathered on the bridge and talked excitedly and egged on the would-be hunters. The cormorant scorned them all. He did not even bother to fly away.

But the Bulgarians and Greeks had been roused and broke into lively discussion of fishing, mainly in Greek. The Bulgarians would spread nets in the stream at night, since the stream was theirs up to the Greek bank, and then in the morning the two sides would share out the haul.

Yet after a few minutes, the formal chill fell again. The guards drifted off, a little shamefaced, away from the bridge, to more hours and weeks and months of boredom and suspicion and hate.

The post-war barrier between Greece and her northern neighbours would not have existed if British troops had not landed in 1944 and prevented E.A.M. from taking power.

The barrier was not altogether a new one; what was new was its height and impenetrability, now that it was not only a frontier between Greece and the rest of the Balkans but also a frontier between the Western sphere and the Eastern sphere.

Apart from the Balkan alliance against the Turks in the early days of the Balkan wars in 1912, the Greeks had never liked or trusted the Bulgarians or the Yugoslavs or Albanians. Even if their particular enemies were the Bulgarians, they cared little enough for their supposed allies, the Serbs or Yugoslavs who, they thought, were insecure guardians of the Monastir Gap, traditional road into Greece for invaders from the North—including the Germans in 1941. There was also the long-standing suspicion that the Yugoslavs wanted Salonika, and would sooner or later accept it as a bribe from one of the greater enemies of Greece.

The Greeks bitterly resented the tiny independent Albania which was created just before, and consolidated after, the 1914-18 war, because it was allowed to keep territory where Greek-speaking members of the Orthodox Church were living, and because it could always be used by a bigger country as a springboard for invasion of Greece. Between the two wars the idea of partitioning Albania between Greece and Yugoslavia was often discussed unofficially. But nothing was done: Albania became a member of the League of Nations. Then in March, 1939, Italy invaded Albania. The Greeks chose to believe that the Albanians had willingly accepted Italian rule and that their worst fears were realised. When Mussolini launched his attack on Greece from Albania in 1940, the Greeks equally chose to believe that all Albanians were fighting alongside the Fascists. They felt all their earlier resentment at independent Albania was justified. They showed what they hoped when, after counter-attacking and entering the southern Albanian town of Koritsa, they flew Greek flags everywhere in the town.

So for over a generation the general tendency had been for Greece to turn her back on her northern neighbours and to look out into the Mediterranean and towards the West. She was linked with the Mediterranean and the West by her merchant shipping, her traders, and by many thousands of Greeks who had settled in Alexandria and other Mediterranean ports and later in the United States, and who up till the war had sent big remittances home to Greece.

When Greece was liberated in 1944, it would have been hard work to turn most Greeks to friendship with their northern neighbours. But an E.A.M. government, ideologically and politically linked with the new pro-Soviet régimes in Yugoslavia, Bulgaria and Albania, would certainly have forced such a conciliation on the Greeks, however unpopular it might have been at first.

Economically, Greece would have had few positive gains from friendship with the rest of the Balkans during the early post-war years. Her neighbours were too poor and too war-stricken to be able to send her grain and meat and eggs. Russia might have sent her small gifts of wheat from political motives, but not enough to feed her people. But negatively Greece would have been spared certain serious evils. An E.A.M. government, backed up by the pro-Soviet régimes to the north, would have been harsh and oppressive but would have permitted no effective resistance to the administration or to economic discipline. No large-scale guerilla movement could have grown up to disrupt recovery. Such resistance as there might have been could have got no support from the northern neighbours and sought no shelter from them. So Greece would have gained in political and economic stability; and as in 1947 the pro-Soviet Balkan régimes set out on their slow difficult path of economic reconstruction, Greece might have had a frugal but secure share in the general recovery.

On the other hand, Greece would have suffered greater loss than any of the other Balkan countries through being cut off from the West, since she had always been much more dependent economically on contact with the outside world than the more agricultural and therefore more self-sufficient countries to the north. An E.A.M. Greece would presumably have forfeited British and United States aid and relief, and would perhaps have had a considerably smaller slice of UNRRA largesse. There might have been two or three years of near-famine. But at the same time an E.A.M. government might have enforced much fairer distribution of supplies, and might also, using the same stern methods as the pro-Soviet Balkan governments, have made a far more serious start on material reconstruction, than any Greek government ever attempted under British occupation.

Any attempt to draw up a hypothetical balance of gain and loss is, however, unreal. For Greece the choice between West and East is particularly difficult. Greece belongs to both. To cut landward Greece off from the rest of the Balkans and make her a Western strategic outpost against the East is artificial and must end in disaster for Greece. To cut seafaring Greece off from the Mediterranean and the West is equally artificial and means long-term impoverishment, together with the danger of serving as an Eastern strategic outpost against the West.

Greece, to survive as an independent country, needs a firm and lasting compromise both in her international relations and in her internal politics. Yet the Greeks more than most Europeans are the enemies of serious compromise, and like to swing from one passionate extreme to another. Over their heads the big Powers of East and West have quarrelled particularly uncompromisingly. In the post-war years Greece has lost more and more of her independence and become more and more a plaything of outside forces. By 1947 it was clear that no royalist government could survive without strong outside support from the West. Equally, if any E.A.M. or Communist government were to seize power, it could not survive without strong outside support from Greece's Balkan neighbours and strong political and moral backing from Russia.

The Greek people seemed, after the liberation, to have lost their sense of union and self-preservation. Under British occupation they had a good deal better chance of saving some sort of independence and balance than Bulgaria or Rumania had under Soviet occupation. But the Greeks threw this chance away. They have to share responsibility for the consequences with the big Powers of East and West.

12

Trieste: West-East Frontier Post

TRIESTE has, since the closing stages of the war when the Western Powers and Russia started manœuvring for strategic vantage points throughout Europe, been one of the most sensitive points of contact and conflict between East and West. In the summer of 1945, it seemed even more likely than the Dardanelles to be the cause of an open clash. The clash was averted. A year later a compromise formula was found by the big Powers. This in theory made Trieste into a sort of no-man's land and meeting-place between East and West. But when in the following months American and British soldiers made baton charges into crowds of sullen, angry, disciplined Slavs and Communists, in the heart of Trieste, or when Slavs retaliated with stones and hand-grenades, it was hard to believe that the compromise was anything but an uneasy truce, leaving the real struggle for Trieste to be fought out later.

During the disputes and haggling between East and West in 1945 and 1946, Trieste came to be lent a quite inflated strategic and economic importance by both sides. In the West people believed that, if Tito's Yugoslavia were allowed to annex the city, then Yugoslavia would master the Adriatic, Russia would use this mastery for political penetration of the Mediterranean, and Italy would fall into Communist hands. Some with even more lively imaginations foresaw a fleet of Russian warships, based on Trieste, disputing Anglo-American naval control of the Mediterranean.

In the East, responsible people appeared to believe that the Anglo-Americans, if Trieste fell into their hands, would use it as a base for the penetration of the 'democratic' or pro-Soviet countries of the Balkans and Central Europe by selfish and imperialist economic interests and monopolies, and that Western political penetration and intrigues, aimed at overthrowing the new 'Eastern' governments, would go hand in hand with economic exploitation. Trieste would become an Anglo-American 'colony' and starting-point for a network of espionage and subversive action reaching out far into the Soviet sphere.

Whether, in fact, the top men on either side ever really conceived such ambitious plans for Trieste, outsiders obviously could not tell. What they could see quite clearly was that in practice Trieste was incapable of playing such a big rôle in either Western or Eastern politico-economic strategy. Neither as a port nor as a naval base nor as a keypoint in communications with the Balkans and Central Europe was Trieste equipped for great things. If the big Powers should ever decide to fight over Trieste, they would be fighting over a mirage. Meanwhile, by their somewhat unreal attempts at compromise they seemed more likely to kill Trieste economically than to develop it for the good of the rest of Europe.

Inside the 'Trieste Free Territory'—created by this unreal compromise—there would always be the seeds of civil war. The 'Westerners' —the mass of non-Communist Italians and a handful of anti-Communist Slavs—and the 'Easterners'—the mass of the Slavs and the Communist or pro-Communist Italians—would always watch each other nervously and suspiciously. Each side would live in fear of an armed coup of some kind, with outside backing, by the other, and would make its own counter-preparations in advance. Each would seek to gain any possible political or economic advantage over the other. Chances of a settled life or constructive work seemed small.

Trieste, in the last phase of the war, was the object of the most undignified scramble between rival Allied forces that took place anywhere in Europe. Elsewhere a demarcation line between East and West, limiting the advance of the Russian and Anglo-American Armies, had been agreed beforehand. Over Venezia Giulia, or Julijska Krajina—the inter-war Italian frontier province of which Trieste was the centre—it was soon clear that no precise agreement had been reached.

The British and Americans knew well that Yugoslavia's claim to part at least of Venezia Giulia was an old one, and was neither the invention of Marshal Tito's régime nor a purely Moscow-prompted element of Soviet strategy. The claim had been raised by the new-created Yugoslavia at the 1919 Peace Conference, when Venezia Giulia was one of the fragments of the Austro-Hungarian Empire which had to be awarded to a new owner. At that time the new Yugoslavia was much weaker than victorious Italy, who could moreover produce a trump card in the secret wartime London Agreement by which Britain pledged most of the eastern border of the Adriatic Sea to Italy. The Yugoslavs quickly had to yield up Trieste itself to Italy, although the struggle over the more southerly port of Fiume trailed on until settled to Yugoslavia's disadvantage by direct Italian-Yugoslav negotiations in 1924.

The official Yugoslav claim to Venezia Giulia then lapsed. But the Slovene patriots of Trieste and the area—mostly lawyers, teachers and professional men—kept up the fight on a local basis, against great odds and in the face of steadily increasing persecution under the Italian Fascist régime.

The Italians forbade all manifestations of Slav language, culture or

o

national feeling. They tried to de-nationalise the Slovenes and Croats—
the Yugoslavs of northern and southern Venezia Giulia respectively—
as thoroughly as possible and to make them good Italians. Many of the
leaders of Slav resistance were arrested, tried, imprisoned, deported or
shot. Others left Trieste for Yugoslavia and settled there, trying to keep
alive the Yugoslav demand for Trieste. But the inter-war governments
of Yugoslavia, though they received the exiles kindly, were not ready to
offend powerful Fascist Italy.

In the early spring of 1941, as Hitler began moving south-east, it
grew clear that Yugoslavia was bound to become involved in war,
either with or against Italy and Germany. Britain suddenly took a lively
interest in the Balkans. The British Government did not pledge Venezia
Giulia to Yugoslavia; but it seems that some sort of mild assurance was
given that the Yugoslav claim would at least be reconsidered by the
victorious Allies at the next peace conference. This assurance was
exploited to the full by successive Royal Yugoslav governments in exile
in Cairo or London between 1941 and 1944. When Tito founded his
rival régime inside Yugoslavia and gradually developed his political
programme, he also naturally put forward a strong claim to Trieste.

When in 1941 Yugoslavia was invaded and dismembered by the
Germans, Italians, Hungarians and Bulgarians, Italy seized the Dal-
matian coast and part of Slovenia, set up a puppet kingdom of Croatia
under an absentee Italian King, Aimone, Duke of Spoleto, and claimed
a kind of overlordship over Montenegro. The Italian occupation forces
reacted violently and brutally to all resistance in these areas. But they
tempered violence with the macchiavellian tactics of employing certain
groups of Yugoslavs to persecute or fight against other groups: at first
Croat nationalists against Serb nationalists, later the anti-Communist
Chetniks against Tito's Communist-led Army of National Liberation.

The Yugoslavs in the Italian-occupied areas first learned to hate the
Italians more than ever before. Then, as Tito's partisan army grew
steadily stronger and managed to exploit the Italian capitulation of
September, 1943, to win temporary control of most of Dalmatia and
part of Venezia Giulia, they learned to despise the Italians as poor
fighters.

After the Italian surrender the high-level policy of Tito's army was
to enrol any Italians who were willing to fight the Germans and to
maintain a few Italian formations, such as the so-called Garibaldi
Division, within the Yugoslav Army of National Liberation. This policy
was expected to have particularly important results in Venezia Giulia,
where there was a big Italian population mixed in with the Slavs.

But it was never really successful. The lower ranks of Tito's army
could never overcome their instinctive dislike and contempt for the
Italians. The Italians on their side could never wholly trust the Yugoslavs, and few had much enthusiasm for fighting with anyone against
anybody. In Venezia Giulia the Italians particularly mistrusted the

Yugoslavs because of the old Yugoslav territorial claims. Apart from a handful of Communists, the few young Italians of Trieste who wanted to fight the Germans went off to the Venice or Padua areas or to the Osoppo to join Italian partisan groups.

So in the last months of the war the partisan groups which operated against the Germans in Venezia Giulia and even crossed into Udine province to the west were practically all formed of the Slovenes and Croats of Venezia Giulia, fighting under the supreme command of the Yugoslav Army of National Liberation. Most of them were fighting what was primarily a local nationalist struggle: to win Trieste and Gorizia and all Venezia Giulia as far west as the River Tagliamento for Yugoslavia. Their hour of triumph and their reward would come when they could march victoriously into Trieste and raise Tito's red star flag on the citadel.

But from the other side the British Eighth Army on the Italian front was pressing slowly and painfully up the east coast of Italy and was presumably planning to swoop through Venice eastwards to Trieste, in order to open a gateway into Austria from the south.

This was the position when Field Marshal Alexander, as Supreme Allied Commander Mediterranean, went to Belgrade to visit Marshal Tito, Prime Minister of the new Yugoslav government just recognised by Britain, early in 1945. His purpose was to get agreement on a demarcation line in Venezia Giulia, to be fixed beforehand between the Yugoslav forces advancing from the east and south and the Anglo-American forces advancing from the west in order to pinch out the Germans in the Trieste area.

Talks started between the two leaders on a military basis, in terms of requirements for a British advance into Austria. Ultimate territorial claims were left aside. But by this time the Venezia Giulia question had become part of the much wider question of delimiting the Eastern and Western spheres in a conquered or liberated Europe. Alexander's visit to Belgrade coincided roughly with the Yalta meeting of the Big Three. While definite agreement was obviously reached at Yalta, any agreement discussed in Belgrade appears—in spite of Alexander's later accusations against Tito—to have been left hanging in mid-air. In any case Tito believed that he had kept ample room for manoeuvre. In fact, the German collapse was quicker than could be foreseen at the time of the Belgrade meeting and Tito could claim that circumstances had changed.

In the last days of April, 1945, the crumbling of the German armies in the south came suddenly. The Eighth Army, headed by the New Zealanders under General Freyburg, raced along the Adriatic coast to reach Trieste from the west. But the Yugoslav IX Corps, converging on the city from south and east and north, got there first.

The Yugoslavs entered Trieste on April 30th and within two days held all the city except for one or two strong points where the German garrison was holding out in hope of surrendering to the British. It was not until May 2nd that New Zealand armoured cars drove in along the main highroad from Italy. They were greeted with noisy relief and joy by the frightened Italians, who thought they had come to save the city from the barbarous Slavs. Slovenes of Trieste never really forgave the New Zealanders because some of their vehicles were draped with Italian flags as they drove in. From the first days the feeling in Trieste was that the Anglo-Americans were the allies and protectors of the Italians against the Slavs.

For forty-five days the Yugoslavs remained in occupation of the city itself and the greater part of Venezia Giulia, while high-level negotiations went on to induce them to withdraw peacefully. On May 19th, Field Marshal Alexander issued a message to his troops which by implication accused Tito of bad faith and compared Yugoslav methods with Nazi methods. His words created great bitterness throughout Yugoslavia and strengthened the feeling that the British favoured their enemies, the Italians, above their allies, the Yugoslavs, who had made such big sacrifices during the war. But the British and United States Governments brought heavy pressure to bear on Marshal Tito, who got no open backing from Russia and had in the end to yield.

Agreement between the three governments was signed on June 9th. On June 12th the Yugoslav troops, boys and girls among them, marched out of Trieste in good order, singing their partisan songs. They withdrew behind the line which came to be known as the Morgan Line, circling round the city to the south and east and then running up north to the Austrian frontier. The Yugoslavs kept the bigger though economically less valuable part of Venezia Giulia, and with it strategic command of Trieste. But Trieste and its immediate surroundings, the shipbuilding town of Monfalcone to the west, and Gorizia, a mainly Italian market town in the hills to the northwest, together with a number of Slovene villages north and northwest of Trieste, were handed over to Anglo-American occupation. The old Austrian naval base of Pola, at the southern tip of the Istrian peninsula, was also handed over by the Yugoslavs, and became a tiny Anglo-American enclave linked with Trieste by an authorised high road running for about seventy miles through the Yugoslav occupation zone.

The Italians of Trieste were jubilant when the Yugoslavs left, and gradually recovered their nerve. Many of them were ardent Italian nationalists; many belonged to the middle-classes and owned property in one form or another. They had found occupation by 'Slavo-Communists' terrifying. The Yugoslav troops had been partly Slovene and Croat peasants from Venezia Giulia; but many had been Dalmatians or Bosnians—the toughest veterans of the Yugoslav partisan war, who had been through inhuman hardships. They were not likely to feel kindly towards the easy-living comfortable Triestini. The IX Corps gave stern orders against looting and unseemly behaviour and called for strictest discipline—particularly since British and New Zealand officers were watching in Trieste. But their men were mostly very young; and the Bosnian Moslems even to the Slovenes seemed strange wild men.

The Italians seem to have greatly magnified whatever looting did take place, which was probably very much less than might have been expected in the circumstances. A year later, there were very few stories about raping circulating in Trieste. But what frightened the Italians most was the big number of summary and arbitrary arrests carried out by the Yugoslavs, especially in Trieste itself. Anyone might be stopped in the street and asked brusquely for his identity papers: if these did not satisfy, he would be carried off and held by the Yugoslavs for a shorter or longer period. Other Triestini were simply removed from their homes and vanished. Soon rumours spread that the Yugoslavs were carrying out mass executions outside the city at night. Very few of these were ever verified, and most of the great 'foiba' scandals—discoveries of rotting corpses in the 'foibe' or deep clefts in the limestone uplands behind the city—fizzled out inconclusively. But it seems certain that around 3,000 or 4,000 Triestine citizens were found to have disappeared after the Yugoslavs left—though much higher figures were put around by the Italians—and very few ever turned up again.

On the Yugoslavs' side it must be said that for them Trieste had both before and during the war been a hot-bed of Fascism and the home of many whom they would consider war criminals. They knew or believed they knew that the Anglo-Americans were curiously lenient to Fascists and former Fascists; they had themselves stern ideas of justice. Also, for the Slovenes of Trieste area there must have been a number of particularly bitter personal grievances and wrongs committed by Italian petty officials and policemen and others, which they felt they were justified in paying off. Finally, there were at that moment in the Trieste area a big number of fugitives from Yugoslavia of one kind or another, who feared retribution for opposition to Tito's national liberation movement. These were men whom the Yugoslav authorities naturally wished to clean up.

But the Italians were not inclined to find any excuses for Yugoslav harshness and Yugoslav excesses. The wealthy and middle-classes in particular were filled with panic, indignation and resentment. They turned with a sigh of thankfulness to their new British and American governors who, they believed, had come to restore the old order and to hold back the Slav hordes from the East.

Some at least of the British and American officers of Allied Military Government started off in the summer of 1945 with the best intentions of strict impartiality and benevolence to all. A few even started with a prejudice in favour of the Yugoslavs and against the Italians. But most soon found it was very much easier to understand the Italian mentality and way of life than the Slav, or Slovene, mentality.

The Italians were easy-going, liked a comfortable pleasant life, and had most of the universal middle-class prejudices plus a certain gay tolerance and cynicism unusual in Anglo-Saxon countries. They were as a rule gratifyingly friendly and hospitable to the Anglo-Americans. They were perfectly ready to help in the task of administration and military government. Italian women were charming, well-dressed, sophisticated and amiable. At a later stage, certain Triestine business and private interests started trying to corrupt individual officers of Allied Military Government, but did so with sufficient man-of-the-world tact and delicacy to avoid giving offence. Sometimes their efforts were successful, and so drew tighter the bonds between Italians and Anglo-Americans.

The Slovenes on the other hand were nearly all suspicious, reserved, full of moral righteousness and a sense of moral grievance. They were suffering from a deep-rooted national and social inferiority complex, combined with a newly-won sense of superiority born of their resistance record against the Fascists and the Germans and of the successes of Tito's national liberation movement. Their leaders definitely discouraged fraternisation between Slovenes and British and American troops; few Slovene girls were willing to be friendly with the soldiers; the small Slovene middle-classes did not offer hospitality to the officers. Above all, the Slovenes would not collaborate in the work of Allied Military Government—or at least not on Anglo-American terms.

The task of setting up an efficient and popular local administration in the Anglo-American occupation zone was the most awkward one facing A.M.G. They found in existence two administrative machines: those relics of the old Italian Fascist administration which had survived under the German occupation following the Italian collapse in September, 1943; and the new Slovene administration set up by the partisan forces and the Yugoslav national liberation movement from the end of 1943 onwards.

Tito's partisans did the same thing in Venezia Giulia as in Yugoslavia. Wherever a district was temporarily liberated, they aimed at creating civil administrative bodies. As a political, and at first also a governing body, a 'Liberation Front' was set up for the Slovene Coastland—or northern part of Venezia Giulia—and for Istria—the Croat-inhabited southern part. These Liberation Fronts were linked with the overall Liberation Front of Yugoslavia, and sent delegates to attend national liberation movement conferences in Yugoslavia. Their leading members were either Communists or Slav nationalists, especially members of the old Slovene Liberal Party, together with a few non-party intellectuals. Most belonged to the small Slovene intelligentsia of Trieste, which had always been intensely active and intensely proud. Below the Liberation Fronts, the partisan forces set up liberation committees in all the Slovene villages that came under their control, while other liberation committees worked clandestinely in cities or areas that remained under German control.

During the war the main military task of these Fronts and committees was to 'mobilise the masses' to join or help the partisans. They also had the wider political task of 'educating the masses' in the ideas and aims, political, social and national, of the Yugoslav national liberation movement. They had in particular to find a synthesis between Communist ideas and strategy and the narrow burning nationalism of the non-Communist Slavs—the villagers were mostly devout Catholics, instinctively mistrustful of communism, while the leading townspeople were mostly Liberals, also dubious about Communism. For wartime purposes, at least, they found this synthesis in fervent Yugoslav nationalism, and established extraordinary unity and discipline. They also created the essential organs of local administration, based on 'people's committees', and in particular their own school system.

By the end of April, 1945, when the Germans collapsed, the Slavs already had a skeleton political and administrative organisation in being. This was used and developed by the Yugoslav Army authorities during the forty-five days. It was extended to Trieste itself. Here the P.N.O.O.—'Council of Liberation for the Slovene Coastland'—took power as executive counterpart to the older Liberation Front of the war period. It was, in fact, the government of the area, controlling lower administrative organs.

Under the Anglo-American-Yugoslav Agreement of June 9th, an undertaking was given that in the Anglo-American zone use would be made of any Yugoslav civil organisation which the Supreme Allied Commander Mediterranean considered to be working satisfactorily.

It took A.M.G. less than two months to decide that the existing Slav organs were not working satisfactorily. A.M.G. also declared that they were not representative—as in Trieste city they almost certainly were not. By Military Government Order No. 11, A.M.G. set out to set up their own system of local government. This split up the Anglo-American Zone into areas; each was to nominate an Area President to be responsible to A.M.G. At the head there was to be a Zone Council, to which the various political bodies, Slav and Italian, were to nominate representatives.

The Slovene leaders decided at this point not to co-operate with A.M.G. who, they felt, had acted in bad faith in refusing to recognise any of the existing Slav organs of administration. They also objected that they would not get fair representation on the Zone Council: all Slavs were united in a single organisation, and so could only get one representative, whereas there were six Italian parties all of which could claim representation.

So the Slovenes went into opposition to A.M.G.; and from August, 1945, onwards, their general strategy was to boycott, and where

practicable to obstruct, A.M.G. and its organs and orders. P.N.O.O.—
or later the almost identical political organisation, U.A.I.S., the 'Italian-
Slovene Anti-fascist Union'—remained in existence as a kind of shadow
government functioning independently of A.M.G. Many of the Slovene
villages in the Anglo-American Zone continued to be governed, in
practice although no longer in theory, by Slovene village committees,
taking their orders from P.N.O.O. and U.A.I.S. The Giulian Communist Party provided the cement holding the whole structure together
in opposition to A.M.G. The British and American officers came to
feel that the one aim of the Slovenes was to obstruct, irritate, annoy and
humiliate A.M.G.

The local government organs set up by A.M.G. remained almost
purely Italian. The few Slovenes who dared collaborate with A.M.G.
were regarded by most of their own people as outcasts, if not traitors,
and were threatened with popular justice. The A.M.G. organs remained
somewhat lifeless bodies, mainly advisory in their functions. They were
not even much respected by the Italians. They were not elected; and
they were probably not representative of the Italian population since
A.M.G., trying to take a middle way, had excluded extreme nationalist
elements. The President of the Zone Council, Engineer Gandusio,
though not a widely-known popular figure, was an intelligent far-seeing
man who was personally respected by leaders in all parties. Yet in
practical power he was not much more than a figurehead. All decisions
of any importance rested with A.M.G.

In so far as A.M.G. administration was effective, it was administration by British and American officers posted in Trieste and in the
smaller towns throughout the Zone, acting through locally recruited
A.M.G. employees. If the Supreme Allied Commander could claim
that the former Slovene administration was unrepresentative, the
Slovenes could equally claim that A.M.G. administration was 'unpopular' in the sense that it did not spring from the people.

Another deep grievance with the Slovenes was the legal system set up
by A.M.G.

A.M.G. held that, as an interim measure, the only just thing was to
adopt Italian law as existing previous to September 8th, 1943—the date
of the Italian capitulation. The Slovenes complained loudly that this
was Fascist law and should be abolished at once, to make way for a
more anti-fascist and 'popular' system of law. Italian lawyers, on the
other hand, said that in practice the Fascist régime had made relatively
few additions to the pre-fascist law of Liberal Italy, and that these
Fascist additions had been removed or suspended under A.M.G.
However, the Slovenes claimed that on principle it was an issue of deep
moral significance.

Another Slovene grievance was that Slovene had not been made
equal with Italian as the official language of the courts. This was a
matter of prestige rather than practical importance. All the Slovene

lawyers of Trieste could plead most eloquently in Italian, and had done so for years; most of their clients, however humble, could talk Italian of a kind. No Italian lawyers or judges could talk Slovene. Further, under A.M.G. any Slovene had at least theoretically the right to speak in court in his own language and to use an interpreter to translate into Italian. But the Slovenes thought this humiliating.

More serious was the Slovene grievance over the police force set up by A.M.G., the 'Venezia Giulia Civil Police'.

When A.M.G. took over in June, 1945, the only existing force was the 'People's Guard', or 'Difesa Popolare' created by the Yugoslav authorities during the forty-five days. This was an impromptu force, unpaid and inevitably ill-equipped and trained. (A director of one of the chief shipbuilding concerns complained bitterly that during the forty-five days hundreds of his workers had been recruited for the Difesa Popolare. He had not only lost their labour but had also had to pay their keep while they served in the Difesa Popolare, which he looked on as a gang of bandits.) The chief job of this force was political: to clean up Fascists and other people hostile to the Tito régime and its Trieste representatives. It was loathed by most Italians.

A.M.G. decided to disband and disarm the Difesa Popolare and replace it by the Venezia Giulia Civil Police. The new police was born on June 24th, 1945. This force was recruited locally. Theoretically anyone, Italian or Slovene, could volunteer. A few recruits came from the Difesa Popolare or from among former partisans; but most came from the old Italian Carabinieri or other Fascist Italian police and gendarmerie services. Before a man was accepted he had to come before a selection board of British and American officers. After that he was screened by the military security authorities for his political record; nevertheless, some men who had served in the Fascist Republican Army managed to slip into the force.

The Venezia Giulia Civil Police, like the administration in general, came to be predominantly Italian. This was not really the fault of A.M.G. or of Colonel Gerald Richardson, the Scotland Yard officer who headed the Police. A.M.G. wished in theory to use Italian police in Italian-speaking areas and Slovenes in Slovene areas. But when the Slovene leaders decided in August, 1945, to boycott A.M.G. administration, most pro-Tito Slovenes withdrew from the Civil Police. A certain number of Slovenes remained in the force or were freshly recruited, but were nearly all anti-Communist and anti-Tito men. When posted in Slovene villages, these men were usually looked on as natural enemies, though in exceptional cases they seemed to get on well enough personally with the villagers.

The new force was trained originally by N.C.Os of the British Military Police, later by British and American police and army officers. About seventeen British officers—eight from the Metropolitan Police and two from the City of London Police—and six American officers held the chief commands in the force. The Civil Police was in theory a purely non-political body of men modelled mostly on the British police. For the first eighteen months their uniform was of American type; but at the end of 1946 Colonel Richardson proudly introduced a new navy blue uniform almost identical with the uniform of the City of London Police.

Nevertheless, the dark mobile faces under the slightly comical helmets were totally un-British—just as the swarthy, unshaven, rolling-eyed men who sat in the back rooms as inspectors of the criminal investigation department were often enough pure Neapolitan, un-British in ideas no less than in face. The force as a whole had its political bias.

This again was not really the fault of A.M.G., but sprang from the whole temperamental and political clash between Slavs on one side and British, Americans and Italians on the other. The Slovene leaders took very little time to declare that the new force was 'unpopular' and contained many 'fascist elements'. In Slovene-Communist demonstrations it often seemed that the crowd deliberately went out of its way to break the nerve of the police.

The rank and file of the policemen were many of them young, inexperienced men with Southern temperaments, and it was not hard to make them lose their heads, panic, and react with violence. Then their British and American superior officers, with the traditional police *esprit de corps,* would protect their subordinates in order to maintain the moral of the force.

A typical incident, though more grave in its results than the average, happened on March 10th, 1946 in Servola, a mainly Slovene village on the southern outskirts of Trieste. The police authorities had apparently been notified that trouble was brewing there. (The exact circumstances remained obscure, but it seemed that the village priest objected to an attempt by local Communists to fly the red star flag from the church tower.) Two lorryloads of Civil Police were sent to the village square in front of the church, where they found an excited crowd of villagers, summoned by the tolling of the church bell. The crowd pressed around the lorries in what seemed to the police a threatening mood, and shouted slogans which were at least unflattering. Toni, the village idiot, apparently set spark to powder by lurching towards one of the lorries. Some of the policemen huddled on the lorry then lost their heads and fired— they claimed later—over the heads of the crowd. But two people in the crowd were killed and others injured. No arms inspection was carried out by superior police officers after the shooting.

At the end of July seven of the policemen on the lorry—all very young men—were brought to trial before an A.M.G. court in Trieste. The case against three of them was quickly dropped, for lack of evidence. The other four were found not guilty. The President of the Court, an American lawyer, Colonel John Weber, ruled that the accused could not be held individually responsible, since it could not be proved whose bullets had caused the deaths; nor could they be held collectively responsible, since the firing was the outcome not of deliberate intent but of the emotional hysteria prevailing both among the crowd and the police.

The story went round Trieste that after the acquittal the seven policemen were sent on holiday, to cheer them up after their trying experiences.

From July, 1946, onwards—the month of the twelve-day general strike called by the Slovene and Communist leaders, and also the month of a curious outburst of anti-Anglo-American feeling on the part of the Italians—British and American military police, or troops acting under military police command, were more and more often used to reinforce or replace the Civil Police. The morale of the Civil Police had been shaken. The Americans and British were particularly employed to make the first charges with batons, truncheons, staves or rifle-butts against any big crowd of Slovenes and Communists holding a demonstration which had not been authorised by A.M.G.

The Americans, with their tin helmets rammed over their eyes and their shiny brown boots, sometimes chewing a large damp cigar, carried out the job with a mixture of outward whooping gusto and inner nervous uncertainty. The British, red-faced and trying to grin off their embarrassment, weighed in silently with grim sheepishness.

The methods used by the British and more particularly the Americans, though they seemed aggressive, bullying and unnecessarily humiliating to the crowd, were less likely to result in serious injury than the more temperamental reactions of the Civil Police. Bad bruises were the most usual casualties. The Civil Police were left with the easier job of cleaning up and dispersing the scattered remnants after the main crowd had been broken up.

The Civil Police and even sometimes the American and British military police did occasionally act against Italian demonstrators as well as against Slovenes and Communists. But—except in the over-heated days of July, 1945, when the blood of the British troops was aroused by Italian interference with their Italian girl friends—police and military handling of Italians was noticeably more tolerant and kindly than their handling of Slovenes and Communists. There was a feeling that the Italians were not really to be taken seriously, that they were just high-spirited and unruly. On one day early in November, 1946, for instance, the police actually arrested fourteen young Italians who took a leading part in big unauthorised demonstrations in Trieste; but by the evening they had all been released. Slovenes, once arrested, might wait in prison for several days, and usually came to trial for disturbing the peace.

After eighteen months of A.M.G. administration, the working of the police system had, inevitably, come to reflect the general clash of forces in Trieste. The Anglo-Americans might have made greater efforts to keep impartial and 'neutral'; but no occupying Power could have created a truly non-political, non-partisan police force in Venezia Giulia.

Schooling was an issue on which A.M.G. accused the Slovenes strongly of ingratitude and obstruction. It was certainly a subject on which there was complete misunderstanding between the Anglo-Americans and the Slavs.

The Italian Fascist government had forbidden all schooling or instruction in the Slovene language or in Slovene literature or history. This ban was an important point in their programme of denationalising and Italianising the Slavs of Venezia Giulia. For the Slavs, it was one of their most bitter grievances against the Italians.

When from 1943 onwards the Slav partisan movement grew strong and the Liberation Front and village liberation committees came into being, one of the jobs which they did with most enthusiasm was to set up their own improvised Slovene schools, openly in 'liberated' villages and clandestinely in occupied districts. Here Slovenes taught in the Slovene language about Slovene national history and literature and the Slovene national struggle. Most were not highly-educated or qualified teachers: no Slovene teachers had been trained under the Fascist régime. The schools were amateurish, and were also highly political. History was taught mainly in terms of Tito's national liberation movement and the partisan war in Yugoslavia. Tito's portrait was displayed everywhere, and the names of Lenin and Stalin cropped up fairly often. But there was an almost religious enthusiasm about these schools; after all, they were the first Slovene schools in the Trieste region for over twenty years.

During the forty-five days of Yugoslav occupation, P.N.O.O. had its own education authorities which extended the Slovene school system and started preparing their own text-books. One primer, in particular, was decorated with the usual portrait of Tito, with five-pointed red stars, and with pictures of little boy partisans, or 'pioneers', carrying tommy-guns, all in gay colours.

When A.M.G. took over in June, 1945, they felt that they would show impartiality and even generosity by reversing the old Fascist ban and creating Slovene schools wherever Slovenes were living. Ethnographical maps of the Anglo-American Zone were prepared with scrupulous fairness, and used as the basis for allotting Slovene or Italian or mixed schools. A young American Methodist, Captain John Simoni, set to work with enthusiasm. Slovene secondary schools, technical schools and training schools for teachers were planned as well as a network of primary schools.

But there were two big stumbling-blocks in the way of understanding between A.M.G. and the Slovenes.

First, A.M.G. insisted that their schools must follow a strictly 'non-political' syllabus. This at once ruled out the P.N.O.O. system of teaching and the P.N.O.O. text-books. A good many of its Slovene teachers were also ruled out on the grounds that they were not qualified.

Then, by a perverse fate, the only man whom A.M.G. could find to act as their Slovene adviser on Slovene schooling was a certain Professor Srecko Barraga, who was known to be strongly anti-Tito and anti-Communist. He had been in Ljubljana, capital of Yugoslav Slovenia, during the German occupation, and there was little serious doubt that he was associated with the German-sponsored anti-Communist organisation, the White Guard. He fled from Slovenia to Italy at the time of the German collapse. Although according to his own lights he was probably a sincere Slovene patriot, sincerely interested in education, his employment by A.M.G., even in an advisory capacity, was provocative and laid the Anglo-Americans open to strong attack by the Slovenes.

A Ljubljana People's Court tried him in absence and sentenced him to death as a war criminal. A.M.G. did not accept this verdict on its own merits, but asked for documentary evidence of Barraga's guilt. The Ljubljana Court did not feel called upon to supply documents; and Barraga remained the leading employee of A.M.G. in Slovene educational affairs, under Captain Simoni. He gave the Slovene leaders an additional excuse for boycotting the A.M.G. school system.

But the main battle was the battle of the text-books. A.M.G. prepared their own charmingly-coloured and strictly non-political text-books. These contained no reference to the Yugoslav national liberation war or the partisan struggle. No Communist leaders appeared in them. These text-books, together with the general A.M.G. school syllabus, were to be used in all A.M.G.'s Slovene schools.

At the end of the first school year, in July, 1946, A.M.G. found that in a big number of their Slovene schools the teachers had in fact ignored their syllabus and text-books, and used the old 'Tito text-books' and the old teaching methods of the partisan days. The Slovenes on their side said that it was an insult to be asked to keep silent about their great liberation war. A.M.G. suspended or threatened with dismissal those teachers found guilty of going against A.M.G. instructions.

At the beginning of the second school year, in October, a fair proportion of the suspended teachers were in fact re-engaged—it was difficult to train up enough new teachers in time—but were transferred to other villages. A certain number of new A.M.G.-trained teachers, guaranteed strictly non-political, were sent out to the villages where posts had been left vacant.

The Slovene leaders chose this moment for a campaign against the transfer of teachers and against the new teachers. Fierce proclamations were bill-posted in the Slovene villages, denouncing Simoni and Barraga and declaring that the A.M.G. school system was riddled with Fascists. 'Parents' Committees', consisting mainly of fiercely maternal mothers and spurred on by tough broad-shouldered girls who had been partisans, were mobilised in the villages. On the first day of the school-year, a dozen teachers were turned out of the schools by the villagers. The transferred teachers were accused simply of 'not being one of us', or 'people of whom we know nothing'. The new A.M.G.-trained teachers were accused of being Fascists or White Guardists, or of having taken no part in the national liberation war.

The squabble developed into an outcrop of 'parents' demonstrations and clashes between village mothers and the Civil Police, school strikes, and incidents over the forcible removal by the police of portraits of Tito from village schoolrooms. Two new 'non-political' schoolmistresses, who had been sent by A.M.G. to Opčina, a big Slovene village bordering on Trieste, and had been turned out because they could not show U.A.I.S. membership cards, were conducted back to the school under police escort and started work under police protection. A.M.G. threatened to close down schools that continued to offend against regulations, and to requisition the school buildings for the use of British or American troops during the winter months.

By this time A.M.G.'s noble intentions had been almost hidden from view in a petty struggle of wills. The misunderstanding and clash over Slovene schools were tragically typical of the whole clash of opposing temperaments and aims.

Most important of the internal struggles in Trieste was the struggle within the labour movement.

The labour struggle cut across the national conflict between Slavs and Italians, but followed the general line of the main conflict between East and West. The Anglo-Americans at times became deeply involved in the struggle.

The organisation of labour in the Trieste area was a vital issue for the Slavs. They themselves were weak in numbers, and would form a small minority in Trieste Free Territory. Somehow or other they must win over at least a section of the Italians. Their best chance was to win over the Italian workers and bring them under Slav-Communist leadership in a powerful trade union organisation. Such a union might play a decisive part in settling the ultimate fate of Trieste.

Conditions in the Trieste area favoured the Slavs. During the last generation economic power had been more and more concentrated in the hands of a small group of capitalists controlling the key industries, notably shipbuilding and mining. These capitalists, even if in some cases of Slav national origin, felt themselves to be Italian, were closely allied with Italian capital, and had drawn fresh Italian capital into the Trieste region. They were also closely allied with the Fascist government.

On the other side there was a relatively large number of industrial

workers concentrated in a relatively small area who, whether Italian or
Slav, were robbed by Italian Fascism of all normal workers' rights.
These conditions favoured the growth of Communist feeling among the
workers, and also the growth of the belief, among Italians as well as
Slavs, that Italy, under whatever government, stood for reaction and
the oppression of the working-class. On this ground it was relatively
easy to sow the seed of the conviction that the new Yugoslavia of Tito's
national liberation movement was the protector of workers' rights, and
that workers, even Italians, would have a better chance of freedom and
prosperity in the new Yugoslavia than in the new Italy.

During the war a clandestine, Communist-led workers' movement
called 'Unità Operaia' had been formed in the Trieste area, combining
both Italians and Slovenes. As Tito's partisans pressed steadily closer
to Trieste, Unità Operaia formed close contacts with the local Liberation
Front, which in turn was closely linked with the partisans.

When the Yugoslav Army entered Trieste, from the nucleus of Unità
Operaia a single trade union organisation 'Sindicati Unici' was formed
to combine all workers, both Italian and Slovene, throughout the old
Italian province of Venezia Giulia. In Trieste city the majority of its
members were Italians; outside the city, the majority were Slovenes.

Sindicati Unici was formed on the model of the unitary all-embracing
trade union organisation of Tito's Yugoslavia, which was, in fact,
roughly the Soviet model. There was a pyramid of committees from the
factory or workshop, up through directing committees for each industry
or undertaking, to a regional executive committee at the top.

During the forty-five days, Sindicati Unici was built up on the open
assumption that the Trieste area would go to Yugoslavia. Communists
held most of the key posts. The most outstanding was Ernesto Radich,
a veteran Italian Communist and a sincere fighter for workers' rights.
He had real influence among the Italian workers.

When in June, 1945, the Yugoslavs withdrew from Trieste and the
Anglo-American Zone was created, Sindicati Unici adapted itself to the
new situation by splitting off—at least in theory—that section of the
organisation which remained in the Yugoslav-occupied Zone. S.U. in
the Anglo-American Zone also modified its statute. Originally this had
contained two paragraphs speaking of the organisation's aim as 'the
strengthening of democracy in Yugoslavia'. Now these were changed
to innocuous non-political phrases about 'the improvement of the
conditions of the working-class'.

But it was clear enough that behind the scenes S.U. in the Anglo-
American Zone remained closely linked with Belgrade and with the
policy of Marshal Tito's government.

For a few weeks after A.M.G. took over, S.U. remained the only
labour organisation in the Anglo-American Zone. In June and July,
1945, fresh elections were held for factory committees and higher committees. These replaced the first elections, held immediately after the

Yugoslavs entered in May, in which in most cases the old clandestine committees of Unità Operaia were simply 'acclaimed' as S.U. committees, and in which a good many irregularities occurred. In the new elections, there was theoretically secret voting; but dissidents claimed that there was intimidation and pressure on the voters.

Towards the end of July the trade union movement split. A rival organisation to S.U., 'Sindicati Giuliani' was formed, representing the more nationalist-minded and less Left-wing of the Italian workers. It was said that its formation was partly a political move on the part of the Italian political groups combined in the Italian 'National Liberation Committee' of Trieste led by Colonel Fonda. Partly, also, it must have been a natural reaction to the Slav nationalist tendencies and the authoritarian methods of the S.U. leaders. One reason given for the split was that the founders of Sindicati Giuliani had discovered that S.U. was still taking orders from Belgrade and was being used as a tool for Yugoslav nationalist policy in the Trieste area; and that it was therefore neglecting the workers' interests.

S.U. retorted that the new rival body was a purely Italian nationalist organisation which, by splitting the workers' movement, was sabotaging the workers' interests. It found support for this argument when S.G. started pressing for affiliation with the Italian General Confederation of Labour in Rome—whereas S.U. could righteously if disingenuously claim that it had no organisational link with the Yugoslav trade union organisation in Belgrade. The Italian General Confederation of Labour at first opposed S.G.'s request, and, under Italian Communist influence, pressed for the formation of a single non-nationalist autonomous organisation in the Trieste area. But in the spring of 1946 it gave way and S.G. was affiliated with Rome.

In the intervening months, during the winter of 1945-46, there had been long but abortive negotiations in Trieste between S.U. and S.G. for the reunion of the two organisations. S.U., in particular Ernesto Radich, took the initiative in these talks. At moments the two parties seemed on the verge of agreement; but—according to the S.U. version— 'outside political influences', meaning Italian nationalist elements, intervened to prevent it. Yet during these months of abortive haggling, the two organisations did at times conduct joint negotiations with the employers on purely labour questions, and achieved certain very definite gains over wage rates.

The breakdown came in March, 1946. S.U. wanted to proclaim a purely political general strike as a protest against the Servola shooting incident in which two members of a Slovene crowd had been killed. S.G. refused to join in the strike. S.U. then voted a resolution saying that its representatives would never again sit at the same table with representatives of S.G. Ernesto Radich, who apparently was against the policy of mixing national and political questions with labour questions, left his post in S.U., which thus lost one of its outstanding men.

Relations between the two organisations became openly hostile when, four months later, S.U. called another general strike on political grounds. Trieste Italians had burst out into violent anti-Slav demonstrations and had wrecked and gutted a Slovene bookshop, after Italian cyclists in a round-Italy bicycle race had been stoned by Slovene villagers near Trieste. The Slovene leaders considered that A.M.G. had not reacted strongly enough against the Italian demonstrators. S.U., jointly with the pro-Tito political organisations, therefore called a general strike to protest against A.M.G.'s tolerance of the resurgence of Fascism and 'neo-fascist elements'.

S.G. refused to join in the strike. Its members in most cases tried to go on working. Streets leading to factories and shipyards were picketed by S.U. workers who prevented blacklegs from going to work. Non-strikers' families were threatened. But owing to S.G.'s abstention, the general strike was only about two-thirds effective.

It was at this point that A.M.G. became heavily involved in the labour struggle. Impatient advocates of strong-arm methods won the day. A.M.G. broke the strike by issuing summonses against the members of the strike committee, which included not only S.U. leaders but also political leaders. Among them were some of the most outstanding figures of the whole Slav-Communist movement, for instance, Frank Stoka, a Trieste fisherman and a great talker, and Giorgio Jaksetich, a veteran of the Spanish civil war and an Italian partisan leader who had collaborated with the Allied armies. The members of the strike committee refused to obey the summons to appear in court and went underground. From then on, since A.M.G. in spite of repeated demonstrations refused to revoke the summonses, they lived 'illegally' when in Trieste and only appeared publicly when they crossed into the Yugoslav-occupied Zone.

The immediate result of the A.M.G. action was that S.U. and the organisations associated with it on the strike committee called off the strike after it had lasted twelve days. They claimed, untruly, that they had won a victory by abolishing neo-fascist elements from the scene. In reality, it was a tactical success for A.M.G.

However, the trouble was not over. The S.U. workers went back to work, but took vengeance—or disciplinary action—against the 'black-legs'. For three days there were clashes in the main shipyards between 'strikers' and 'non-strikers'. 'Strikers' stuck up black lists of those they considered the ringleaders among the 'non-strikers', and a number of 'non-strikers' were beaten up in quiet corners of the yards. In one case the shipyard office of the S.G. was attacked and wrecked. On the other side some members of S.G. armed themselves with grenades and pistols when they went to work, and it was alleged that armed gangs of Italians were allowed into certain shipyards to protect the 'non-strikers'.

At this point the shipyard owners, 'Cantieri Riuniti del' Adriatico' of which Signor Augusto Cosulich, a conservative-minded industrialist of the old-fashioned type, was managing director, declared a lock-out in the Monfalcone and San Marco yards—the two biggest yards of the Trieste area. A.M.G. again intervened—much to the satisfaction of the owners—and put the two shipyards under Allied military control. Lieutenant-Colonel J. E. Foden, a British officer with experience as an industrialist, was placed in charge.

On July 19th the yards reopened. A platoon of the British Royal Artillery 4th Medium Regiment, together with a platoon of American soldiers of the 88th Division, were stationed outside each of the yards, ready to carry out any order from Colonel Foden to enter and arrest 'any person who committed any act of violence or any act calculated to disturb law, order or safety'.

The threat alone was enough. Colonel Foden was left in charge of the yards for twelve days. During this time there were no incidents, although the Slovene-Communist press protested against A.M.G.'s 'colonial methods'. At worst there was a mild tussle of wills between Colonel Foden and the Monfalcone workers over the removal of the red star flags which the workers insisted on flying from the highest crane. In the end, Colonel Foden climbed several hundred steps and removed them himself, without opposition.

But when military control was withdrawn, trouble started again. During August members of S.G. were beaten up almost daily in the Monfalcone yards. On the other hand, a few more members of S.G. were found carrying grenades into the yards. On August 26th, A.M.G. intervened yet again, more strongly.

This time Allied troops were posted inside the yards. At Monfalcone, a vast rambling shipyard where there were over 7,000 workers, twenty-five British soldiers and twenty-five of the Venezia Giulia Civil Police entered. Armed only with wooden pick-staves, they patrolled the yards in couples—one British soldier and one civil policeman. The workers were angry and declared a 'white strike'. This meant that they just sat and stared and made more or less threatening remarks at the lonely couples of intruders. There were a great many pieces of scrap metal lying around which the strikers could use as weapons, and patrolling was a rather nerve-racking job for the soldiers. But their nerve held; there were no clashes; after two days the strike was called off. Work started again; there were no more beatings. A.M.G. successfully maintained the system of patrols on a more or less permanent basis, in spite of the protests of S.U. It was another tactical defeat for S.U.; but it did not really weaken its power.

In November, 1946, international developments over Trieste opened a new phase in the labour struggle. It became clear that Marshal Tito would in the end have to yield to the creation of a Trieste Free Territory and abandon his claim to annex Trieste. S.U. had to prepare for the big political rôle it was called on to play in the Free Territory. Helped by a recommendation made by the World Federation of Trade Unions, calling for trade union unity in Trieste, S.U. renewed negotiations with S.G., which was unenthusiastic but could not refuse.

A joint 'conciliation committee' drawn from the two organisations, was formed. It was to work out plans for collaboration or fusion. It got very little way with planning fusion. But on November 23rd, surprisingly, S.U. and S.G. took their first joint action for six months. They combined in backing a strike of 1,200 Trieste tramway workers, called to enforce a claim for a 30 per cent. wage increase and other demands. A.M.G. found themselves negotiating with the new 'conciliation committee' of the two organisations. A face-saving formula convenient to both sides was found; the strike was called off, but the tramway workers' basic demands were granted.

This joint action by S.U. and S.G. was, however, a flash in the pan. Wider agreement did not follow. Negotiations dragged on and on during the following months. The balance of forces between the two bodies was too uneven, and outside influences were too disturbing, for compromise to be reached.

In the winter of 1946-47, S.U. claimed about 80,000 members compared with about 30,000 members of S.G. S.U., with its Communist leadership, was far better organised and more energetic than S.G. It enforced strict discipline on its members, if necessary, it was said, by intimidation. It strengthened its position by fighting not only for political aims but also, with great toughness, for improvements in working conditions, and could boast of concrete gains. It had a perfectly clear line of basic policy, presumably inspired by Belgrade, even if it sometimes had to make tactical retreats before Anglo-American pressure. It had everything to gain from a merger with S.G., since it would always be the stronger partner. It could therefore in the long run dictate the policy of the merged organisation. By a merger it could also eliminate a rival whose existence would weaken its own political influence and bargaining power in Trieste Free Territory.

Equally, S.G. had many motives for holding out against a merger and for fighting for its independence. It could not count on backing from the Italian General Confederation of Labour in Rome, which was under Communist influence, nor from the World Federation of Trade Unions, but it could get political support from the Italian parties in Trieste and from powerful quarters in Rome.

In the long run S.U. stood to win the day. If it did so, it would become sole representative of a labour force of over 100,000 people, or perhaps over one quarter of the total population of Trieste Free Territory, Italians and Slavs combined. In the economic field, it would be in a very strong bargaining position to hold in check the small group of capitalists who had so far controlled Trieste, and might even break their power. Politically, it could throw in all its weight on the side of the 'popular' forces in the Assembly and Government of the Free Territory —that is, the pro-Slav, Eastern forces—and against the Western forces, which would be represented as the agents of Anglo-American capitalist imperialism and 'colonial exploitation' of the working masses.

S.U. could, in fact, become one of the decisive factors in preventing Trieste from becoming a permanent Western outpost and in turning it into an Eastern outpost against the Western Powers.

Closely linked with the labour question was the even more important question: what chances had Trieste of becoming economically prosperous.

When in 1946 the big Powers decided to create a Trieste Free Territory, the leading men in Trieste started trying to work out whether or not the Free Territory could become self-supporting and so capable of independent existence. It was soon clear that the answer could not be found in terms of the resources of the Free Territory and the efforts of its people, but only in terms of the attitude of the hinterland countries and of relations between the big Powers.

Ernest Bevin, in idealistic mood, had a vision of Trieste as the natural transit port for the trade of Central and South-eastern Europe, prospering on this traffic.* But this vision presupposed a pacified and united Europe and, in particular, the benevolence of Yugoslavia.

In practice, it seemed by the end of 1946 much more likely that Czechoslovakia, Hungary, the Balkan countries and perhaps also Austria, all of which formed the economic hinterland of Trieste, would remain firmly enclosed in the Soviet sphere, cut off by well-spiked political barriers and trading with the West on a strictly limited scale only. If Trieste Free Territory were believed to be predominantly under Anglo-American influence, exerted either directly or through the United Nations Organisation, then these hinterland countries would be unlikely to make any but very restricted use of Trieste as a trade outlet.

They would in no case be dependent on Trieste. The Central European countries, particularly Czechoslovakia, could use the newly developing Polish ports of Stettin, Danzig and Gdynia, with which she would have canal and river links. For purely Mediterranean traffic, and as an outlet for the Balkan countries, there would be Fiume—chief port of Hungary in the days of the Austro-Hungarian Empire, bereft of its natural functions by annexation to Italy in 1924, and awarded by the Paris Peace Conference in 1946 to Yugoslavia.

Fiume had suffered a good deal of war damage, and eighteen months after the end of fighting the port was still partly blocked by mines. The Yugoslavs had not done much to get the port working again. But their

---

* By 1948 Bevin seemed to have changed his mind. Speaking in the House of Commons on January 22nd, he said: 'In Trieste we have difficulties. We had hoped that the method of international agreement would be allowed to work, and so what should have been a great experiment in post-war international collaboration has only been a continuing source of friction and bother.' Two months later, the Western Powers decided that Trieste Free Territory was unworkable and proposed that Trieste should go back to Italy.

friends in Trieste firmly believed that, if Tito called for the effort, Yugoslavia could restore the port within two years, and could in the same time, through volunteer labour, double the railway leading north from Fiume to San Pietro del Carso, and from there to Postumia and Central Europe. Yugoslavia could also improve the railway running east from Fiume to Zagreb, and from there north-east to Hungary or south-east to Belgrade and the Balkans. At the end of this time, Yugoslavs calculated, Fiume port could carry a volume of traffic sufficient to satisfy the needs of Central Europe and the Balkans.

If Yugoslavia offered particularly easy freight rates and waived customs formalities for traffic from the Soviet sphere passing through Fiume—at the same time denying any such advantages to traffic passing through Yugoslav territory to Trieste—she could strangle Trieste port much more effectively than Poland strangled Danzig after the first world war.

Yugoslavia could use her control of the main landward communications leading out of Trieste Free Territory to tighten this stranglehold. The main double-track north-easterly railway from Trieste to Postumia and Central Europe would run through Yugoslav territory. So would the single-track line running north to the Austrian frontier at Piedicolle, which also linked with the double-track line running north-west from Gorizia to the Italian junction of Udine. Only one line from Trieste would run clear of Yugoslav territory. This was the main double-track railway running west to Venice and also linking by single-track lines with Udine and the track running north from Udine to the Austrian frontier at Tarvisio. There was also a high road running through Italian territory west and then north to Austria, by roughly the same rather roundabout route. But otherwise the main high roads would run through Yugoslavia.

So Yugoslavia would have a very strong economic, as well as strategic and military, grip on Trieste Free Territory, and could starve it of its port traffic.

The Yugoslavs could also, in a minor way, take more direct steps to starve out Trieste. The Free Territory—a city of over a quarter of a million people with a tiny, mostly barren, hinterland—could never be self-supporting in food. It could get some vegetables and fruit from the Capodistria area, which would be just within its southern border; but this area, which had been allotted to the Yugoslav occupation zone in 1945, had come under strong Yugoslav influence and might be unfriendly to Trieste city. Normally the Italian province of Udine would be the city's chief supplier of fruit and vegetables, and it would have direct connections with Trieste; but there was a small Slav minority and a strong Communist Party in Udine province which might try to sabotage supplies to the Free Territory.

In any case, the main food supplies for Trieste—meat, butter and eggs—would naturally come from the hinterland which under the peace treaty was to become Yugoslav. And a blockade on food supplies was a measure that had already been tried, on a small scale, by the Yugoslav occupation authorities against the Anglo-American enclave at Pola in November, 1946. It might be repeated, on a larger scale, against the Free Territory.

Yugoslavia could also starve the Trieste shipbuilding yards of the timber which they normally got from the hinterland. During the A.M.G. period supplies from the Yugoslav Zone came spasmodically and rarely, and the yards had to seek timber elsewhere. The same was true of the brown coal of the Arsa mines in Southern Istria, used in the furnaces of Trieste workshops: even during the A.M.G. period the Yugoslavs had at times threatened to stop deliveries, and they could always do the same again in the future.

Finally the Yugoslavs, acting through S.U., could make the lives of the Trieste capitalists a burden. If there were too many labour troubles and if the workers demanded wage rates too high to allow for quick easy profits, the capitalists could easily be driven to transfer their interests away from the Free Territory.

Up till 1947 there was no clear evidence that Yugoslavia's leaders had decided on a policy of strangling Trieste Free Territory. It was commonly said in Trieste that Yugoslav agents, acting through third parties, were buying up housing property in the city, presumably to accommodate Yugoslav commercial and financial agencies in the future. Some Triestini believed that Marshal Tito's government would find Trieste Free Territory useful as a link between Yugoslavia's strictly State-controlled economy and the capitalist world. Yugoslavia was obviously still waiting to see how the Free Territory would turn out, and how far it could be brought under Eastern influence. But the threat of strangulation was held in readiness. It was not an empty one.

On the other side, Italian business interests, inside and outside Trieste, were speculating on the hope that the Western Powers would, for political and strategic reasons, advance big loans to the Free Territory, that American business and financial interests would pour money into Trieste, and that there might be at least a few years of rosy prosperity in a heavily-subsidised Trieste. They did not believe that such prosperity could last, but thought there might be a chance of quick and easy profits.

Certain Italian interests were influenced not only by hopes of gain in Trieste, but also by fears of inflation and economic decay in Italy, of the growing strength of the Italian Communist Party, and of the prospect of Italian labour legislation imposing severe burdens on capital. A Western-subsidised Trieste, they believed, might remain an island of old-fashioned liberal economy, in which capital could make hay while the sun shone.

Less reputable interests believed that Trieste Free Territory would be a glorious no-man's land in which there would be endless chances for evading customs formalities, currency regulations and company laws, and for indulging in high-level smuggling and black-marketing on an international scale.

For all these reasons, there was a considerable influx of capital from Italy proper into Trieste banks during the later months of 1946. In Trieste itself an exceptionally high number of new companies was registered; for the moment most of them existed on paper only, but registration would give a basis for starting up mushroom enterprises if there were a boom in Trieste Free Territory.

Several wealthy and well-placed gentlemen of Trieste were most anxious to start up a casino, to draw wealthy foreigners to Trieste, and also to draw off money from the austerely-controlled hinter-land countries. High-sounding honours and decorations were offered to high A.M.G. officials to win favour for the project. But A.M.G. stayed firm in its refusal. The plan was also frowned on by Monsignor Santin, Catholic Bishop of Trieste. But its promoters still had hopes of getting their scheme past the government of the Free Territory.

Another plan of the same kind, often discussed in Trieste, was to introduce an easy quick divorce law in the Free Territory, which would attract wealthy foreigners, especially from Catholic Italy, where no divorce was allowed. This project also agitated the Catholic clergy of Trieste; but they were not likely to have the last word in the matter.

As for Trieste's outlook as a smuggling centre, the ground was already being prepared during the A.M.G. era. Anti-Tito refugees from Yugo-slavia, who had settled in Trieste and wanted to make money quickly, were especially active. During October, 1946, for instance, the Civil Police, investigating a big counterfeiting racket which was smuggling forged Yugoslav notes into Yugoslavia, seized faked dinar notes totalling nearly half a million dinars; it was said that the total of faked notes in Trieste might reach several millions.

In the same month the police, trying to clean up the Trieste end of a big dope-smuggling ring, based on South Tirol, seized over 280 phials of cocaine—or 'enough to kill half Trieste', as one official said.

American security police in Trieste spent much of their time trying to shut down the vast and highly organised illegal traffic in American cigarettes and other goods diverted from American military stores. They were only partly successful.

Charges made by Fiorello La Guardia, then Director-General of UNRRA, during a visit to Belgrade in the autumn of 1946, that a big quantity of UNRRA goods destined for Yugoslavia were being syste-matically filched in transit through Trieste, led to lengthy investigations and the holding of a formal UNRRA court of enquiry. The court's findings were never published. A.M.G. officials repeatedly declared that only one half of 1 per cent. of UNRRA supplies went astray in Trieste.

But there was an uneasy feeling in the city that even if the charges were very much exaggerated, they had had some foundation.

Other more purely local rackets sprang up in Trieste. On November 13th, 1946, there was a shooting affray in one of Trieste's most crowded shopping and café streets. A man named Ercole Miancic, who had the reputation of being the city's biggest racketeer, running a successful extortion and protection racket on Trieste shops and businesses, died later of his wounds. But in the affray he had shot one policeman through the throat and wounded another before he fell.

After eighteen months of Anglo-American administration, a senior A.M.G. official serenely estimated that over and above Trieste city's official population of 260,000, there were upwards of 100,000 people living 'illegally'—that is, they were not registered in any city records or with the police, and had no identity papers or ration cards. Another officer, speaking unofficially, estimated the illegal population at nearly a quarter of a million.

Unless therefore a very thorough purge and clean-up were to be carried out when the Free Territory was instituted, the ground would be ready for the development of Trieste as centre for many internal and international rackets. But these, though they might bring profits to a few, could obviously not bring prosperity to the city.

Trieste's prosperity depended mainly on two things: the port traffic, and the shipbuilding industry.

The volume of port traffic, as suggested above, would always be decided largely by outside factors. Trends during the A.M.G. period were not particularly promising. According to figures published in July, 1946, traffic passing through Trieste port during the first four months of 1946 was 54.3 per cent. of the figure for the same period of 1938. Practically all this traffic was goods arriving by sea; very little was exports from the hinterland. Nearly all the goods arriving by sea were exceptional: they were either military supplies for the Anglo-American occupation forces in Venezia Giulia or for the British occupation zone of Austria, or else they were UNRRA supplies for Yugoslavia, Czechoslovakia, Hungary and Austria.

When in the first half of 1947 these exceptional supplies dropped off, the volume of traffic through Trieste fell sharply too. There was not the normal commercial traffic with Central Europe and the Balkans to replace them. By the end of 1946 there was a small trickle of goods from Yugoslavia passing through the port, but practically no trade from Central Europe.

In November, 1946, A.M.G. sponsored, as a pioneer move, a very small-scale scheme for a motor lorry service by road from Trieste to Vienna, carrying gift food parcels to Austrians on the outward trip and bringing back commercial goods from Austria and Czechoslovakia on the return journey. The chief aim was to open up small commercial exchanges with Central Europe. 'We are just breaking the ice—sort of guinea-pigging the thing through a little,' A.M.G.'s chief transportation officer said. But even this scheme, small as it was, was hamstrung by frontier and customs formalities and restrictions and red tape on transit through the Soviet occupation zone of Austria. These were a minor foretaste of the difficulties in the way of restarting a flow of Central European trade through Trieste.

The Trieste area shipbuilding yards—the chief industry of the area—showed some signs of returning prosperity under Anglo-American administration. But it was doubtful whether this trend would continue in the Free Territory.

The single big shipbuilding combine in the area, 'Cantieri Riuniti del'Adriatico', controlled the biggest shipyard, at Monfalcone fifteen miles west of Trieste, the smaller San Marco and San Rocco shipyards and the San Andrea engineering works in Trieste itself, and certain linked subsidiary undertakings elsewhere in Venezia Giulia. The Cosulich family, headed by the shrewd, elderly, mistrustful Augusto Cosulich, was the chief power in the combine, which was also closely associated, through the Economo family, with certain important Trieste insurance interests which traditionally did business throughout Central and South-eastern Europe. The Cosulich-Economo group was, in fact, the most powerful capitalist group of the Trieste area. It linked Trieste with Turin, Genoa, Clydeside, the City of London, with private or governmental shipping interests in Scandinavia, Egypt, Argentina and elsewhere, and, through the associated insurance interests, with Eastern Europe.

The question was whether this important group, which had flourished under Austria-Hungary and under Italian Fascism, and had not done at all badly under the German occupation of 1943-45 or under A.M.G., would find it practicable or profitable to carry on in Trieste Free Territory, or would decide to transfer their interests elsewhere.

At the end of 1946 they were still undecided. Allied bombing had reduced the productive capacity of the shipyards by about one-third. The San Marco yard had in 1946 a daily capacity of 30 tons of steel hull production compared with a pre-war figure of 50 tons. The Monfalcone yard was employing 7,750 workers compared with 10,200 workers in 1940. But A.M.G. had advanced some loans for repair of bomb damage and a start had been made on repair work. Although constant labour troubles and general uncertainty about the future of Trieste had been a brake on recovery, it was announced in November, 1946, that foreign shipowners had placed orders for twenty-eight ships of a total tonnage of 120,000, and that there was already work enough on order to employ the shipyards until the end of 1947.

On the other hand, the settlement imposed by the Italian Peace Treaty made the Trieste capitalists pessimistic. The Monfalcone yard, specialising on passenger ships, large tankers and refrigerator cargo vessels, would be cut off from Trieste and left to Italy. So would one or two other subsidiaries. Division from Italy would also make necessary a redistribution of capital: the majority of the shares of C.R.D.A. were in Italian hands, outside the borders of Trieste Free Territory.

Most of all, the Trieste capitalists feared Italian competition, after separation from Italy. Between the two wars, the Trieste shipyards had been strongly backed by the Italian government, which placed big orders for warships and submarines. If in the future C.R.D.A., isolated in a tiny Free Territory, had to go into free competition with Italian shipbuilders, for instance those of Genoa, their outlook would be precarious.

For that reason, experts of C.R.D.A., during 1946, pressed strongly for a customs and monetary union between Trieste Free Territory and Italy, and a guarantee of electric power supplies from the Venice area and for special facilities on Italian railways for the supply of raw materials. They had, however, little chance of obtaining their requests.

Trieste capitalists had not much hope that Anglo-American capital would interest itself, on a private basis, in Trieste shipbuilding. The Trieste yards would, in their small way, be in competition with British and American shipbuilders. So they could only hope for support from the West on a governmental level, given for political motives. Failing this, it seemed fairly certain that the existing Trieste capitalists would sooner or later quit the Free Territory and leave it to fall economically into Eastern hands.

Western financial and economic support, given directly or through the United Nations or the International Bank, was one of the two key questions to the economic future of Trieste—the other being the attitude of the hinterland States.

It was obvious that Western support, to be effective, would have to be on a fairly large scale. During the Moscow four-Power Conference of March, 1947, Anglo-American experts estimated that the deficit in the finances of a Trieste Free Territory over a three-month period—for example July-September, 1947—would be 5,000,000 dollars or £1,250,000. On this basis the four Foreign Ministers agreed that the future governor of Trieste should be authorised to ask the United Nations for aid in foreign exchange up to 5,000,000 dollars.

At a rough guess, therefore, the annual deficit in the finances of Trieste Free Territory, during the first years of its existence, was likely to be somewhere around 20,000,000 dollars or £5,000,000. But this figure would not include the subventions required by Trieste industries, for instance the shipyards, if they were to recover prosperity. The Western Powers would find it a considerable burden—in proportion to the size of the object—to keep Trieste Free Territory a going concern under Western influence.

The rival political organisations which would compete for power in

Trieste Free Territory could be split up fairly simply into the Easterners and the Westerners.

There was a tiny group of Trieste autonomists, who tried to remain somewhere in the middle of the road. They called themselves the 'Fronte dell'Independenza per il Libero Stato Giuliano' and were run by a somewhat dilettante Triestine, Carlo Tolloy. During the A.M.G. period, the 'Fronte' ran its own weekly newspaper and claimed 3,000 members—probably an excessive figure. Nobody took it seriously, except when the Easterners chose for obscure reasons to attack Tolloy as an agent of Western imperialism.

On the side of the Easterners, the chief body was originally P.N.O.O. But this title had somehow a vague Slav flavour, and during 1946 the Easterners realised more and more strongly that it was vital for them to conciliate the Italians. So their chief organisation came to be U.A.I.S. —the 'Italian-Slovene Anti-fascist Union'. In practice there was very little difference between P.N.O.O. and U.A.I.S.; the same men ran both. U.A.I.S. was very closely linked with S.U., the trade union organisation, and with other subsidiaries such as the youth organisation (G.A.I.S.), the women's organisation (D.A.I.S.), and the partisans' organisation (A.P.G.). Most closely of all it was linked with the Giulian Communist Party, formed in August, 1945, as a party independent both of the Italian and of the Yugoslav Communist Parties, but obviously following the Belgrade line.

Often the same men held parallel posts in U.A.I.S. and the Giulian Communist Party. In the early days Boris Kraigher, a young Slovene Communist intellectual, was secretary both of the Regional Committee of U.A.I.S. and of the Giulian Communist Party. In 1946, after Kraigher had gone to Ljubljana to take up a leading post in the government of the Yugoslav federal unit of Slovenia, both these positions were taken over by an older Slovene Communist, Branko Babic.

The more highly-coloured figures among the leaders of the Easterners disappeared from public life when A.M.G. issued summonses against the general strike committee in July—Stoka, Jaksetich, Regent, Ukmar and others. This disappearance left, as the leading Italians on the Eastern side, Giuseppe Pogassi, President of the Trieste Council of Liberation, a not very serious professional man who talked a great deal, and a young Communist from Italy proper, Alessandro De Stradi.

De Stradi had a simple, open, friendly way of talking, a charming boyish smile, and seemed honest and sincere in his political beliefs. Although he followed the party line in declaring that Trieste should by rights go to Yugoslavia, he seemed convinced that Trieste Free Territory could work successfully—provided, of course, that the Western Powers did not impose a 'colonial governor' or make Trieste a base for 'Anglo-American imperialist expansion'. He was persistently cheerful about the chances of collaboration between the Easterners and the non-Communist Italian parties of Trieste in the Free Territory government and assembly. He was, naturally, refreshingly free from the rather stifling Slav nationalism which most of the Slovene Communists allowed to peep out from under their wider social ideology.

Babic, for example, was a silent reserved man, but was, outsiders felt, intensely Slovene under the skin. When he held a press conference for foreign and local (mainly Italian) journalists, he refused to speak a word of any language except Slovene, although he could perfectly well speak Italian. He always stressed Slovene national complaints against the Italians and A.M.G., rather than the broader issues of the joint Italian-Slovene class struggle. In the lesser officials of U.A.I.S. and P.N.O.O., who were mainly Slovene, this national fervour was even more obvious.

It seemed almost stronger among the Slovene Communists than among the non-Communist Slovene nationalists who collaborated with them in U.A.I.S. and P.N.O.O. These non-Communists were usually Liberals; the most outstanding ones were distinguished Trieste lawyers and intellectuals, respected and even liked by leading non-Communist Italians.

Their position was rather a tragic one. Many of them had fought for the Slovene cause in Trieste throughout their lives. Some had suffered imprisonment or deportation or internment under Italian Fascism. Some had friends or relatives who had been shot or executed by the Italians. They had lived to bring about an end to Italian nationalist domination of Trieste and to win national freedom for the Slovenes. They tended to be romantics and enthusiasts. Yet when the time came they lost the leadership of the Slovene movement in the Trieste area.

It was inevitable that, after Russia came into the war in 1941, they should join up with the Slovene Communists in what developed into a branch of Tito's national liberation movement. It was their only hope of achieving their life-long aims. They joined with eagerness and self-sacrifice.

But often they were men who by upbringing and culture had a Western rather than a Slav orientation. They were Liberals of the Western type who had too much personal integrity to camouflage themselves as Communists. At first the national struggle to win Trieste for Yugoslavia—for any Yugoslavia, whether Communist or non-Communist—united them fully with the Communists. They were also very useful to the Communists, since they were men of standing in the city and had good contacts in the outer world. But by 1946 they were beginning to be pushed into the background. When high-level Communist policy decided that the fight over Trieste must be shifted from a national to a class basis, their position became more and more awkward.

Then, in November, 1946, Tito made to the Italian Communist leader, Palmiro Togliatti, his startling if not altogether serious proposal that Trieste should remain with Italy—under certain conditions. This offer, even when it was rejected by the Rome government, left the Slovene nationalists bewildered and helpless and, at least in their inmost hearts, resentful. Most of the Slovene villagers felt in the same way: at first they simply could not believe their ears; then they felt confused and angry; it took several days before they regained their half-religious faith that Tito, however mysterious his ways, knew best. The Slovene Communists, though just as nationalist at heart, might be used to these sudden twists and bends of policy; the non-Communist Slovenes were not. It seemed only a matter of time before the leading non-Communists would be caught out in 'disloyalty' to the Easterners, or would quite simply be eliminated from Eastern ranks.

Skirmishing uneasily on the borderline between the Easterners and Westerners were two unhappy groups, the real strength of which it was difficult to guess.

One—much the larger—was formed by the anti-Tito, anti-Communist Slovenes. Nearly all of them would have liked to join a non-Communist, Western Yugoslavia but feared an Eastern Yugoslavia. They were mainly staunch Catholics, led by old-time clericals and priests, though there were a few Liberals among them. A few Slovene villages north of Trieste were known as 'white' villages, in contrast with the usual 'red' villages. But most of the anti-Tito Slovenes were afraid to show themselves openly: the Eastern organisations were too powerful and all-seeing.

However, in the latter part of 1946 a small anti-Tito Slovene party was formed—probably with a little discreet Anglo-American encouragement—called Slovene National Democracy. It was violently anti-Communist, but its practical programme was vague. It was strongest in the mountainous, remote Collio district north of Gorizia, bordering on the Italian province of Udine, where, perhaps, closeness to the Western sphere gave courage. But although the party was strongly anti-Eastern in general principle, it was also sufficiently anti-Italian in prejudice to make it difficult to fit it neatly into the Western camp.

The other unhappy group was the small number of old-time Italian Communists who had found it difficult to accept wholeheartedly the Slav nationalism of the Slovene Communists and later of the Giulian Communist Party, with its close ties with Belgrade. Either they were genuine internationalists, or else they felt that their own natural ties were with Rome and the Italian Communist Party. Ernesto Radich, the original leader of S.U., probably belonged to this way of thought, and there must have been others among the Italian workers of Trieste. They could not be neatly fitted into the Eastern camp.

The Westerners of Trieste were originally combined loosely in an Italian 'Committee of National Liberation' which came into existence, as a revival of an earlier attempt to form an anti-fascist group in the city, not long before the Germans were driven out of Trieste. The Committee's leader during 1945 and most of 1946 was a handsome lean and melancholy reserve colonel of the Italian Army, Antonio Fonda, a non-party man but a strong Italian nationalist. He had lost a son fighting in the Italian Army in Russia. The main aim of the Committee during the last days of German occupation was to keep Trieste out of the hands of the Slavs; and its leaders were accused of negotiating for this purpose with the German garrison commander in April, 1945. But it was too feeble a body to play any important part during the military phase. And during the forty-five days of Yugoslav occupation it was too frightened to do anything effective.

After A.M.G. had been established, the Committee settled down into a vague political association, united by militant Italian nationalism, of the Trieste branches of the six Italian parties, Christian Democrat, Socialist, Action, Liberal, Republican and Democratic Labour. Although the Christian Democrats had a staunch Catholic following, it was the Action Party and the Socialists who were the most active—but as Italian nationalists, not as moderate Left-wing parties. Outside the political parties, the Committee had fairly close unofficial ties with the non-Communist trade union organisation S.G. It also had links with the hundreds of Italian refugees from the Yugoslav occupation zone of Venezia Giulia who settled in Trieste and provided explosive material for nationalist activities. The chief Trieste branch of the Action Party and the Trieste headquarters of the refugees' association shared the same offices.

The mystery was, who exactly was responsible for organising the gangs of Italian youths who, in times of tension, patrolled the main streets of Trieste singing nationalist songs and formed the advance guard in every Italian nationalist demonstration; and who, also, provided the stores of grenades and machine guns which were periodically discovered by the police in Italian hands. The Committee of National Liberation several times disclaimed responsibility. There were suspicions against the Action Party, particularly when in December, 1946, a stock of arms was found in their Trieste offices. But it was usually said that a young Italian nobleman had been sent by certain powerful quarters in Rome for the task of organisation. If so, he never appeared in public.

In Gorizia, there was something of the same mystery. A youngish, neurotic, excitable Italian of Gorizia, an ex-officer of the Italian Air Force called Corsini, whose father-in-law ran a prosperous motor transport company, could often be seen in the chief café of the town, the Café Garibaldi, or in the Corso, conferring with his subordinates, who directed the gangs of young Italians who led the periodical anti-Slovene demonstrations in Gorizia. But it remained a secret exactly who was backing Luigi Corsini. In Gorizia, as in Trieste, the local Italian Committee of National Liberation disclaimed responsibility.

Some of the most intelligent and responsible Westerners of Trieste deliberately stayed outside the Italian Committee of National Liberation. Chief of these was Engineer Gandusio, President of the Zone Council. He was an anti-fascist of long-standing, who claimed to have been one of the founders of an earlier Trieste Committee of National

Liberation, formed in 1942, even before the battle of Stalingrad showed the way the war was turning. In the following year he was arrested by the Germans and spent two years in concentration camp at Dachau. When he was released and came back to Trieste, he found that the new Committee of National Liberation was a 'kindergarten', and stayed aloof.

He was the man in Trieste most trusted by the Italian Government, and often visited Rome for consultations. Since he had little faith in the Committee of National Liberation, he was probably not surprised when at the end of 1946 it fell into disfavour with Rome.

Gandusio, although nominally a member of the conservative-minded Italian Liberal Party, was one of the few Italians in Trieste who saw the need of a general move to the Left. Just as the Peace Conference decision to create Trieste Free Territory made the Easterners decide to shift the struggle from the Slav national plane to the social and class plane, so it led far-seeing Italians like Gandusio to a similar determination. They feared a general swing-over by the Italian workers of Trieste to the Eastern camp, if the Westerners could offer nothing but worn-out Italian nationalist slogans. The Italian parties, they believed, must develop genuine social programmes.

So Colonel Fonda lost his leadership of the Committee of National Liberation; a system of rotating presidents was instituted as an interim measure; but early in 1947 the Committee more or less fell into disuse. The Italian parties themselves became rather more active, drawing into three rough groupings of Right, Centre and (somewhat mild) Left. The Uomo Qualunque—the new Italian party of strongly Fascist colour—which had been allowed to start up in Trieste in the later part of 1946, naturally joined the Right grouping.

This was the general framework in which, in the first half of 1947, negotiations were held between Easterners and Westerners to reach agreement on the formation of an interim government and assembly in Trieste Free Territory when it came into being.

The iniative apparently came from the Easterners. In October, 1946, U.A.I.S. had taken a false step by launching, without preparation and prematurely, an invitation to 'all sincere democratic forces' to form a 'United Front of Democratic Action' on the basis of Italian-Slav collaboration in a programme designed to prevent the Free Territory from becoming an Anglo-American 'colony'. This was a naïve attempt to win over moderate non-Communist Italians. It failed utterly. So the Slovene leaders made a fresh start with the 1947 negotiations.

The chief issue was, how many representatives the Easterners and Westerners should have in the Free Territory bodies. The original demand of U.A.I.S., made in November, 1946, was that the Easterners should have two-thirds of the representatives. Their theory was that the Slovenes could claim one-third and those Italians who belong to U.A.I.S. another third, leaving the remaining third for the Westerners.

On the Western side it was pointed out that according to available statistics, considerably more than two-thirds of the population of the Free Territory would be Italian, and that it was absurd to claim that one half of the Italians belonged to U.A.I.S. Therefore the Westerners— the non-Communist Italians—should have two-thirds of the representatives, leaving the remaining third to the Easterners—the Slovenes and the Communist Party.

During the 1947 negotiations the Easterners seemed surprisingly reasonable, and at one point apparently agreed roughly with the Western point of view on representation. Lesser difficulties arose over the Uomo Qualunque. The Easterners claimed that the Qualunquisti had no right to representation, since they were 'neo-fascist'. Even over this, agreement seemed possible. But in the early summer of 1947 negotiations were suddenly suspended—apparently by the Westerners.

No explanation was given on the Western side. But it was likely that the new active anti-Communist development of United States foreign policy, shown particularly in the 'Truman doctrine' towards Greece and Turkey, encouraged the Westerners of Trieste to wait and see. Later on, they might get an even better bargaining position as the Truman doctrine extended its scope to other parts of Europe.

Relations between Easterners and Westerners in Trieste would always trail in the wake of relations between Moscow and Washington-London. A local interim agreement might be reached in Trieste, but would have little lasting force unless it rested on high level agreement between the big Powers.

Even in that case, it would be difficult for Easterners and Westerners to join in making Trieste a real no-man's land, a true neutral zone between the Eastern and Western worlds. Differences of temperament, conception and method were large. Internal compromise in Trieste would most likely mean internal deadlock and paralysis. And a paralysed Trieste, kept alive only by spasmodic injections of Western aid, could very well topple over, sooner or later, into the waiting arms of the Eastern Powers. It would then be resuscitated as a Balkan outpost of the Eastern strategic and political defence system in Europe.

13

Portrait of Trieste

THE Trieste neighbourhood, during the A.M.G. period, was an odd mixture of gaiety and grimness, sophisticated profusion and simple poverty, easy-going tolerance and rigid earnestness, careless kindliness and sudden brutality. It must always have contained these contradictions, and always would. The clash of Italian and Slav, the contrast between the rich coastline and the bare uplands, made them inevitable. But while Trieste was a point of international conflict, they became more than usually sharp.

The first thing most foreigners saw, coming from the West, was the two-mile stretch of coast road from Miramare—the fantastic little sham château once a toy of the Habsburgs—leading into the sprawling commercial city and port, with their jumbled, pretentious, nineteenth-century buildings.

In summertime the seaward side of the road, which ran along the shore, had a frieze of golden-brown, well-fleshed young bodies. The young men and girls, the young mothers and children, of Italian middle-class Trieste seemed to have all the time in the world to swim or splash or paddle, shouting and laughing, to sit on the low sea-wall or on the kerbstone sunning themselves and chatting and flirting, or to lean gracefully against one of the trees that shaded the high road.

Ice-cream sellers trundled up and down the road lazily, doing easy trade. Bathers lapped up their ice-cream cornets or chewed grapes. On the landward side the hill rose steeply from the road, terraced with vines and fruit trees. Here and there a comfortable villa was tucked into a hollow in the hillside, bedded in a walled garden of sub-tropical trees and flowering shrubs. On the sea, canoes bobbed up and down on the slight swell. Further out a speed-boat churned up its long creamy wash, or a sailing-boat with daffodil-coloured or rusty brown sails leaned over in the light breeze. Further out still there were a few fishing boats.

But most of the fishermen went out at night. As dusk fell, the bathers vanished behind a tree or a bush on the landward side of the coast road to get dressed, and then bicycled or took a bus back into the city, or drove home in a small open Fiat. A few strollers still wandered under the trees listening to the plash of the little waves on the stones. The

Trieste lighthouse, high on the hillside, lit up its rotating yellow beam,
and was answered from Yugoslav-occupied territory by the Capodistria
lighthouse, away to the south on the far side of the great sweeping bay
which formed the windy north-east corner of the Adriatic. Then, on a
still night, the bay would be filled with the little yellow twinkling lights
of a scattered fleet of fishing-boats.

In the city, the better-off Triestini sat eating all kinds of delicious sea-
food: lobsters, sole or red mullet fried in oil, *scampi* (little prawns fried
in batter), tunny fish. Men with great baskets did the rounds of the
restaurants peddling the little local oysters—squeezing a dollop of
lemon juice on each—and shell-fish. For the palate jaded with fish,
there were always big juicy steaks or platefuls of spaghetti or fluffy
omelettes or crisp salads. There was plenty of cheap red and white wine:
the best came from the Verona district. Sometimes the restaurant door
opened and a melancholy, once-handsome old man, a former opera
singer, came in and sang his earlier successes in a hoarse broken voice
to his guitar.

After dinner the most lively street in Italian Trieste was the Viale XX
Settembre. Double lines of chestnut trees shaded the narrow double
roadways on each side; in the middle was a flagged open space for
strollers and for painted iron café tables. Down each side there were
shops, still lit at night, showing fur-coats and handbags and nylons and
frocks, cinemas with neon lights, crowded cafés with brilliant windows,
and ice-cream bars gleaming with chromium and mirrors.

In the lamplight, young Italians, boys and girls, wandered under the
trees, talking and laughing loudly, up the gentle slope of the Viale and
down again. Somewhere up at the top there was a fun-fair, and near it
the pony-trotting race-track. But the best entertainment was in the
Viale itself—to stare and be stared at, to crack jokes and laugh, to walk
arm-in-arm six abreast singing Italian patriotic songs, to make pert
remarks about the red-faced British soldiers, often mildly tipsy, who
strode and lurched among the throng.

Some of the cafés, with their red plush seats and their ornate gilt-
framed wall mirrors, had their own little five-man orchestra, thrumming
out Italian and American dance-hits, amplified metallically by com-
peting loudspeakers. From time to time a café singer, man or girl,
would step up on the little platform to the café microphone, and in a
voice hard but somehow melodious and rhythmically insistent would
sing a popular Italian nationalist song. The more ardently nationalist it
was, the more enthusiastically everyone in the café applauded it. Sometimes an amiably drunken British soldier lurched up and tried to seize
the microphone to bray out hoarsely a sentimental song of his youth:
he was equally amiably, if a little scornfully, edged away.

At the lower end of the Viale was the special meeting-place of the
young Italian toughs, students and schoolboys, who formed the core of
the nationalist gangs. They sat, trying to look grim and self-important,

at the little outdoor café tables, and put on conspiratorial airs. Sometimes at a mysterious summons they all moved off to some arranged
meeting-place to make a demonstration or start up trouble of some
minor kind. But on the whole they seemed to like it better if they could
just sit and plot.

This, usually, was the only touch of grimness in the Viale XX
Settembre. It was hard even to take the Italian gangs seriously—until
you had seen them hunt down and beat up some lonely Slovene or
Communist in a back-street.

Sometimes, there might be a civil or military police raid on the Viale.
One night in 1946 both ends were sealed off and the police made a
thorough comb-out of everyone in the street. But no one ever learned
the exact purpose of these police searches, and they seemed to most
people exciting rather than frightening.

On one solitary occasion in July, 1946, there was the sudden flare-up
of bad feeling between the Italians and the British troops, as happened
periodically in other Italian towns such as Padua and Venice and
Mestre. British soldiers pouring out of the cinemas in the Viale XX
Settembre and elsewhere took off their belts and used them on any
Italians who provoked them. But this flare-up seemed quickly forgotten.
Mutual tolerance and good humour, mixed with some mutual con-
tempt, soon flowed again like smooth oil.

Italian Trieste was normally a place of careless, lackadaisical ease.
But Italian Trieste stopped short, suddenly, on the hill-slopes that rose
sharply around the city. On the uplands behind the city—the Carso—
almost everything changed.

There was still sunlight. It was harsh and merciless at midday in
summer, beating on the stony scrubby dry Carso, where a few scrawny
beasts grazed hungrily. It was obviously hard work to scratch enough
earth together to grow crops and fruit.

A small Slovene village on the Carso, off the high road, was a cluster
of strongly-built rough stone cottages and small houses. They looked
huddled together for defence against an unfriendly world. Windows
were narrow; they seemed to want to keep out prying strangers. Streets
were sometimes so twisting and small that a cart could not get through.

On the main roads the villages were larger, more open and expansive,
and might have an inn where, before the war, Italian Triestini would
go and have supper in the garden, in the cool of a summer evening, and
stare out at the great blue shadowy ridge of the Vipacco away to the
north-east. But from 1945 onwards most Italian Triestini feared the
unfriendliness of the Slovene villagers and kept away.

Some things all Slovene villages had in common. One was a big
baroque-style church, more Austrian than Italian in character. In 1946,
one wall of the church had painted up on it in large letters the village
roll of honour in the anti-fascist struggle and the partisan war: so many
partisans killed, so many men shot or executed by the Fascists, so many

imprisoned, deported or interned. Usually the total figure was around one hundred, in bigger villages more than that.

Then there was a building with the Slovene red star flag flying over it, the 'Narodni Dom' or 'People's House'—home of the local committees of the various Slovene organisations subsidiary to P.N.O.O. and U.A.I.S. Outside there was a big notice-board with notices of the meetings, elections and cultural and sports activities of the village and district 'People's Committees'.

Usually there were other red star flags flying in the village too—perhaps one over the schoolhouse. And on any big wall there were Slovene slogans painted up: 'Tito is Ours, we are Tito's'; 'We want Tito'; 'We want Yugoslavia'; 'Trieste is Ours'; 'We want to be the Seventh Federative Republic' (of Yugoslavia). Sometimes, very faded, there were still the worn-out slogans of the first days of liberation, 'Long live our Allies', even 'Long live the New Zealanders'. But these had never been repainted.

The newer slogans issued by the Slovene-Communist organisations after the Big Four decision to create Trieste Free Territory—'We do not want a colonial governor', 'Trieste must not be an Anglo-American colony'—seldom got as far as the villages; they did not spread beyond the outskirts of the city. The villages stayed in the nationalist phase.

Perhaps the older and more sedate Slovene villagers, by the end of 1946, had begun to feel a little sated with the great Slav propaganda and political campaign, to long for peace and quiet. But they did not really count. The people who mattered were the young ex-partisans, the grim angry-looking boy with two red badly-healed stumps for arms, the brawny broad-shouldered deep-chested girl with strong cheek-bones and jutting obstinate chin. The young people were fierce and intolerant, and they were the ruling force in the villages. They represented the 'people'.

Most of the village priests followed the 'people'. They were not Communists. They were good Catholics. But they were many of them staunch Slovene nationalists of old standing. In any case, few thought it wise to go against the village.

If the Church did not stand up against the Slovene-Communist organisations and the village 'People's Committees', it was unlikely that anyone else would.

In Trieste, Italians and Slovenes had their own separate amusements. The Italians liked opera and concerts, in as grand a style as possible. They were pleased when A.M.G. restarted open-air Italian opera within the battlements of the old citadel, up above the city. They thronged there—together with a few Slovenes—in their thousands, and sat till past one o'clock in the morning, even in a high wind, listening not too attentively to Verdi or Puccini or even a programme of Viennese music and Strauss waltzes. If an Italian virtuoso or conductor came to Trieste, the large impressive Teatro Verdi would be crowded with well-dressed gentlemen and ladies who clapped and cheered with prolonged gusto and enthusiasm. They liked to make every concert a big social occasion. Afterwards they went away and tore the performance to pieces with the most biting criticism. It was all very agreeable and civilised and Western.

The Slovenes had their 'cultural evenings' in their local cultural circles. Perhaps in a long low room, festooned with paper streamers in red, blue and white—the Slovene national colours—a serious and earnest audience of Slovenes of all ages, usually family parties, gathered, paying a very small entrance fee to hear a visiting Slovene choir from Ljubljana, singing Slovene national, religious and above all partisan songs. The people in the audience were well-scrubbed, with shining apple-cheeked faces and sturdy bodies, neatly but unelegantly dressed, mostly of the artisan or lower-paid clerk type. They listened intently in utter silence and stillness, with devoted eyes fixed on the platform. Obviously such evenings were both a deep, communal, emotional experience and a national and political celebration.

In the rare intervals, rather surprisingly, the men burst into the bar attached to the meeting-place and poured down a good deal of beer and wine and stronger local drinks, talking heartily and cheerily. Everybody knew everybody. But after this relief, they filed back into the main room to listen with the same intense devotion as before. For them culture was a solemn act of Slovene faith.

There was the same sort of difference of atmosphere between Slovene-Communist and Italian demonstrations. The Italians rushed in with gusto, as though the whole thing were rather a rag; nothing was very highly organised on a mass scale; only a few ringleaders were needed, and there would soon be plenty of boys and young men to flock after them and join in the spirit of the thing. Suddenly, the Italians might panic or turn vicious; then they were seized by an ugly, if rather schoolboy, mood of brutality, even cruelty. But it soon passed like a summer storm. Usually, Italian demonstrations were a kind of game—if sometimes the game took the peculiarly nasty form of a man-hunt.

Slovene-Communist demonstrations were highly organised; instructions were sent around to key-men in advance; Slovenes came for miles from the countryside, even from the Yugoslav-occupied zone. The crowds were disciplined, up to a certain point restrained, sullen, self-righteous, injured and aggrieved. When the police or the military broke up the crowd, or when there was a direct clash with the Italians, the odd extremist might throw a grenade, or one group, in retaliation, might hurl paving stones and chunks of wood at the police or the troops. But more characteristic was the disciplined mass which, at a word, marched off in procession, singing partisan songs, very seldom answering the jeers of Italian bystanders, held rigid by a communal sense of moral superiority.

Demonstrations in the Trieste neighbourhood left curiously vivid flashes of memory in the minds of outsiders.

American soldiers whirling their rubber batons and whooping as they loped into a Communist crowd in the Piazza Garibaldi in Trieste; men in the crowd hurling back flower-pots of gaily-coloured flowers from the stands around the little cherub-crowned baroque fountain as they scattered and ran; men showering stones and bits of scrap metal from a thirty-foot high ramp near the Piazza Garibaldi down on the Civil Police in the roadway below; the police taking cover in side-streets and firing a volley of shots up at the ramp, while the stone-throwers ducked behind a protecting wall.

A young American soldier, in the falling dusk of a dusty street in the 'red' fishing village of Muggia, kicking a young Communist on the ground who had tripped over his banner and fallen as he fled.

Two Civil policemen, in the hot afternoon sun in the main square of Monfalcone, having a stand-up fight, truncheons against bare fists, with a single dark muscular girl Communist, taller than they; the girl crying angry frustrated tears as she pummelled the police.

The empty hot square of Monfalcone, littered with torn and broken banners, the moment after the police had charged a Communist crowd; a young boy sneaking out into the great empty space to rescue a banner; a policeman chasing him and tearing up the banner and stamping on the remnants.

Gorizia: a policeman with a bloody face stumbling out of the cloud of smoke that rose from a clump of bushes just after the sharp bang of an exploding grenade, in the 'Park of Remembrance'; nearby, little Italian girls in white frocks, with the Italian national colours draped round them, running away frightened from the marble Italian war memorial where an Italian mass had just been held. About twelve young Italians chasing a man and pulling him off his bicycle, beating him over the head till the blood streamed as he knelt in the road begging for mercy; a civil policeman joining in the beating. Italian boys with long staves charging down a street of Slovene shops, all hastily shuttered, and tearing to pieces every bicycle or hand-cart left in the empty street; Italian youths swarming in through a first-floor window to track down a man who had taken refuge inside a house.

Also Gorizia: a small open green car with a Yugoslav number-plate speeding down the main Corso as Italian bystanders shouted and yelled and threw stones and bits of wood and café chairs and iron café tables; two Yugoslav officers in the car ducking and shielding their heads with their arms.

Still Gorizia: a Slovene harvest festival procession of ox-carts and lorries, carrying tableaux showing Slovene agricultural and sports

activities, running the gauntlet of the main Corso; young Italians, boys
and girls, jeering and cat-calling and whistling, and shouting 'prostitute'
at a marching group of young Slovene girls in white; small boys throwing conkers at the procession; men throwing firecrackers under the
carts; two white oxen rearing and twisting away from the smoke and
noise; a small girl on the ox-cart bursting into tears, her companions
looking scared but singing a Slovene song. A tableau on one lorry
showing a Slovene partisan with a noose being slung round his neck by
a tin-hatted German soldier; as the lorry passed, willowy young Italians
jeeringly raising their arms in the fascist salute and shouting 'Duce,
Duce'.

A Sunday morning in Trieste, just after mass; crowds of Italian
schoolboys and students and a few young toughs gathering outside the
cathedral on the citadel hill above the city and the shining sea; suddenly
the crowds forming into long streams and cascading like waterfalls
down the hillside, down the steep white flights of steps into the heart
of the city; a British regimental sergeant-major, grinning under his
clipped moustache, trying out his newly-trained squad of local mounted
police against the thousands of young Italians massed in the Corso; the
horses wheeling about, intricately but quite harmlessly, among the
crowd which yielded and flowed back again; Italian boys and girls
jeering at the British R.S.M., shouting almost laughingly, 'India,
India'.

The funeral procession of an Italian Communist worker, dead as the
result of a demonstration, the coffin draped in the red flag, winding
slowly up the steep twisting narrow streets leading from the heart of
Trieste to the 'red' suburb of San Giacomo; the priest, at the head,
chanting wearily; the insistent funeral beat of the drums following the
coffin; the mourners, in heavy black clothes, sweating in the early
evening sun; working men and women leaning out of the windows of
the tall rickety houses, some crossing themselves devoutly and praying,
some giving the clenched fist salute.

The satisfied voices of an American major and a British captain after
two hours' hard work breaking up a peaceful if unauthorised demonstration. 'Well, old boy, I think we've shown the flag all right to-day.'
'I should say we have.'

The city of Trieste was not entirely made up of fervent Italian
nationalists, fervent Slovenes and fanatical Communists. As a big port
and a meeting-place of different races, it was the kind of place to breed
tolerant half-hearted cynics, strange mixed types.

There were a fair number of people of mixed Italian-Slav blood, or
with a strain of Jewish or German or Hungarian, even Armenian or
Greek, blood, who did not feel that they really belonged to one side or
the other in the great nationalist struggle.

Then there were the over-forty-fives: many of them sighed for the broad easy prosperous days of the Austro-Hungarian Empire. Some with mild nostalgia would point to the antique fragile figure of an ex-admiral of the Austro-Hungarian Navy who still did his daily constitutional up and down one of the shadier streets of Trieste. He was a precious relic of the good old days.

Even among the out-and-out nationalists and political extremists there were on both sides some extremely human and fallible people.

There was the prominent pro-Tito business magnate, a charming man-of-the-world of Croat origin, said to be one of the economic experts most trusted by Marshal Tito's government. He was also said to be one of the most wily and wary operators in Trieste. But he had a blind spot. One day a former girl friend introduced to him an Englishman who said he was Jack Wise, a British soldier. Jack Wise produced documents supposed to show that he had large credits with the Bank of England. The magnate, on the strength of the documents, advanced him large sums in Italian currency. It was only when his loans had reached the 1,500,000 lire mark that the magnate had enquiries made in London. He discovered that no such man as Jack Wise was known there. Yet Trieste is famous for the smartness of its business men.

There was the seventeen-year-old Italian schoolboy, Paolo, of a 'good' Trieste family. He was just beginning his matric exam. when he was called away from school by what turned out to be a bogus telephone message saying that his mother had been taken dangerously ill. Paolo after leaving school vanished from Trieste for three days. He turned up one evening, very worn and weary, and told his anxious family—and the British security police—that he had been kidnapped in a Trieste street by a mysterious car and carried off to the Yugoslav-occupied zone. By luck and daring, he said, he had managed to escape at a cross-roads and had made his way painfully back to Trieste on foot.

It was obviously yet another 'Slavo-Communist' outrage. The British police accepted the story. But something in the boy's manner made his uncle doubt him; and Paolo broke down. The true story was that he himself, afraid that he would fail in his matric, had arranged the fake phone call. After leaving school he had met his girl friend and had gone with her to the pleasant Italian town of Udine and spent a couple of days in her company. He thought the cover-story of the kidnapping particularly good because his chief examiner was a strong Italian nationalist and would probably be delighted to let the victim of a Slav atrocity pass his matric with honours, in absence. At the same time Paolo had hoped to become a hero among his nationalist school friends.

But Paolo was not quite a good enough liar.

Then there was Guglielmo Berlot, the Communist barber of Trieste. He was a willowy, rather consumptive-looking young man with great shifty black eyes and a flowing moustache. He was brought to trial after the police had raided a house in Santa Scala Street in Trieste and had unexpectedly found a curious collection of documents, mostly signed reports, which seemed to reveal the workings of a Communist campaign of intimidation intended to enforce the general strike of July, 1946, on Trieste shopkeepers and market stallholders and café owners.

Berlot admitted in court that some of the documents—hand-written scraps of paper—were signed by himself. But he denied aggrievedly that they proved that he had taken part in any planned campaign of intimidation. He was, he said, a close but impartial observer of human nature. During the general strike he had found it interesting to watch objectively in the Trieste fruit and vegetable market and see how men reacted when their stalls were thrown over and broken up. He had then scribbled down descriptive notes on odd bits of paper. He needed them for his next book: it might be either a big historical work on Trieste or a work of fiction; he wasn't sure. Most probably fiction. The publishers, unfortunately, had already turned down two books of his.

The A.M.G. court somehow or other did not believe Berlot's explanation, and sentenced him. But presumably the sentence was suspended. A few weeks later, Berlot was still walking about Trieste, more willowy and wandering-eyed than ever. Perhaps he was collecting fresh material for his book.

There was also the middle-aged, solid Italian worker who took part in a rather listless Slovene-Communist demonstration outside A.M.G. headquarters in Trieste, one summer evening after work. Nothing much was happening: a delegation from the crowd was repeatedly asking to see Colonel Alfred Bowman, the benign and dashing Los Angeles lawyer who was Senior Civil Affairs Officer. But everyone knew that the Colonel had gone home to his hillside villa, where he could sit on the terrace and imagine himself in California, at least an hour earlier. The Italian worker was talking to two of his Communist comrades and said:

'Of course, these demonstrations are a fine thing, and of course we all want Trieste to go to Yugoslavia. But sometimes it seems that we aren't getting anywhere. If nothing comes of it all, I suggest that we ought to go to Naples. They say that the black market there is wonderful —much better than anything here in Trieste.'

His friends agreed.

14

Conclusions

FROM the spring of 1947 onwards the political and economic clash between East and West over the Balkans and the whole of Eastern Europe came more and more into the open.

America's policy—mainly for internal political reasons—took a far more active and outspoken form. President Truman pledged aid to Greece and Turkey to strengthen them both militarily and economically. He made it quite clear that he believed both these countries directly threatened by the menace of Eastern aggression from without, and Greece also by Communist aggression from within. American aid was given on a frankly anti-Soviet, anti-Communist basis.

Russia, although she did not at once react openly, acted on the assumption that America wanted not only to prop up the anti-Communist régimes in the border countries on the western side of the dividing line between the two spheres of Europe, but also to undermine and weaken the pro-Soviet régimes on the eastern side of the line. So Russia speeded up and intensified the measures she had already undertaken to guarantee that she would have a cast-iron system of friendly and unopposed governments on her side of the line, even after the withdrawal of the Red Army from the border countries.

This meant that all leading politicians in these countries, whose loyalty to Moscow was in any way doubtful and who might become pawns in the American game, had to be discredited and banned from political activity. In outstanding cases they had to be executed or imprisoned.

America broadened the Truman doctrine into the Marshall plan, which held out rather vague hopes of American economic aid to any country which joined with other European countries in grasping it. Moscow and the Communists of the Soviet sphere interpreted the plan as a device to take mean advantage of the grave economic difficulties of the countries of the Soviet sphere, and to seduce their peoples and the non-Communist sections of their governments away from loyalty to Russia. The Oppositions in these countries seized on the Marshall plan with wild and unrealistic enthusiasm as offering not only economic but also political salvation, and tried to use it for their own political ends.

The pro-Soviet governments of Eastern Europe, some regretfully, some defiantly, turned down the Marshall plan. They cut themselves off from economic relations with the West except by the narrow way of bilateral trade negotiations with Britain and the Western European countries. At the same time they quickly strengthened and extended the network of bilateral trade agreements between the countries inside the Soviet sphere. These agreements aimed at fullest mutual aid in carrying out each country's long-term economic plan for recovery and indus- trialisation, and at making the East as nearly as possible economically independent of the West. They were reinforced, in the closing months of 1947, by a network of politico-military agreements between the Eastern European countries, aimed not only against renewed German aggression, but also against aggression from any third party. This obviously implied that they were directed against the 'Anglo-American imperialists'.

At the same time the pro-Soviet governments took final steps to liquidate the pro-Western political oppositions in their own countries. In Bulgaria Nikola Petkov and his Agrarian Party were destroyed; in Rumania Maniu and the National Peasant Party were removed. These two parties, which had a wide following among the peasants in the two countries, had been the only formidable opposition to the new Com- munist-controlled governments.

Simultaneously, the non-Communist members of these governments either were eliminated or else became more and more mere fellow- travellers in a Communist-driven train.

The Communist policy underlying this clearing of the political scene was openly revealed when the formation of the Cominform, with head- quarters in Belgrade, was announced at the beginning of October, 1947. This made it plain that the period of 'anti-fascist' coalitions was finished and that the Communist parties were to act alone and forcefully against the 'Anglo-American imperialists' and their agents, real or supposed. The three years' uneasy truce in the Balkans was at an end.

On the western side of the borderline, the Greek government of Maximos was replaced by the Sofoulis coalition, but the policies of both were fundamentally the same: with American aid, to liquidate the Markos rising and with it the Communist Party.

In the execution of this policy, several thousands of Greek Com- munists and near-Communists were arrested in 1947. Numerically, political arrests in Greece were probably on a good deal larger scale than in Rumania or Bulgaria. But the Greek government had more excuse for such action than the Rumanian or Bulgarian governments. The Greek Communist Party was obviously behind the Markos guerilla movement, which was making the British-trained Greek Army look silly and was becoming a real menace to the Greek State. The Bulgarian and Rumanian peasant parties had neither the chance nor perhaps the wish to organise big active and armed illegal resistance movements, although they might theoretically have got wide popular backing. At most they probably conspired rather feebly and, in spite of the unpopularity of the new régimes, quite harmlessly from the point of view of the Communist-controlled governments and of Moscow. The Communists were either naïve or disingenuous if they took seriously the schoolboy fantasies secretly hatched by one or two enthusiastic Americans in the Balkans. The Bulgarian and Rumanian Oppositions were dangerous only as potential fifth-columnists in case of 'hot war' between Russia and the West, but not until then.

On the level of the Big Powers, Russia, before the United Nations, defended Yugoslavia, Bulgaria and Albania against the charge that they were helping the Markos movement in Greece, obstructed the plan to leave a permanent United Nations commission to watch the Greek frontiers, and attacked the Greek anti-Communist governments. America and Britain protested through diplomatic channels against political arrests and the suppression of the National Peasant Party in Rumania, and against the arrest and execution of Petkov and the suppression of the Opposition press in Bulgaria.

Britain, America and France decided at the beginning of the summer of 1947 to ratify the satellite peace treaties, including those with Bulgaria and Rumania. The Western Powers presumably hoped that when the Red Army left, Soviet and Communist influence in these countries would be weakened and pro-Western forces would have more freedom of action. Russia delayed ratification for another four months. Presumably she was unwilling to withdraw her troops until she thought her political and economic influence secured against all Western attempts to undermine it.

Before the end of 1947 Russia had withdrawn the Red Army from Bulgaria. She could keep troops in Rumania until an Austrian settlement was reached, since Rumania was stated to lie on her lines of communication with Austria. But by that time Russian occupation forces were no longer politically necessary in either country; relative security had been established.

In the closing months of 1947 the Russian-American-British Control Commissions in Bulgaria and Rumania were dissolved. The armistice period was ended.

Over the creation of Trieste Free Territory, the Big Four haggled aimlessly throughout 1947. The immediate dispute was about the appointment of a United Nations governor for the Free Territory. Russia objected to America's candidates and America objected to Russia's.

Trieste itself simmered uneasily. It had two big sensations in the spring and summer: the murder of an Englishman, Brigadier de Winton, at Pola by a fanatical Italian nationalist and former Fascist, Maria Pasquinelli, and a big scandal over corruption in the Public Works Department of Allied Military Government. In the autumn, the coming into force of the Italian Peace Treaty did not bring the Free Territory to life as it should have done. It only meant that the Anglo-Americans, on withdrawal from Italy, remained in occupation of that sector of the Territory which had always been included in their zone, while the Yugoslavs kept the sector which they had always held since their withdrawal from Trieste city in June, 1945.

Yugoslav attempts to gain a foothold in Trieste city itself, or a share in the running of the Anglo-American sector of the Free Territory, were rejected by the Anglo-Americans with firmness and pained surprise. The Yugoslavs then formally accused the Anglo-Americans of mal-administration in their sector. There was the usual exchange of acid notes.

Inside the Free Territory, there was political deadlock. On the economic side, there was stagnation; Fiume made the first moves to capture Trieste traffic. The delay in bringing the Free Territory to life seemed to help the Eastern rather than the Western forces in Trieste.

Russia's political strategy in the Balkans in 1947 had, it seemed, a simple aim. The Russians wanted to consolidate their grip on those countries already lying inside their sphere; and they wanted to cause as much trouble as possible in the border areas still in Western hands, Greece and Trieste. At worst this policy would embarrass the Western Powers. At best it might cause Western public opinion to tire of apparently pointless squabbling and constantly increasing commitments, and so might force the Western Powers to withdraw from the border areas.

The policy of the West did not seem to have any such clear-cut aim. It appeared piecemeal rather than systematic. Two convictions were probably behind it. First, that the Russians and the Communists make themselves more and more unpopular the longer they are in power anywhere, so that general reaction against them must steadily grow. Second, that the rigidity and inexperience of economic planning of the Soviet type, together with lack of certain raw materials and industrial equipment, must cripple economic recovery in the Soviet sphere. This in turn would mean that the countries of the Soviet sphere must inevitably get poorer and poorer and more and more in need of outside aid.

So in the end—the Western belief seemed to be—it would either be possible to pull down the barrier set by Russia across Europe, or else the Soviet sphere would become so involved in its own difficulties that, even if the barrier were maintained, it would be perfectly harmless to the West.

As purely personal views, the following guesses can be made about the future:

1. It is true that the Russians and the Communists will get more and

more unpopular in countries such as Rumania and Bulgaria, in proportion as they take stricter and stricter measures to abolish any last relics of political opposition and to enforce economic control and discipline. A new generation will have to grow up before the Soviet-Communist way of life is acceptable. But this unpopularity will not hamper them much. Their organisational drive and their security methods are so thorough and sweeping, if rough and ready, that popular discontent will be more or less harmless—particularly since all its likeliest leaders and organisers have been removed. Whether or not the Western Powers go on trying to intervene in the Soviet sphere, the Eastern forces will be able to consolidate themselves.

The worst the Russians and Communists have to fear is widespread passive resistance by the peasants. But they have learned something from what happened in the Ukraine in the 'thirties, and will probably just manage to avoid any such development in the Balkans.

2. Even though the Russians and Communists may consolidate the new régimes in the Balkans, this does not mean that everything will go smoothly or quickly. Particularly in Rumania, there are too few experienced, competent and honest men in the ranks of the Easterners to run the new political and economic machine efficiently, or even to abolish corruption. Also, some of the good men—and altogether there were few enough of them—have been on the Opposition side and have been driven further and further into purely negative obstruction, or have been eliminated altogether. Assuming that the new régimes survive, these men are lost to the service of their country. Because of shortage of leaders, organisers and experts, it will take ten years or even a generation before the new machines can work smoothly.

3. For similar reasons, the ambitious two-year plan for Bulgaria, and the parallel plan when decreed for Rumania, cannot hope to achieve their ends of recovery, rapid increase in agricultural production, industrialisation and electrification in the short time-limit set. Again it will take ten years or far more probably a generation before these Balkan States can become modern countries with balanced economies resting on a thriving industry as well as a thriving agriculture. It will be equally long before there is any overall rise in the average standard of living.

4. The economic plans of the Soviet-controlled Balkans will also mean a number of years of strictest discipline and stern self-sacrifice for all, and, in the long run, the elimination of the existing middle-classes and of all but the smallest private enterprises. Life will be very hard and hardship will increase discontent, which in turn will slow down, though not stop, the carrying out of the economic plan. On the other hand, there will not be economic breakdown. The new economies will rest on solid foundations, even if the structures are built painfully and sometimes by inhuman methods.

5. Russia will not make economic sacrifices for the countries lying in

her sphere. She will merely help the pro-Soviet governments to maintain their control if ever it is threatened from within or without. Her trade agreements with these countries will be if anything more in her own interest than in theirs.

6. Border areas on the western side of the dividing line, like Greece and Trieste, have a far more uncertain future than those on the eastern side, because the policy of the Western Powers is far more incalculable.

But it is already certain that, whatever might have been achieved in Greece in 1945, from 1947 onwards unrelenting Communist pressure inside and outside Greece will make it impossible for any moderate, energetic and progressive forces to take power and carve out a prosperous middle way. Any American efforts to foster such forces will fail, as Britain's did in 1945 and 1946. The Communists, if they cannot rule in Athens themselves, will either force power into the hands of the extremists of the Right or else force moderates to become extremists, as happened with Sofoulis. The Communists will also force the extremists into more and more repressive policies and actions. The extremists will be less and less able to maintain themselves without increasingly large Western—primarily American—political, economic and even direct military support.

In Trieste the development will be a little different because there may, at least theoretically, be United Nations control. But the general trend will probably be the same. To keep pro-Western forces in control or even in being, the West will have to give increasingly strong support.

7. The border areas on the Western side, partly because they will not have stable and energetic governments, partly because of Eastern pressure, will not achieve economic stability and discipline, and will not be able to become financially and economically self-sufficient. The Western Powers, mainly America, will have to subsidise them more and more and more heavily to keep them from bankruptcy and to keep them inside the Western sphere. If, as they may, the Western Powers ever relax their efforts, they will give the Eastern forces in these border areas their chance. The East-West dividing line across Europe is more likely to shift westwards than eastwards.

There is still the bigger and deeper question: will the ordinary man or woman, not as a political or economic animal, but as a human being, find life more worth living on the Eastern or the Western side of the border?

There is the choice between imposed purposefulness and free-for-all aimlessness; between rigid control of the human being in all his actions, and—at least in Greece—anarchy which leaves the human being at the mercy of his enemies; between a sure if hard minimum of social security at the price of a big sacrifice in human freedom, and social insecurity which puts the individual at the mercy of social parasites, racketeers and speculators. It will not be a pleasant choice for the border peoples.

At best, on the Eastern side the individual can, if he chooses, comfort himself with blind faith in daydreams about a future in which he will belong to a socially just, free and universally prosperous community—however much human injustice, oppression and poverty he may see around him at the moment. On the Western side the individual is free to make hay if and when the sun shines, or to revel in the melancholy delights of pessimism, scepticism and daydreams about the beautiful past when it does not.

But so long as the border lands between East and West are an area of conflict and tension, on neither side of the border will it be possible to live the life of a real human being.

Set and printed in Great Britain by Tonbridge Printers Ltd.,
Peach Hall Works, Tonbridge, in Times ten on eleven point

AUSTRIA

Gorizia
Monfalcone
Trieste
Ljubljana
San Pietro
Fiume
Zagreb

YUGO

ADRIATIC SEA

ITALY

Bari

TRIESTE AREA

Gorizia
Monfalcone
Trieste
Ljubljana
San Pietro
Fiume
Pola

MEDI